DATE DUE

Caviar

❧

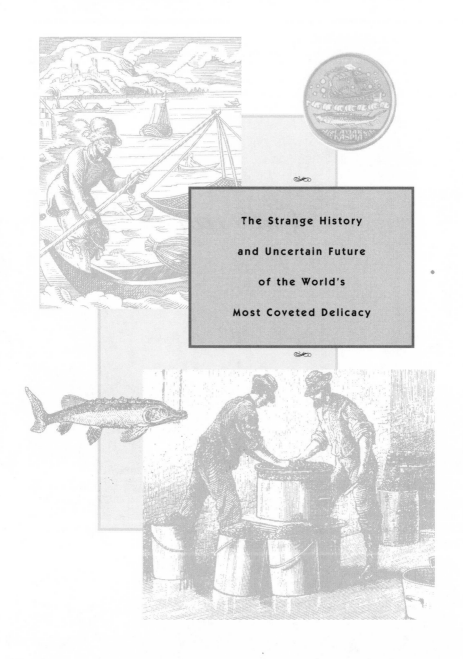

The Strange History

and Uncertain Future

of the World's

Most Coveted Delicacy

Caviar

· · · · · ❧ · · · ·

Inga Saffron

Broadway Books
New York

Broadway Books titles may be purchased for business or
promotional use or for special sales. For information, please write to:
Special Markets Department, Random House, Inc.,
280 Park Avenue, New York, NY 10017.

PRINTED IN THE UNITED STATES OF AMERICA

BROADWAY BOOKS and its logo, a letter B bisected on the diagonal,
are trademarks of Broadway Books,
a division of Random House, Inc.

visit our website at www.broadwaybooks.com

First edition published 2002.

Designed by Donna Sinisgalli

Map illustrated by Laura Hartman Maestro

Library of Congress Cataloging-in-Publication Data
Saffron, Inga, 1957–
Caviar : the strange history and uncertain future of the world's most
coveted delicacy / by Inga Saffron.—1st ed.
p. cm
Includes index
1. Caviar.   I. Title.

TX385 .S24 2002
641.3'92—dc21   2001049962

ISBN 0-7679-0623-3

1 3 5 7 9 10 8 6 4 2

For Sky,

who loves caviar,

and for Ken,

who doesn't.

Contents

•

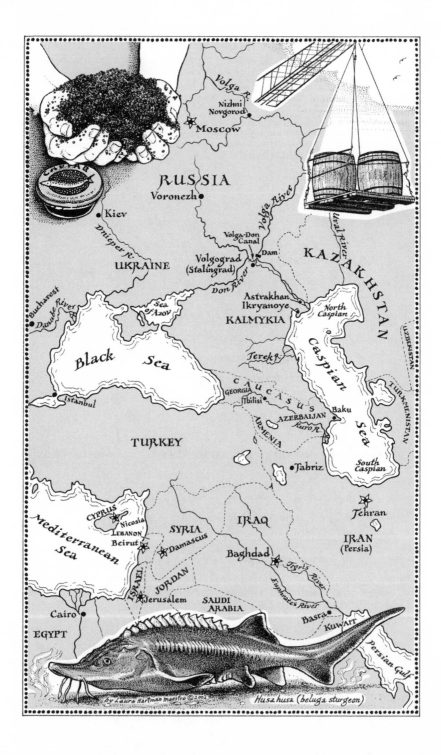

Husz husz (beluga sturgeon)

by Laura Hartman Maestro ©2002

Prologue

•

CAVIAR DREAMS

The roe of the Russian mother sturgeon has probably been
present at more important international affairs than have
all the Russian dignitaries of history combined. This
seemingly simple article of diet has taken its place in the
world along with pearls, sables, old silver, and Cellini
cups.

—JAMES BEARD

I had been living in Moscow for just a few weeks when I first ate what
M.F.K. Fisher once described as "almost enough caviar."

I had tasted caviar perhaps twice before coming to Russia in 1994
as a correspondent for the *Philadelphia Inquirer,* but in microscopic portions. The first time was during my freshman year at college. A friend
who later became my husband took me to a restaurant in Greenwich
Village that specialized in omelets. It was really a diner with preten-
sions, but to a seventeen-year-old new to New York it seemed elegant
and grown up. Scanning the menu, I was stopped by the caviar-and-
sour-cream combination. Until that moment, it had never occurred to
me that caviar was something I might long for. But sitting in that

hushed room, as the fading winter light fell on the edges of the Formica tables, and I contemplated whether the meal amounted to a date, I knew that caviar was exactly what I wanted.

The omelet, when it arrived, had a trail of sour cream flowing from its edges. Beneath the crust of cooked eggs, I can recall seeing a few scattered black dots swimming in a yolky pool. About the taste, I remember nothing, except that I liked it. The absence of a more specific memory has not colored my feelings about caviar one bit. Caviar is not just about taste. Those glistening black globules are a culinary Rorschach that unleashes our deeply held notions about wealth, luxury, and life.

Although I did not eat caviar again for many years, it was the food that most embodied my idea of Russia, at least as I understood it from nineteenth-century novels. Tasting caviar again in Moscow, I felt as if I could detect within each round egg the whole lost universe of St. Petersburg literary salons and country estates, just as a McDonald's hamburger might offer Russians a brief intimacy with life on the suburban strip. In America, caviar had been something abstract. In Moscow during the early 1990s, caviar was sold everywhere, even by sidewalk peddlers. I could not get my fill of the stuff.

In the beginning, I bought my caviar in a fancy food store on the Arbat. The dusty jars, which still bore the stamp of the nonexistent USSR, had recently been relegated to a back shelf. In their place were elaborate pyramids of Lipton tea, European chocolates, and other mysterious foreign imports, which were then considered by Russians to be the height of sophistication. But caviar was the only product in the store that held any attraction for me. Then I met Magomed.

Magomed was a Daghestani from Mahachkala, a port city on the Caspian Sea in southern Russia, where most of the world's caviar-producing sturgeon live. A dark, wiry man, he always arrived at my door wearing a tracksuit and looking a little sweaty and unshaven, as if he had spent the night on the train with a traveling soccer team. I received my first phone call from him a few weeks after I began working in Moscow. He was nervous about speaking on the telephone, like a lot of people in Russia. He rushed through his name, as if we were old acquaintances. It would be better if he stopped by my office, he hissed. This didn't strike me as unusual. Generations of foreign correspondents before me had been contacted out of the blue by dissidents, spies, crackpots, and other mysterious people with stories to tell.

Magomed arrived with two sturdy plastic bags rather than a story. I would have to piece one together later. He grinned happily as he removed a large blue can from his bag and placed it on my desk for inspection. Briefly distracted by his dazzling mouthful of lacquered gold teeth, I mistook the can for a tin of Danish butter cookies, then all the rage in Moscow, until my eyes fell on the familiar words *Malossol* and *Russkaya Ikra*—mildly salted Russian caviar. With a chef's flourish, Magomed whisked the lid away. A plateau of shiny black caviar stood in the void. It was vastly more caviar than I had ever encountered in my life.

By then, my Russian assistant had wandered in to see what was going on and was stopped in her tracks by the view. Magomed urged us to try the caviar. We took some teaspoons and dug in. I rolled the eggs over my tongue, allowing the taut spheres to detonate a few at a time, hoping to harbor the taste for as long as possible. The salty-buttery richness filled my mouth, nuclear in its intensity. New and different tastes came in explosive bursts, as the initial fishiness gave way to more complex flavors and aromas. I was reminded of other rich foods—olives, pine nuts, smoked salmon. But it was the physical sensation, the way the firm casings of the eggs gave way as they popped against my tongue and cheek that dominated the experience. What I realized was that caviar was something you experienced in your mouth, not your stomach. Compared to Magomed's caviar, the stuff I had been buying on the Arbat was junk, as bland and featureless as jelly.

So, I bought my first kilogram of contraband. I handed Magomed $125 in American bills for the tin. Later, the price would rise to $150 for two pounds—small change, I knew, compared to what Americans were paying in specialty shops, where jars that could fit in the palm of your hand were displayed like jewels on slivered ice. If I ever bothered to ask Magomed where his caviar came from, or how he transported it to Moscow, I'm sure I settled for the vaguest of answers.

That first evening, I ate caviar by the spoonful. For dinner, we had caviar with blini and sour cream. In the morning, I layered my two-year-old daughter's toast with caviar. Even my husband, a confirmed fish hater, felt compelled to join in. When friends visited our apartment, I passed around crackers mounded with caviar. If we had not managed to empty the entire tin by Magomed's next visit, my housekeeper would feed the leftovers to her cat.

We were hardly the only foreigners consumed by the desire to consume caviar. Magomed and his partners had acquired a copy of a telephone directory listing Moscow's expatriates, and they went through it as systematically as American telemarketers. At dinner parties in foreigners' apartments, the host would invariably emerge from the kitchen bearing a mayonnaise-sized jar of Magomed's caviar, another of sour cream, and a skyscraper of blini. The guests would lather on the caviar and sour cream and eat until they were stuffed. One correspondent we knew was so obsessed that he would sneak home at lunchtime to eat his caviar straight from the jar, like peanut butter.

It was around this time that caviar also began to seep into America's food consciousness in a big way. Caviar had always been available from gourmet shops in America, but it took a bit of effort and knowledge to locate it. That situation began to change soon after the Soviet Union and its trade restrictions fell apart in 1991. Caviar stores opened in big cities across the United States. Buying caviar became a straightforward commercial exchange. The cans and jars were stacked prominently in glass display cases. You read the price list and made your choice. A clerk would wrap your purchase in an ice pack and hand it to you in a little shopping bag, often with the store's logo printed on it. Soon you could get reasonably good Russian caviar in airport terminals, via the Internet, even in suburban supermarkets. You could also buy a lot of congealed black goo. You might hear people on the train talking about how much they were ordering for New Year's Eve or see ads for caviar in newspaper food sections. Middle-class people began to think of caviar as an aristocratic indulgence they could afford.

It was a wonderful fantasy while it lasted. The reality was that caviar was never meant to be a delicacy for the masses, as easy to obtain as a box of chocolates. Sturgeon, the prehistoric-looking fish that produces the coveted black roe, is a large, ponderous beast, ill prepared by nature for an age of industrial fishing. They are incredibly easy to catch in the big gill nets used by fishermen who work the rivers that drain into the Caspian and Black Seas. When you land a female, you don't just take home a belly full of caviar, you eliminate the future.

Caviar derives its mystique from its intense flavor, high price and, most of all, its renowned scarcity. Its reputation helps to fuel our desire. In our minds it remains the snack of the tsars. Throughout the world, you only have to say "caviar" to convey the idea of aristocratic decadence; the television host Robin Leach did just that every time he introduced the lives of the rich and famous, with the promise of "champagne fantasies and caviar dreams." These associations were so firmly embedded in our collective imagination that Russian caviar remained a luxury product through seven decades of Communist rule.

. . .

IN THE mosaic of Russian culture, caviar is merely a luminous fleck. A simple dish, made by mixing salt into sturgeon's eggs, caviar has been a fixture on the national table for at least a millennium. Perhaps because Russians perceive their identity through the lens of those black orbs, they have jealously guarded the delicacy for much of their history, controlling the caviar trade with a zeal that far exceeded its monetary value to the nation. For more than four centuries, the Russian state determined how many sturgeon could be caught, how much caviar could be made, and how much of that could be sold abroad.

The Soviet system was famously unable to manufacture a decent television set or adequately gauge the domestic appetite for sausage, yet somehow it managed a sophisticated cartel that produced and marketed this gourmet delicacy to a select, affluent Western clientele. Along with Iran, the Soviet Union completely controlled the world caviar market for much of the twentieth century. Although they were no environmentalists, the Soviets managed the sturgeon in a way that seems enlightened compared with today's destructive fishing frenzy. Thanks to the Communists, caviar remained a delicacy for the few.

The disciplined cartel collapsed with the Soviet Union, which was reconstituted as fifteen separate nations. Today five of them border the Caspian, all eager to squeeze money from the rivers. Russia is no longer capable of running a state caviar industry. Its processing plants and boats have been sold cheap to local entrepreneurs—or, depending on your viewpoint, Mafia thugs. In the region around Astrakhan, the center of Russian caviar production since the sixteenth century, anyone who can wield a hook and line is effectively a caviar producer. Those trawling for sturgeon are often unemployed men who have few options other than stealing from the waters that feed them. Out on the water under the cover of night, they dream of hitting the jackpot, catching not just any sturgeon, but one fat with eggs. If they're lucky, they might gross twenty dollars from a night's work, a large sum in the Russian provinces.

It is difficult to pinpoint the exact moment when caviar stopped being the centerpiece at Moscow dinner parties. The intervals between Magomed's calls grew longer, and during a stay in Azerbaijan, which fronts the Caspian Sea, a glum United Nations official I happened to be interviewing predicted that we would be the last generation to indulge our taste for caviar. The claim struck me then as excessively alarmist. There is plenty for sale in Moscow, I countered. "Yes, and it's selling here at the bazaar for thirty dollars a kilo. That's the problem," he said. In the skewed reality of post-Soviet life, no one was surprised that something so scarce should sell for so little.

Caviar had entered my life suddenly, but its disappearance was more gradual. While I was no longer indulging regularly, I never stopped thinking about caviar. For a short time, caviar made us believe that we were all aristocrats. I didn't want to believe in a world without caviar. But half a decade later, the possibility was no longer outlandish. It was time to get the story Magomed never told me, to find out where this rare delicacy had come from, and whether there would be any left for my daughter's children.

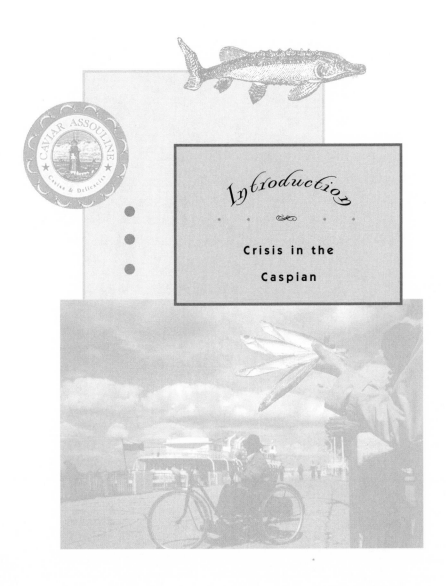

CAVIAR ASSOULINE

Caviar & Delicacies

Introduction

· · ❧ · ·

Crisis in the

Caspian

In the nature of things, that fabulous food caviar must be
a rarity, or it does not fulfill its function.
—MAGUELONNE TOUSSAINT-SAMAT,
A HISTORY OF FOOD

*T*he Russian poet Velimir Khlebnikov once lamented in a letter to his avant-garde circle in St. Petersburg that he loved his hometown of Astrakhan dearly except for the heat, the provincial indifference to literature and, most of all, "the fact that everything here revolves around fish." When Khlebnikov listed the city's deficiencies in 1913, his friends would have understood that the fish in question was sturgeon, and what Astrakhan revolved around was caviar.

Today, the hot exhaust of steppe air still blasts Astrakhan in the summer, and the city still lacks a decent bookstore, but the pungent fish odors that so vexed Khlebnikov are noticeably absent. Along the Volga River quays, where caviar makers used to slit the bellies of giant sturgeon as they puckered desperately for air, there is no sign of the old wooden packing houses, operated before the Russian Revolution by famous names such as Dieckmann & Hansen of Hamburg, or Romanoff of New York.

Soviet planners long ago moved the messy business out of sight, and the Volga River's banks are now lined by a graceful promenade. These improvements might have appealed to Khlebnikov's sense of irony, especially since the poet's family had been among Astrakhan's most prominent caviar traders in the nineteenth century. Instead of waiting for the shallow-bottomed barks to arrive at the quays with flapping fish, you can watch schools of hormone-charged teenagers strolling up the promenade, following the same course once taken by the sturgeon struggling up the Volga to spawn.

Fortunately the Soviets never managed to rub all the life out of Astrakhan, or extinguish fully the beating heart of a natural trading town. Astrakhan was once an important stop on the Silk Route, where Chinese caravans and Venetian merchants haggled over exotic wares. The whitewashed kremlin built by Ivan the Terrible still presides above the old city, supported by stones taken from the palaces of the Golden Horde in Sarai, the magnificent capital built by Batu Khan, the Mongol warlord who ruled Russia in the thirteenth century. As Astrakhan's main street slopes down to the Volga, the bourgeois "Style Moderne" apartment buildings of the twentieth century give way to stout, nineteenth-century merchants' houses adorned with lacy woodcarvings, all relics of the city's previous life as the center of the world's caviar trade.

On a May night in Astrakhan, I hurried with my friend Mira to join the parade along the quays. Before we had gone more than a few steps along the river, we were both overpowered by the irresistible scent of grilling food, floating up from the outdoor restaurants that lined the embankment.

"It's sturgeon *shashlik*," Mira announced, eyes shining. Shashlik, a

Slavic variation on shish kebab, always sends Russians into raptures, especially when it involves thick chunks of golden sturgeon.

We walked into the first restaurant we saw. Mira paused to ask the grillman if he was serving sturgeon.

"Not yet," he muttered, turning away to concentrate on the lines of pork and lamb kebabs dripping their fat into the coffin-shaped grill.

"What do you mean, 'Not yet?' Isn't it the season?" she persisted, knowing perfectly well that it was the height of the spring sturgeon run, when the mature fish leave the Caspian Sea and migrate up the Volga to lay their precious eggs. Mira was a professor of linguistics at an elite Moscow university, as well as a shashlik-lover, so she seemed to feel a professional obligation to explore the grillman's semantic ambiguity.

"We might have it later," he answered. He was looking at us now. His caramel-brown skin and black hair indicated he was from one of the ethnic groups that populate southern Russia, perhaps an Armenian or an Azeri. Winking, he flashed a smile of Caucasian gold. "All right, come back in twenty minutes," he said.

We chewed over this mysterious exchange as we walked and waited. Why all the fuss? We were just trying to order the local specialty in a restaurant, yet we felt as if we were setting up a drug deal. Perhaps if we had dared to ask for caviar, then all this hush-hush, come-back-later business would have made sense. The international caviar trade had become a lucrative and nasty black market enterprise in the years since the Soviet monopoly went under. But who wanted sturgeon meat outside of Russia? We knew that sturgeon stocks in the Caspian were suffering as a result of the frenzied poaching, yet the fish was still served all over Russia.

As we approached the restaurant garden again a half hour later, Dima the grillman hustled us to a back table shadowed by a leafy tree. Up front, a petite singer with distinctly Mongol features belted Russian pop tunes over a recorded track, while a group of women in skyscraper heels undulated languidly among the tables, as if under the spell of a snake charmer. Two plates arrived heaped with mountains of sliced onions. Carving out an exploratory tunnel, I uncovered cubes of golden brown sturgeon embedded in the tangled mound. I took a tentative bite. Within the crunchy carapace, the meat was buttery, mellow, sweet, chewy, the seafood equivalent of a fine beef fillet. I was surprised that an endangered species could be so delicious.

We were finishing our beers when Dima stopped by to inform us that we should pay him separately for the sturgeon. Handing over the equivalent of eight dollars, we pressed him to explain his earlier reticence. By now, we had guessed that our meal was prepared from contraband sturgeon caught by poachers. But Dima just smiled away our questions. It was time to come clean about our motives. Could Dima introduce us to one of these poachers, I asked?

His face clouded over with anger. "Those barbarians," he seethed, startling us with his accusing tone. "Don't you know they've already destroyed the sturgeon? Soon there will be none left." He returned to his grill, still scowling at the prospect, yet still ready to participate in the sturgeon's destruction.

DIMA WAS right about the sturgeon's future. After a decade of economic turmoil in Russia, the Caspian sturgeon was in serious trouble. For years, scientists had warned that the sturgeon was being wiped out by caviar poachers and uncontrolled fishing. But Russian officials either ignored the advice, or insisted that stocks were still abundant enough to justify a limited amount of commercial fishing.

There was little doubt that more caviar was being consumed

worldwide than ever. Even as sturgeon meat was going underground in Astrakhan's restaurants, caviar was becoming a standard item in the refrigerator cases of Western supermarkets. While I was in Moscow in the spring of 2000, I was able to buy a 100-gram jar—over two ounces—of very good osetra for twelve dollars in an upscale, Swiss-owned supermarket—and was then chided by my Russian friends for overpaying. But in Astrakhan, the epicenter of the international caviar trade, people had begun to think of caviar and sturgeon as relics of the past. On the same night Mira and I went hunting for sturgeon shashlik, huge crowds flocked to an outdoor concert sponsored by a Russian petroleum company to celebrate the first gusher of oil in the waters near Astrakhan. People told us that everything in Astrakhan now revolved around oil, the new source of riches from the Caspian.

Caviar had once been the source of Astrakhan's wealth. Sturgeon are found throughout the Northern Hemisphere, but nowhere in such numbers and variety as in the Caspian Sea. Its mildly saline waters contain a concentrated soup of sturgeon, including the three species most prized for their eggs: the beluga, the Russian sturgeon, and the stellate. These great gray beasts are marked by waves of sharp crests called scutes that run along their spine and sides, dramatically sloping snouts, and fleshy lips located on the undersides of their chins. They look as prehistoric as they are. Sturgeon have hardly changed in appearance since the days of the dinosaur.

Every spring, these ancient fish leave the Caspian Sea and begin their arduous journey up its tributaries to spawn. In doing so, they make themselves vulnerable to the thousands of fishermen who lie in wait along the riverbanks. Some sturgeon travel up the Volga River, toward Astrakhan, while others head east to the Ural River in Kazakhstan, or west to the Kura River in Azerbaijan. But whichever route they take, the

fishermen are there, drawing their huge nets across the water like floating fences, in the hope of catching a ripe female with a belly containing
a fortune in eggs.

Not all sturgeon eggs are alike. Each species produces its own dis-
tinctive roe. The beluga's gray eggs are nearly as big as ball bearings
and buttery in taste, and cost more than any other kind. The Russian
sturgeon give somewhat smaller but more intensely flavored beads that
are labeled osetra. The slim, streamlined stellate produces the briny,
pinhead sevruga eggs. Russians also like the small-grained roe of other
Caspian Sea sturgeons such as Shipp and sterlet, although these are
rarely sold in the West. Perfectly good black caviar can be made from
many of the twenty-seven varieties of sturgeon.

During the nineteenth century, in fact, most of the world's caviar
supply came not from the Caspian region, but from the rivers flowing
into the Atlantic Ocean. In the summer of 1913, when Khlebnikov ex-
iled himself to Astrakhan, the bustling Caspian port had only just over-
taken New Jersey's Delaware River as the world's main source of
sturgeon caviar. Until then, the roe of the Atlantic sturgeon and the
shovelnose supplied most of the world's caviar, although it had never
attained the quality of the Caspian varieties. With the American waters
fished clean, caviar companies flocked to Astrakhan's riverfront to satisfy the European craving for caviar. They quickly established canner-
ies and fleets of fishing boats.

By the time the Communists came to power in 1917, Astrakhan had
become the leading producer of caviar in the world. The Communists
nationalized the family-run caviar houses. But they were inexperienced
and caviar production fell drastically, and the delicacy seemed about to
go the way of the Romanov dynasty. But once the Communists mastered the production of caviar, the trade resumed on the same level, and
with the same customers, as before the revolution. The Soviet govern-

ment centralized production in a single, massive, but surprisingly efficient state monopoly that maintained high standards of quality control. Amid the profound political changes that followed the Soviet collapse in 1991, little attention was paid to the parallel collapse of the state-controlled caviar industry. Within a year, the trade had reverted back to private firms, as if the Communist regime had been a brief interruption. The state's boats and processing equipment were parceled out to a new generation of private Russian producers, all convinced there were plenty of sturgeon still in the sea.

EVGENY APTEKAR was one of those optimists. He had fallen into the caviar trade by accident in the mid-1990s, after losing his construction job. With factories shutting down all over Russia, it was clear there was no future in such work. But he wasn't sure what to do next. He was still in his twenties, lean and blond, with doughy features leavened by twinkling blue eyes. He tried working as a shuttle trader, traveling to places such as Turkey and Dubai to buy cheap consumer goods that could be sold back home in Russia.

After a few trips abroad, Evgeny decided that shuttle trading wasn't worth the effort. He realized that he could do better closer to home. Just a few blocks from where he lived in Astrakhan, a surviving caviar factory still turned out the one Russian product that the world wanted. He bought a few cases, took them on the train to Moscow, and sold the whole lot of caviar in a day. In time, he developed a list of foreign customers, dispensed with the long trips to Moscow, and started shipping caviar in quantity directly from Astrakhan to distributors in Europe and America.

By the end of the 1990s, Evgeny was a legal, recognized caviar wholesaler. His company, Karon-TM Ltd., produced and packed its own caviar. As his business grew, Evgeny gradually expanded into all aspects of caviar production. He bought a fleet of boats, a collection of nets, and some used canning equipment, then hired fishermen to work the Volga for sturgeon. His firm employed 350 people around the Astrakhan region. Evgeny moved his office into an old merchant's house in downtown Astrakhan. He had one of his former construction buddies install air conditioning, to help make the scorching Astrakhan summers bearable, and decorated his office with a collection of antique samovars. Business was so good that Evgeny could afford to send his two daughters to boarding school in England. After a decade in the caviar trade, he had a huge stake in the sturgeon's survival.

I had heard good things about Evgeny from Western dealers, and when I met him in Astrakhan, I understood why they liked him. Unlike many Russians who went into business after 1991, he did not model himself on characters in *The Godfather*—no gold chains, no thick-necked bodyguards, no thuggish posturing. When I walked into his office, he was wearing a pair of faded Levi's and a white crew shirt, and tapping steadily into a computer.

The caviar trade had become a form of high-stakes gambling for many Western importers. They were continually being ripped off by their Russian suppliers, who might promise fresh beluga and then deliver sour sevruga. You could make a quick profit that way, but Evgeny had long ago decided that he was in the caviar business for life. The best way to keep his Western customers, he believed, was to give them what they wanted.

Even with the best of intentions, that was not easy in Russia. Shipments were held up at customs while inspectors demanded bribes. Bureaucrats took weeks to process his manifests. But Evgeny learned to deal with them. His regular customers included Dieckmann & Hansen,

Germany's largest caviar house, and Caviarteria, a rapidly expanding New York firm.

In Astrakhan, Karon was still a small producer trying to become a big one. "You can only survive for a short time as a trader. You have to broaden your operation to survive," Evgeny said. By the spring of 2000, he was making plans to open a small sales office in New York. But just as his company was ready to expand, the Russian government announced it was going to crack down on the caviar trade.

During the chaotic years of the early 1990s, virtually everything was for sale in Russia. Anyone could go fishing for sturgeon and anyone could export caviar. That's how Evgeny got his start. But the free-for-all had taken its toll on the Caspian sturgeon population. Under prodding from the world's environmentalists, Moscow agreed to regulate the fishing. Evgeny learned that all caviar producers would need to buy a license to export their caviar abroad, where it could fetch as much as $500 a pound wholesale, ten times more valuable than in Russia.

That was just the first of many new rules. At the beginning of the spring fishing season in 2000, the Russian government realized that export licenses alone weren't enough to stop the poaching. Moscow would also have to limit fishing. For years, scientists had been urging Moscow to set realistic catch limits reflecting the true state of the sturgeon population. Evgeny learned that Russian scientists had fixed the total catch at just five hundred tons. The catch would be divided among a few big caviar producers, who would have to bid for a share of the total at a government auction. The winners would be assigned a quota based on their share.

Evgeny was determined to win a share of the catch. Without his own legal quota, he would be out of business. On the day of the auction, all the big producers submitted bids. Evgeny bid high. He felt he had taken his business too far to give up. Just to be on the safe side, he also submitted a bid for a share of Turkmenistan's catch. Turkmenistan, which hugs the eastern shore of the Caspian, had also agreed to introduce similar controls. Both of Evgeny's bids were successful, and he was assigned two catch quotas. His company was now one of just a dozen producers legally allowed to fish for migrating Caspian sturgeon. Evgeny thought his two shares would elevate him to the top tier of caviar producers.

By May 2000, midway through the main fishing season, Evgeny's expectations were far less grand. Instead of enjoying record sales, he felt he had made a terrible mistake. He told me he was starting to worry about catching enough sturgeon to recoup the cost of his investments in the fishing shares. Everyone knew that new government regulations hadn't stopped the poaching, yet he was still surprised at how much his daily catches had fallen. He wasn't at the panic stage. But he could not help noticing that his biggest competitor, a firm called Russkaya Ikra, had sent home all the employees from its processing plant because it had no roe to pack. Evgeny was also hearing rumors that an Armenian caviar firm based in Astrakhan was having trouble filling its quota. Every day, Evgeny received the daily catch reports from his Volga fishing stations. The numbers were terrible. Unless things picked up, Evgeny realized he wasn't going to be able to make his quota, either.

There was a way to make up the difference, Evgeny knew, but it wasn't quite legal. His fishermen were allowed to trawl only for sturgeon migrating up the Volga. But because sturgeon spawn only once every few years, there were still plenty of adult fish swimming around the Caspian Sea. Since he had already paid for his share of the sturgeon catch, Evgeny thought that the government should let him make up the difference by allowing fishing in the Caspian. But first he would need to talk to the scientists at the Caspian Fisheries Research Institute. They were the ones who monitored the Caspian sturgeon population and set the catch quotas. Only they could make it legal to fish in the sea.

BY CHANCE, I had already arranged to see one of the institute's top sturgeon specialists, Raisa Khodorevskaya. I had seen her name mentioned in dozens of scientific papers about the Caspian sturgeon, and I was eager to meet her.

The Caspian Fisheries Institute was created during Astrakhan's nineteenth-century caviar rush, and it had been incorporated into the Soviet Union's ambitious scientific program. But like all Soviet research institutes, it had fallen on hard times. The lobby was dark when Mira and I arrived in midmorning, and we fumbled through the unlit halls to Raisa's office. She was waiting for us in a large bare room at an old wooden school desk. Like many Russian scientists she worked without the benefit of a computer. Raisa was a warm, broad-hipped, broad-faced woman, with a natural inclination to cluck maternally at her visitors. She waved us in as she went to search for some chairs.

Raisa had devoted more than three decades to tracking the Caspian sturgeon. She was the first scientist to recognize the sharp drop in the catches in the early 1990s. Because she frequently went down to the fishing stations to talk to the fishermen, she knew that the ranks of poachers had swelled. While many poachers were poor villagers who fished out of desperation, poaching had become highly organized in places such as Daghestan. There, poaching gangs worked the Caspian in broad daylight, dragging their nets from large boats. By 1993, she was begging Moscow officials to do something. She wanted Boris Yeltsin's government to follow the Soviet-era fishing regulations. Eventually, her scientific papers on the declining sturgeon population caught the attention of Western environmentalists, who began to pressure Moscow to act.

Raisa's great victory was in helping to convince Moscow to sign an international treaty in 1998 regulating caviar exports. She lobbied the fisheries bureaucrats to reduce the Caspian sturgeon catch to five hundred tons, down from the twelve thousand tons officially hauled from Russian waters in 1990. Because the five-hundred-ton quota meant that only a handful of producers would be able to fish legally for sturgeon, she thought it would make it easier to detect the poachers. As part of the deal, the fisheries police promised to enforce a Soviet-era ban on open-sea fishing.

So, when Evgeny came to her and asked for permission to fish in the Caspian, Raisa was shocked. Raisa objected to fishing for sturgeon in the open sea for the same reasons that environmentalists oppose the clear-cutting of forests. When big trawlers drag their nets across the Caspian floor, they make no distinction between egg-laden female sturgeons, male sturgeons, juvenile sturgeons, or any other species of fish. Their long nets churn up the sea bottom, ravaging colonies of mollusks and worms that provide the bottom-feeding sturgeons with their most reliable meals. Even the Soviet Union, hardly the world's most environmentally conscientious nation, had imposed a ban on open-sea fishing in 1962, when it controlled four-fifths of the Caspian Sea. But with five nations now surrounding the Caspian Sea, it was impossible to get everyone to agree to the ban.

Russian poachers illegally scoured the Caspian Sea along with the Azeris, Daghestanis, Kazaks, and Turkmen. Russia still forbade its fishermen to trawl in the Caspian, but as Raisa knew, it was difficult to enforce the ban when the other countries averted their eyes and let their fishermen drag their nets freely through the sea. Evgeny's complaint was that the restrictions were unfair to law-abiding Russian producers like himself. He had followed the rules. He attended the auction and bought the right to fish. And yet the poachers who paid nothing could fish where and when they liked. Evgeny told Raisa that he would accept all sorts of controls if she would just relax the ban. Beginning to sound desperate, he promised to accept size limits, time limits. He even swore his fishermen would throw back juveniles. But Raisa wasn't buying any of it.

As a fish biologist who had studied the intimate habits of sturgeon, she knew how little time was left. Raisa believed that only a total ban on fishing would save the sturgeon. She had reluctantly accepted the five-hundred-ton catch quota, but only because it was the best compromise she could get from Moscow. It came as no surprise to her now that Evgeny couldn't catch his fill. She had predicted the crisis all along.

There was something else that worried her. The quota was expressed in terms of fish, not caviar, even though it was the eggs that drove the whole business. Producers like Evgeny paid the government for so many tons of sturgeon, but it was only caviar that they wanted. The male sturgeon and the immature females were just slightly better than worthless, as far as they were concerned. Among the fishermen, they were derided as "empties," while a sturgeon with a belly full of eggs was called a "cow." The empties were supposed to be counted toward the five-hundred-ton quota the same as the cows. But by May, Raisa was hearing alarming reports that the fishing companies were quietly discarding the males so they wouldn't be counted toward the quota. That meant that the actual legal catch was more like a thousand tons. As a result, female sturgeons were becoming even rarer than males. "Right now, only fifteen percent of the fish going upriver are females," Raisa confided to me when I mentioned Evgeny's proposal. "If the private companies take only females, what will be left?"

Intellectually, Evgeny understood the situation. He belonged to the new generation of caviar traders who realized you couldn't just keep taking from the sea. He was building a sturgeon-breeding farm, and this effort had endeared Evgeny to the institute's researchers. Together with Raisa and other scientists, Evgeny had supported Russia's decision to put the sturgeon on the international list of endangered species.

Evgeny's motives were not entirely selfless. He would be the first to admit it. He saw the quota system as a way of gaining an edge over the black market producers. The quota made it more difficult for poachers to move their caviar out of Russia. Abroad, caviar was more valuable than gold. Karon was one of just a dozen companies that could legally sell Russian caviar to high-profile foreign dealers such as Petrossian and Caviarteria.

But what use was access to Western markets now without caviar to sell? As the spring season progressed, Evgeny was growing more agitated. The daily totals that his fishermen reported were below his worst estimates. Even more troubling, nearly three-quarters of the fish caught were males.

His fears coalesced a few days after his talk with Raisa. All of Astrakhan's fish processors were grumbling about poor catches in the Caspian. It wasn't just sturgeon, they said, but every commercial species that migrated up the Volga in the spring—pike, carp, herring, even the lowly vobla, or roach, which was dried to the consistency of a wood board and chewed while drinking beer. The worst fears of the scientists were coming true. "Very soon, there will be no black caviar from the Caspian," Evgeny told me, now speaking as sourly as Dima.

But no one was ready to believe that the sea that had fed Russia for centuries was exhausted. Maybe it was just an off year, Evgeny suggested hopefully. Maybe the unusually high spring waters had delayed the sturgeon's spawning run. Maybe the poachers had better nets this year. Evgeny just wasn't sure. Maybe his fishermen weren't telling him everything.

It was one thing to get the daily catch reports by phone, another to be there when the nets were brought in. There were so few sturgeon now, you had to count every one. Evgeny decided it was time to send his trusted fishing manager, Venyamin Ivanovich, down to the delta.

"CIVILIZATION ends here," Venyamin Ivanovich crowed as the asphalt road ended, and he maneuvered his white Audi sedan onto the hard, sable-colored earth of the Caspian steppe, some 150 miles south of Astrakhan. He barely bothered to tap the brake as he took off across the parched grassland. Mira and I braced ourselves for a bumpy ride.

We were supposed to be going fishing for sturgeon, but there seemed nothing in this landscape to suggest the proximity of the lush Volga River Delta. Other than a pair of domesticated camels lounging in the scrub, we had seen no hint of human habitation for more than an hour. After several attempts, I realized there was no point asking Venyamin for a more detailed progress report. Even though he had joined the ranks of Russia's private businessmen, and bought himself a foreign car and a pair of wraparound sunglasses, Venyamin retained the manners of an old Soviet boss. He did not like questions. He preferred to lecture. So he continued to negotiate curves around the wind-carved earthen moguls, talking about sturgeon at his own pace.

Venyamin had no doubt learned the habit of hoarding information during the many years that he worked as the financial director of a Soviet factory. The Soviet Union was full of such steel gray, crew-cut managers. When the Communist system imploded many of them fought to hang on to their positions and prestige long after factories stopped producing anything, and many of them were reduced to joining the abject legions of the elderly who hawked their unwanted factory products on street corners.

Venyamin was one of the lucky ones. He landed a job with Evgeny Aptekar. It was a good match. Evgeny knew how to sell things. Venyamin could run a production operation. He knew sturgeon, too. Having grown up in the delta, Venyamin could tell a cow from an empty at a glance. His role now was to oversee Karon's fishing stations along the Volga, to make sure the caviar was processed correctly, and to keep everyone in the far-flung empire honest and hardworking. He wasn't the top boss anymore, but the fishermen knew enough to address him as "Mr. Director."

Just when it seemed as if Venyamin might drive us all the way across the steppe into Central Asia, a velvety green fissure appeared in the barren desert. The Volga is a startling sight. After the unremitting sterility of the steppe landscape, its banks appear as luxuriant as the Florida everglades. The willows and oaks along its edge rise up from spring floods like water nymphs released from a spell. But about two hundred yards inland is an arid, treeless plain. The contrast in landscapes grows more extreme as the Volga runs south, following its 2,300-mile course from the latitude of Moscow to the Caspian, transporting the melting snows of Russia's heartland to the desert steppe. As the river approaches the sea, it unfurls like an enormous green leaf, veined by hundreds of narrow channels. Europe's longest river becomes Europe's largest wetland, a silty, reed-choked oasis for birds, turtles, wolves, and the largest of freshwater fishes.

Our destination was an old Cossack settlement with the forlorn name of Wolves' Island, some four hours downriver from Astrakhan. The place had been founded, according to legend, in the late seventeenth century by a band of renegade Cossacks who were looking for a place to hide after a failed uprising against the tsar. It seemed as if only a handful of improvements had been made since then. The village now amounted to a few dozen tottering wood houses, so weather-beaten they appeared to merge into the dusty steppe. The fenced yards contained chickens, small gardens, and an assortment of rusted machine parts. The main street was an obstacle course of ruts and dirt mounds. It was hard to imagine the villagers coaxing any crops from the dry steppe soil. Venyamin was right about Wolves' Island. This was the end of civilization.

Wolves' Island owes its existence entirely to its strategic location on the edge of the delta. The village occupies the last scrap of dry land before the Volga pours into the sea. Because every sturgeon hoping to spawn in the Volga must pass through the labyrinth of reeds that encircles Wolves' Island, there is no better place to drop a net for sturgeon.

Writing about this part of the world two thousand years ago, Herodotus was struck by its savage, primal quality. The delta "has forty mouths, all but one issuing into swamp and marshland, where men are said to live who eat raw fish." The abundance of such fish has drawn nomads to the delta since ancient times, but permanent settlers didn't come to Wolves' Island until the Cossacks arrived. The fishing was good and they stayed. Their descendants earned their living supplying the Astrakhan caviar houses. When the Soviet government came along in 1917, the villagers were organized into fishing collectives called kolkhozs. For the seventy years of Communism, the inhabitants of the village supplied the state with black caviar, which was sold to the West for hard currency. With the collapse of the Soviet Union, the dusty, out-of-the-way town might have been returned to the wolves if Evgeny Aptekar had not come along and hired its fishermen to work for Karon.

By necessity, sturgeon fishermen in the Volga Delta worked in teams. While it is possible for one man to catch a sturgeon with a hook and a line, hauling up one of the great gray beasts demands many hands. When open-mesh gill nets were introduced in the late nineteenth century, sturgeon fishing became even more of a team effort. Originally made of cotton, and later of tough nylon filament, these mesh nets themselves could weigh hundreds of pounds. Each team staked out its own fishing grounds, called *tonyas*. No other team could fish there. The tonya fishermen built small huts on their section of the riverbank to mark their turf and give them a place to cook and nap. In the old days, these huts offered a shady spot to make caviar, too.

Down at the Wolves' Island bank, one of Karon's boat pilots had been waiting all morning to shuttle us over to the village tonya, which was located some distance from the village itself. As we entered the delta thicket, I immediately understood why Venyamin needed a professional pilot to navigate the delta. High bulrushes walled in the channel, blocking any view of the delta except for the bands of sky and water. Steering the small outboard through the narrow passages was like driving through a car wash at high speed, only reeds thwacked at the sides of the boat instead of brushes. After the bleakness of the steppe, the ride through the delta was exhilarating. The delta was as alive as the steppe was dead. Blue herons skimmed overhead and marsh ducks poked their heads underwater for fish. Our path was lit by colonies of brilliant yellow lotuses. I found myself daydreaming about how easy it would be for the pilot to cut the motor, glide his boat behind a screen of reeds, and drop a line for sturgeon. Venyamin must have been having the same thought. Nodding amiably at the pilot, he yelled over the roar of the motor, "This guy is one of the poachers." The pilot, a well-tanned young man in army fatigues, just smiled a guilty grin.

For someone working for a legitimate caviar producer, Venyamin had a strange fascination with poachers. He was always telling us stories about how easy it was to get around the fishing restrictions. He even boasted about a friend who dealt in black market caviar. The guy made a good living buying caviar on the Daghestan side of the Caspian and transporting it to dealers in Poland. The Daghestan caviar cost a dollar a pound, a price that was even less in absolute terms than the Cossacks received for their caviar a century ago. But unlike the Cossacks, Venyamin's friend had to pay thousands of dollars in bribes to the highway police to smuggle the contraband through Russia and Belarus to the Polish border. Despite this hefty toll, Venyamin said his friend still managed to take home five thousand dollars for delivering four hundred pounds of caviar to his Polish connection. The Poles earned the big money by moving the caviar into Western Europe or America. Venyamin marveled at the idea of selling caviar without the constraints of government quotas or regulations.

All this talk of caviar must have stoked Venyamin's appetite. When the boat touched the tonya's makeshift dock, he leapt onto shore without waiting for us, roaring, "Where's lunch?"

Nikolai, the tonya foreman, a balding man in his late forties who had been helping the team let out the nets, rushed over to greet his boss. "Mr. Director," he gushed, pumping his hand theatrically. Venyamin gave him a familiar slap on the back and then headed for the kitchen. His inspection tour would have to wait.

No sooner had we sat down at the plank table than Venyamin began passing around enormous bowls of steaming soup, the broth as yellow as the lotuses we had just passed in the delta. I was startled to see the familiar chunks of fish bobbing on the surface. My bowl alone must have contained a pound of sturgeon meat, enough to make the plate I had in Astrakhan look like a snack.

The soup was *ukha*, the breakfast, lunch, and dinner of tonya fishermen, a worthy rival to a Marseilles bouillabaisse and a New England chowder. It was traditional for the tonya cook to keep a pot on simmer, replenishing it through the day with fresh catches. Delta fishermen expect to find sturgeon in their ukha, just as Yankee fishermen expect cod in their chowder. But because of all the eulogies for the sturgeon I had been hearing in Astrakhan, I assumed that ukha would be a thing of the past, that the fish had become too rare to waste on fishermen or their guests.

Sturgeon soup is incredibly filling stuff, perfect for the calorie-consuming work of fishing. The meat is said to have more cholesterol and fat than pork. After half a bowl each, Mira and I could not imagine eating again for days. But soon a second sturgeon course appeared on the table, this time the raw sturgeon that Herodotus described, an entire bucketful. Called *balyk*, it had been sprinkled with salt that morning, packed with layers of onions, and set out in the sun to marinate. If we didn't try some, I knew Venyamin would be annoyed, and he was prickly enough already. I picked up a small chunk of fish. Pairing it with the crusty bread, I briefly considered a new theory for the sturgeon's demise: the fishermen were eating them all. Or maybe Mira and I were to blame. Stuffed as we were, we couldn't stop chewing on the tangy pieces.

Venyamin left the mess room as abruptly as he had arrived and swaggered down to the bank. He wanted to see how many sturgeon the fishermen were bringing in. The mesh was just being let out from a winch bolted to the deck of a small tug. Two fishermen stood on either side of the winch, guiding the net into the water. The net slid in as lightly as a ribbon coming off a spool. Meanwhile, a dozen men from the tonyas stood in the shallow water waiting to grab the slack. When the tug had released the entire net, it would partition an area of the river more than four hundred yards across. That was nearly as long as two city blocks. The mesh of this immense net was hardly bigger than my hand, small enough to catch a herring. To keep the heavy net from sinking to the bottom, a necklace of plastic floats had been attached to the top edge.

Opening such a large net was slow work. It took thirty minutes for the boat to reach the opposite bank. Then it made a U-turn and started back toward us, forming a large corral that stretched all the way to the river bottom. At its full extension, the net fell twenty-two yards below the surface.

The quest for the world's greatest luxury turned out to be exceedingly dull work. River fishing has none of the danger, uncertainty, or romance associated with the ocean kind. It is a mechanical process. All day long, the tug drags the net across the channel, then pulls it in again like a noose. As soon as the fish are removed from its grasp, the operation starts all over again. The fishermen spend most of their time standing around in the chilly water, holding up the edge of the net to keep it from tangling.

Venyamin watched intently as the fishermen tightened the noose. A second winch on shore was taking most of the weight, but the fishermen formed a cordon around the net, using all their strength to keep the fish inside. They didn't want their catch swimming out the top. As the circle grew smaller, we could see silvery fish trapped inside. The net had trapped everything in its path—pike, carp, herring, sterlet, as well as sturgeon. Venyamin cared only about one thing.

"How many sturgeon did you get?" he called to the fishermen.

"Not one," the foreman Nikolai answered officiously.

"I see a stellate," insisted Venyamin. The net was twenty feet away, a tangled mass of wildly flapping fish. "And a Russian sturgeon with caviar," he added.

With a final heave, the men bunched the net into a tight wad. Then, crouching slightly, as if they were raising a medicine ball, they emptied the twitching contents into a shallow boat. Nothing that had been in the river at the moment the net was drawn had escaped. When a few fish tried to jump over the sides of the boat, the fishermen grabbed them with their bare hands and tossed them back into the boat. The men hurriedly sorted the different varieties into crates. But no large sturgeon emerged out of the slimy heap.

Venyamin was twitching as much as the fish. His eyes puffed with fury. This was worse, much worse than his boss, Evgeny, had feared.

Then Nikolai, the foreman, appeared from behind the boat, looking serious. He was swinging two slim stellates by the tails. Empties, he informed Venyamin. Whether they were male or female didn't matter, only that their bellies held no eggs.

Without bothering to inspect them, Venyamin turned to walk away. His whole body vibrated in anger. He had been wrong about the Russian sturgeon. And if that wasn't irritating enough, his men had not caught a single cow all afternoon. He would have to call Evgeny with the news: Karon had used up two more sturgeon from its quota and had no caviar to show for it.

Just then, the sound of laughter prompted Venyamin to turn around. Nikolai was standing ankle deep in the water trying to control a Russian sturgeon almost as big as himself. Its smooth belly glowed a brilliant china white in the afternoon light. On its underside, where its chin should be, a pair of large fleshy lips opened and closed like a blinking eye. Except for those pathetic gasps for air, this powerfully built creature put up no resistance, as if it were already resigned to its fate. Just in case, a fisherman whacked the sturgeon hard on the head with a club. Its lips went slack, but it was only knocked out. Karon was now three fish closer to filling its quota.

"It's with caviar," Venyamin shouted as he bent over the prostrate fish. "You can see the curve in the belly near the genitals," he explained, now more animated than he had been the entire trip. "If the tail is narrow, the caviar is good. You press the belly. It's soft where the caviar is."

How strange that Venyamin could be jubilant over a single female sturgeon. In the nineteenth century, Cossack fishermen hauled in sturgeon by the hundreds. Even in the 1980s, Soviet fishermen routinely found seven or eight sturgeon twisting inside each net they pulled to the surface. Venyamin's crew brought in only half that many sturgeon and only one of them a cow. Her eggs weren't even mature, Venyamin concluded after pressing the belly. He instructed Nikolai to keep the fish alive in a floating cage until the eggs ripened. If the Russian sturgeon yielded twenty pounds of good osetra, the fish would be worth more than six thousand dollars to Evgeny.

The Wolves' Island fishermen were hardly the only ones in the delta who had worked a whole afternoon that day to catch a single female sturgeon. There are hundreds of identical tonyas arrayed along the Volga, from Wolves' Island to the town of Ikryanoye—literally Caviarville—near Astrakhan. I spent a day at a tonya near Ikryanoye where the only sturgeon caught in a day of work was an infant, a mere eighteen inches long.

With all these tonyas spreading their nets like a gauntlet, how did a sturgeon have any chance of making it upriver to spawn? If, by some stroke of luck, a sturgeon escaped the bottom draggers in the Caspian, found its way into the delta, and evaded the river nets and the legions of poachers, it would still have to swim hundreds of miles past Astrakhan to its traditional spawning grounds. And for the biggest of the sturgeon, those grounds were blocked by the Volgograd Dam.

Venyamin signaled that it was time to head back to the village. The tonya's tugboat was inching across the channel, beginning the process of laying the net all over again. Everywhere in the delta, tonya fishermen were playing out the same ritual. During the fishing season, two shifts of fishermen keep the tonyas working round the clock.

Just before we settled back into our boat, Venyamin stopped briefly to talk to the foreman, Nikolai. When he joined us again, I noticed he was holding a sack. The two empty stellates were inside. "Are you going to make ukha," I joked. Back to his usual taciturn self, Venyamin did not bother to answer me.

The fact was, it didn't matter what Venyamin did with them. At that moment, everyone in the boat back to Wolves' Island understood that those two males were never going to be counted in the quota.

Part One

The Invention
of Caviar

1

· · · ❧ · · ·

How to Catch
a Sturgeon

*The Khazars believe that deep in the inky blackness of the
Caspian Sea there is an eyeless fish that, like a clock,
marks the only correct time in the universe.*

—MILORAD PAVIC, DICTIONARY OF THE KHAZARS

*A*ccording to all the usual rules of evolution, the sturgeon should be
extinct already.

Sturgeon are in no hurry to reproduce. They take almost as long as
a human being to reach sexual maturity. While a single fish may carry
millions of eggs in its belly, the odds are that only a single hatchling will
survive into adulthood. That lone offspring will then have to risk its life
to reproduce. Swimming upriver along the same course its parents took,
the young sturgeon will ramble leisurely through narrow channels

where even the least enterprising of its human predators can easily pluck it from the water.

It was not always this way. The sturgeon had already been making its way up the earth's rivers for 250 million years when human beings first appeared. Sturgeon are older than the dinosaurs. They were already ancient when such bony fish as the perch, cod, and striped bass began to appear. Yet, even as the earth cooled, dinosaurs veered into extinction, and mammals came to dominate the land, the dogged sturgeon somehow kept plodding along. It remains a big, slow-moving beast, sweetly curious about the goings-on above its head and lumpenly passive when it runs into danger. Scientists call the fish a living fossil because the sturgeon have changed little over the millennia. A sturgeon caught today could fit more or less neatly into a petrified impression left by its Jurassic counterpart.

Today sturgeon live exclusively in the waters of the Northern Hemisphere. Most sturgeon are anadromous, which means they make their homes in the sea and commute to rivers to spawn. They are usually most comfortable someplace between the two, in the brackish deltas and tidal estuaries where salt water and fresh water collide. These mildly saline border zones nourish immense numbers of small creatures such as worms and crayfish, which keep the bottom-feeding sturgeon well fed. The Caspian's fame as the ideal home for sturgeon is due to the fact that it is more of a salty lake than a real sea. The northern portion of the Caspian, where the Volga spills into the sea, is unusually shallow and warm, and contains the highest concentration of sturgeon in the world.

The sturgeon still looks like an animal that might have cavorted with the dinosaurs. Young sturgeon have a puppy-like cuteness, as well as a curious nature, but with age their features grow more jowly, bloated, and monstrous in size. Perhaps as compensation for its passive nature, the sturgeon's grayish tree trunk of a body is sheathed in a protective bony mantle. Five rows of hard plates, or scutes, run along its sides and spine like ranges of tiny mountains, each peak rising to a point sharp enough to inflict a painful wound on less hard-bodied creatures. To complete their menacing image, sturgeon have big sharklike tails that can deliver a powerful blow.

It is the sturgeon's huge sloping head that seems to mark it as a holdover of another time. The head is out of all proportion to the rest of its body. When viewed from the top or sides, the sturgeon's snout may look no more unusual than a shark's head. But the sturgeon has no powerful jaws to open, no dagger teeth with which to rip its food to shreds. The sturgeon's mouth is tucked far under its chin, close to its belly, and there is not a single tooth inside. Skimming over the sea floor, the sturgeon extends its soft blubbery lips like a hose to vacuum up larvae and mollusks embedded in the silt. Four fat whiskers under its chin act as sensors to identify the choice morsels. Without them, this half-blind, ancient creature would hardly know what its toothless mouth was up to.

Despite its antiquated, tubular mouth, the sturgeon is a machine designed for eating. The word *sturgeon* comes from the German verb *störer*, which means "to root." After nosing around up to its eyeballs in the mud, the sturgeon uses its powerful tail to swoosh the food toward its mouth. It swallows everything whole, even clams in their shells. Sturgeon are opportunistic feeders, happy to stray from their standard diet when something interesting comes along. The bigger sturgeon, such as the beluga, will sometimes go after herring, ducks, even baby seals, while the Pacific Ocean's white sturgeon routinely dines on dead salmon that float downriver after spawning. Sometimes after a frenzy of feeding, the sturgeon will leap joyfully out of the water, like a shimmering phantom from the deep, frightening the life out of fishermen in small boats.

So far, scientists have identified twenty-seven species of sturgeon in the *Acipenser* order. The number is a subject of dispute because scientists are always arguing over what actually constitutes a distinct sturgeon species. The fish that produces osetra caviar, for instance, is called the Russian sturgeon by the Russians and the Persian sturgeon by the Iranians, but scientists now suspect they are the same species, *Acipenser gueldenstaedtii*. The *gueldenstaedtii* also shows up in the Black Sea, off the coasts of Romania and Ukraine. The Romanians call it *nisetru*, while it's just plain Russian sturgeon to the Ukrainians. The two other sturgeon species famed for their caviar, the beluga and the stellate, the mother of sevruga, also happen to be found in both the Caspian and Black Seas.

Many people think a sturgeon is just a sturgeon, but the twenty-seven varieties vary enormously in appearance and size. The beluga, or *Huso huso*, can easily weigh a ton, making it the largest freshwater fish on earth. As it ages, it takes on the aerodynamic proportions of a blimp. Its elongated snout becomes rounder and less pronounced. At the opposite extreme is the svelte sterlet, the *Acipenser ruthenus*, which rarely weighs more than twelve pounds. The sterlet is the only Russian sturgeon that does not venture into the sea. Celebrated for its flesh rather than its eggs, the yard-long fish is still caught in the rivers of Eastern Europe, central Russia, and Siberia.

Because the sturgeon always returns to the same place to spawn, certain species are found only in a single river basin. The Adriatic sturgeon exists only in the Adriatic along the coasts of Italy, Greece, and Albania. The few remaining specimens of the common European sturgeon inhabit the Mediterranean regions of France and Spain. The

Atlantic sturgeon is native to the East Coast of the United States. The Pacific white sturgeon, which nearly rivals the beluga in size, spends all its time in the waters of California, Washington, and British Columbia, trying to satisfy its voracious appetite.

The sturgeon's constant eating makes for a big fish. Since sturgeon never really stop growing, the older ones tend to be immense. The beluga, which may live more than a century, will swell in girth until it is as big around as a man's hug and twice as long as a pickup truck. The largest beluga on record weighed 4,570 pounds and stretched twenty-eight feet. Caught in 1736, it was an empty, presumably male. But some thirty years later, Cossacks on the Ural River recorded a female beluga weighing a mere 2,520 pounds. She reportedly yielded an impressive nine hundred pounds of roe, which would have made her worth half a million dollars at today's prices.

North American varieties of sturgeon can also attain similar gargantuan proportions. A Pacific white sturgeon, the *Acipenser transmontanus,* pulled from the Fraser River near Vancouver in the 1890s tipped the scale at 1,600 pounds, and measured eighteen feet from nose to tail, longer than the dinghy the fishermen used to catch it. The averages are even more impressive than the extremes: in the 1860s, the typical white sturgeon weighed 500 pounds. Such giants would be inconceivable today because few sturgeon are allowed to live long enough to amass such bulk.

No matter what its size, a good deal of a sturgeon's poundage is devoted to reproduction. A female's eggs can account for 15 percent of her body weight. It is not unusual for one female to carry around 10 million eggs. The bigger the mother sturgeon, the bigger the individual eggs. The three giants of the sturgeon family—the beluga, the kaluga, and the white sturgeon—produce dark gray beads roughly the size of the capital O on this page. The roe of the kaluga, which roams the

Amur River between Russia and China, is sometimes passed off as beluga caviar because the two are so similar, although kaluga caviar lacks the brininess of beluga. While the white sturgeon eggs are a little smaller, they have an intense flavor. Size is not everything when it comes to caviar. Large beluga eggs sometimes lack the intense, oceanic zing of more fine-grained varieties. Connoisseurs insist that they prefer pinhead sevruga eggs, which are only half the size of beluga caviar.

Caviar can be made from the roe of any sturgeon except the green sturgeon, a rare species that inhabits the Pacific coast of California. Both its eggs and flesh are said to be poisonous. For much of the twentieth century, only the roe of the beluga, Russian sturgeon, and stellate were considered fit for making caviar. But as the numbers of these sturgeon have dwindled, caviar makers have turned to such scorned varieties as the white sturgeon, the Mississippi shovelnose, the Missouri paddlefish, and the Atlantic Sturgeon.

Sturgeon eggs vary in color, from black to olive green to mustard. Beluga eggs are often grayer than the Russian sturgeon's osetra. The diverse shadings are usually a reflection of what the fish ate and how ripe the eggs were when the fish was caught. A sturgeon taken too early in the spawning cycle, like those caught at sea, will have jet-black eggs, but they will be gooey with fat and won't deliver a satisfying pop when eaten. As the fish gets closer to spawning, its eggs become lighter, tauter, and more flavorful. Fishermen insist that the best caviar comes from fish caught three or four days before spawning. If they catch a sturgeon too early in its migration, they often keep it alive until the eggs are ripe. In the Caspian, where some sturgeon spawn in the spring and others in the fall, caviar made from the spring catch is said to be more flavorful than the production from the fall migration.

For centuries, connoisseurs have been fascinated by the subtle variations in different types of caviar. The rarest and most expensive type is easily identified by its unusual pale, yellowish color. Known as golden caviar, it is the stuff of legend. In tsarist times, golden caviar was so venerated that all specimens were supposed to be delivered to the royal court. Stalin later emulated this practice. Perhaps the rulers saw their own image reflected in the glow of the golden eggs. Scientists now believe that these eggs, if fertilized, would produce albino sturgeon. Despite the high price golden caviar commands, some dealers say that it is actually quite bland, proving that taste is determined as much by the eye as the mouth.

THE STURGEON needs a multitude of eggs because its chances of producing an offspring are incredibly slim. The smallest of the sturgeon do not spawn for the first time until they are more than six years old. But jumbo varieties such as the beluga and kaluga, as well as some northern paddlefish, only reach maturity when they are well into their twenties. Before the days when Caspian poachers scoured the open sea for sturgeon, the juveniles there could at least count on a carefree youth. These days, a sturgeon's life typically ends while it is still a teenager.

When a sturgeon does get a chance to spawn, at least it does not have to concern itself with eating. As it heads upriver, the sturgeon lives mostly off its fat, its mind focused on nature's imperative. Pushing against the current, the sturgeon travels about twenty miles a day for several weeks until it reaches its spawning grounds. Sturgeon are extremely choosy about where they will lay their eggs. The fish's internal wiring demands that it return to the same area, even to the same spot, where it was hatched many years earlier. A stellate born in the Volga River would never consider a trip up the Kura River, although both waterways drain into the Caspian, and both are host to populations of stellates. If a dam blocks the way to a sturgeon's birthplace, it will refuse to spawn. The beluga, for instance, no longer reproduces naturally in the Volga or the Danube because its ancient spawning grounds are dammed.

When the sturgeon finally arrives at the spot where it and all its ancestors were born, the parameters for successful spawning grow even more precise. The sturgeon needs to find a rocky stretch of river to lay her eggs. The water should be shallow, but washed by a strong current.

While fertilization is a highly impersonal affair for most fish, sturgeon do it differently. A nineteenth-century sturgeon expert named John A. Ryder discovered that as the roe sturgeon approaches her spawning place, the male fish will pick up her scent and swim to join her. The males pull up alongside roe fish, pressing their bodies tightly against her abdomen, a behavior that stimulates the female to release her eggs, and the males their fertilizing milt. If the female sturgeon fails to meet a potential mate on the trip upriver, she will rub her belly against the hard rocky surface, and hope a male will come along later to fertilize them. Nowadays, with so few sturgeon around, such serendipity is rare.

Within a day, the fertilized eggs hatch into thousands of frenetic, transparent fish fry. Most will be eaten by bigger fish, including the sturgeon themselves. Pollution and sickness will kill others. Of the survivors, only a handful of fingerlings will have the energy to swim downstream to the sea. Rarely does more than one make it all the way.

Left to themselves, sturgeon might very well continue happily in their inefficient ways. Ovid, who lived near today's Black Sea port of Constanta, called the sturgeon a "pilgrim of the most illustrious waves." Unlike salmon, which die at the end of an exhausting migration, sturgeon live to spawn again. A beluga can produce eggs every seven years; other sturgeon may swell as frequently as every two years. As compensation for its inefficient habits, nature gives a sturgeon as many as ten chances to reproduce over its long life. Since it only needs to generate two adult offspring during its lifetime to keep the population stable, the odds for the next generation are reasonably good as long as the sturgeon keeps traveling upriver every few years.

The trouble is that hardly any sturgeon get to make the trip anymore.

WHEN THE French storyteller, epicure, and traveler Alexandre Dumas stood on the banks of the Volga in the 1850s to observe the caviar harvest, it must have seemed that the sturgeon would never stop coming. At a spot much like the Wolves' Island tonya, Dumas saw an immense log fence blocking the sturgeons' path up the river. It was impossible for the big fish to get past the barrier, built on sturdy pilings sunk hard into the river mud, yet they would not turn around. Bunched up at the fence was a huge traffic jam of flapping sturgeon, most of them beluga.

As they pushed and shoved, the fish impaled themselves on a line of floating hooks dangling in front of the fence. "In less than an hour and a half, we watched them take 120 or 130 fish," Dumas marveled. With the efficiency of workers on an assembly line, the fishermen towed the beluga to the slaughtering pen. These were good-sized specimens, weighing as much as eight hundred pounds. Some continued to twist and gasp even after their bellies were slit and the egg sacks yanked out. The processing was "utterly revolting," Dumas complained, before accepting a gift of caviar taken from the largest sturgeon. There was enough roe from the one fish to fill eight casks, each holding ten pounds.

For such an immense animal, the sturgeon is relatively easy to catch. A sturgeon may balk about being diverted from its migration, but with none of the strength or mettle of a tuna or striped bass. The sturgeon's "resistance is less than that of algae," the Hungarian anthropologist Geza de Rohan-Csermak once observed. An overstatement perhaps, but there is no doubt that sturgeon are an unusually passive fish. Scientists say an injured sturgeon will shut down into a state of suspended animation, as if it believes that playing dead is a better strategy than putting up a good fight.

This does not mean that trapping a sturgeon requires no ingenuity. Until nylon was invented, cotton fishing nets were virtually useless against sturgeon, whose sharp bony plates ripped right through the mesh. As early as the fourteenth century, Volga River fishermen built the log fences Dumas observed in the rivers to corral the fish into a small area. But they still needed a way to pull the trapped sturgeon out of the water. It would never occur to most sturgeon to bite at a baited hook, since they don't snap at their food like perch or cod. Eventually fishermen realized it would be easier to hook the sturgeon by the tail instead of the mouth. They just needed the right kind of hook.

They began experimenting with hooks that could be fixed in place just a few inches above the bottom of the river, where sturgeon usually feed. Instead of using the standard, J-shaped hook, fishermen fashioned multibarbed hooks that looked like tiny anchors. The second-century Greek writer Aelianus, who was fascinated by fishermen in the Danube, explained that the hooks were kept bobbing in place by tying a piece of lung meat to the line. The lung, usually from a bull, was buoyant enough to serve as a float in the days before cork became available. The fisherman would then secure his line to a yoke of oxen standing on the bank.

When a curious sturgeon came along to inspect the float, its constantly twitching tail would invariably become caught on the sharp tip of the sturgeon hook. Other types of fish might take off with the hook still embedded in their flesh, but not most sturgeon. All the oxen had to do was pull it up on the shore. Implausible as this method sounds, it dominated sturgeon fishing from the Volga to the Danube for centuries.

If one such hook was good for catching sturgeon, then a hundred were even better. As the market for caviar increased, the system grew more elaborate. Fishermen strung necklaces of hooks across the channels so that a sturgeon chugging upriver could hardly avoid bumping into the web of sharp prongs and impaling itself. By the middle of the nineteenth century, the mouth of the Danube was so crowded with hooks, ships were unable to pass during the sturgeon season. In the Fraser River of British Columbia, a single firm oversaw a network of twenty thousand hooks. The trouble with these hook lines was that they snared everything that came along, juveniles and mature fish alike, decimating the sturgeon population. Starting with Peter the Great, Russian authorities made repeated attempts to outlaw the hook tackle, which is called *snast*. But even today, the snast remains the method of choice for sturgeon poachers in the Volga Delta, who find them easier to conceal than nets.

The deadly snast is even more effective when combined with the kind of weir that Dumas described. By the eighteenth century, Volga fishing companies were erecting impenetrable wooden fences in the rivers as fast as they could. These fences were as dangerous for the fishermen as it was for the fish. After touring the fishing sites along the Volga in 1770, the Russian naturalist Samuel Gemelin was appalled by the gruesome conditions in which the fishermen worked. To build these weirs, he wrote in a report to the St. Petersburg Academy of Sciences, divers spent seven to ten minutes at a time on the river bottom, pounding the wooden pilings into the mud. By the time they returned to the surface, their noses were streaming with blood from staying underwater too long. The men would rest just long enough to down a shot of vodka, then return to the chilly bottom again. After a few seasons of such work, the men lost their hearing and sight. Many died within a few years of taking up diving.

But like the snast lines, log weirs were strikingly effective. Together, these two innovations turned sturgeon fishing into an industrial process. By today's standards, the catches were enormous. Gemelin reported seeing Volga fishermen take 250 beluga an hour, and estimated the annual catch in that river was between fifty thousand and eighty thousand fish. A century later, Northwest Coast Indians in British Columbia adopted similar wooden weirs. Once the fish were trapped, the Indians liked to stand in their canoes and plunge a harpoon into the fish's flesh. Eventually such dramatic methods were replaced by a sharp grappling hook, which could be used to snag the fish and roll it into the boat.

As materials for making nets became stronger in the late nineteenth century, fishermen gave up their snasts, spears, and fences. Small mesh nets made from tough monofilament are now widespread in the Caspian. Curiously, sport fishermen along the Pacific Coast are the only ones who catch sturgeon with a single baited hook. They cast for white sturgeon the same way they might go after a tuna. The fish actually fights to keep the bait, leaping repeatedly into the air until it rolls over, exhausted.

PERHAPS NINETEENTH-CENTURY Russian fishermen would have captured even more sturgeon if they had not imposed their own peculiar restrictions. These had nothing to do with the efficiency of hooks or sturgeon weirs. Rather, the Russian industry was governed by a web of superstition and tradition that determined when and how fishing took place. In 1861, a state fisheries inspector who went by the signature *A. Ya. Shulz* was astounded by the complex and seemingly irrational excuses the fishermen had invented to justify not fishing. He found that they would refuse to touch their tackle:

"If before their departure to the tonya, or already on their way there, they met a priest."

"If a hare runs across the road, they will knit their brows and come back home, and everybody will consider it quite reasonable as far as circumstances are concerned, otherwise misfortune would have befallen them without fail."

"It is also an omen, if on the way out a stranger asks for money or something in the house."

"Or, if it so happens, that on the way to the tonya, a snake is seen floating across the river, it is considered an attribute of misfortune."

"If they happen to touch a pike with an oar and the pike is then thrown into a boat, as quite often happens, the pike will be cut into small pieces and thrown out of the boat from both sides into the water. Otherwise this meeting is considered to be a true sign of death or serious illness of one of the fishermen present in the boat."

YET SOMEHOW the fishing got done, Shulz marveled. The catch that year was so "mythical" in size, he wrote to his superiors in St. Petersburg, that "it can easily seem incredible to a non-eyewitness." So abundant were the sturgeon in the Volga that undersized fish were dumped in the trash, he reported.

A completely different set of customs prevailed on the Ural River, which also flows into the Caspian. While the Volga fishing was dominated by big companies, independent fishermen still worked the Ural. Most of them were Cossacks, the fierce Slavic horsemen who served as the tsar's border guards. As payment for their military service, they had been given exclusive rights by the tsar to fish in the Ural River during the sturgeon migration. Not even private ships were allowed to sail upriver when the sturgeon were spawning. According to Nicholas Borodine, a nineteenth-century sturgeon expert who was descended from Cossacks, the Ural fishermen were careful not to exhaust the tsar's gift. They intentionally limited the length of the fishing season to ensure that some sturgeon were able to spawn. While their Volga counterparts were fishing madly into midsummer, the Ural Cossacks did not catch their first sturgeon until September 17. On that day, hundreds of Cossacks gathered on the shore with boats and hooks. No fishing could begin until the Cossack *ataman*, or chief, fired a cannon signaling the start of the season. At the shot, some six thousand Cossacks in lightweight barks would all rush together into the same section of the river. Since they had built log weirs to trap the sturgeon, there was not much of a contest. The Cossacks used nets, hook lines, and harpoons to scoop out the trapped fish. By the end of the day, a mountain of sturgeon had been piled on the bank.

The Ural Cossacks were able to hold off their fishing until September because the Caspian Sea sturgeon stagger their migrations over the seasons. While more than half the mature sturgeon head upriver between February and June, the rest wait until autumn to make the trip. Some fish start the trip just before the river freezes and spend the winter hibernating under the ice, standing straight up with their noses in the mud until the thaw. The Ural Cossacks were permitted a few days of ice fishing each year. They gathered by the hundreds with long, hooked spears that could be jammed through holes in the ice and thrust into the sides of the hibernating sturgeon.

For the Cossacks, sturgeon fishing was about more than caviar. They also fished for food. The thick slabs of meat would sustain their families through the harsh winter on the barren steppe. The sturgeon's flesh would be salted in long fillets that can be thinly sliced like smoked salmon. Russians consider the sturgeon's spinal cord, or *visigia*, as much a delicacy as caviar. The cord is ripped out from the sturgeon's backbone, dried, tied into switches, and used to make a strong, flavorful soup. A century ago, fishermen also collected the swim bladders, which were boiled down for isinglass, an early form of plastic immortalized in the surrey song from the musical *Oklahoma*. The isinglass had many other uses, too. It could be distilled to make glue, clarify beer, and stiffen homemade jellies. Until packaged gelatin came along, isinglass was indispensable in the kitchen.

The first thing a fisherman did before tending to any of these products was to remove the precious ovarian sacks from the sturgeon's womb. The operation takes only few strokes of the knife, but unless it is correctly done the caviar will be ruined. Processing caviar requires a quick hand, good judgment, and a certain cold-blooded resolve. The first rule, and the one most often ignored by poachers, is never make caviar from a dead sturgeon. The fish should still be gasping for breath when the knife rips down her leathery belly, otherwise harmful enzymes will seep into the ovaries and flesh. Poachers, who may check their snast lines only every couple of days, are notorious for carving up the dead sturgeon they find floating on their hooks. The enzymes may merely give the caviar a mushy taste, or they can also make the eater very sick.

So exacting is the process of making caviar that it is a specialized profession in Russia. After the fish is landed, a skilled *ikryanchik*—a caviar master—drags the fish to a shady spot. It could be under the nearest tree or a more sanitary processing plant. The ikryanchik snips out the ovarian sacks from the fish's belly and begins to transform the grayish lumps into the delicacy we know as caviar. In smaller sturgeon, each of these sacks would be about the size of a chicken and have the unappealing look of wet cardboard. The ovaries of a beluga may each be as large as a sheep. The ikryanchik must act quickly after he makes the cut. Even eggs taken at their peak can lose their flavor if they sit too long. Some experts insist that the ikryanchik has exactly thirteen minutes, others insist that five-minute caviar is the best. Poachers may waste hours before mixing the caviar, especially when they are trying to avoid detection. The result can be bland and mushy.

Caviar is still an exclusively handmade, artisanal food. The ikryanchik starts by gently massaging the ovaries through a mesh screen so that the individual beads sift slowly into a bowl. The sifting must be done with great care to avoid crushing the eggs. When the beads have been completely separated from the membrane, they are rinsed in salt water. The ikryanchik then mixes in good-quality loose salt, until it reaches about 4 percent of the total weight of the eggs. A good ikryanchik does not rely on formulas, but adjusts the salt to account for the season, type of eggs, and their quality. There are even some buyers who claim they can identify the ikryanchik by the salting, just as wine experts know their chateau.

The resulting caviar is called *malossol*, the Russian word for lightly salted. It will taste great right out of the ikryanchik's bowl, but the eggs will also gain character as the salt penetrates the casings. Virtually all caviar made for export today is malossol, yet people forget this light touch is a relatively recent innovation. In the past, when transportation was slower and less reliable, producers tended to heap on the salt, as much as 15 percent of the volume, to prevent spoilage. Caviar was also pressed into cakes by being repeatedly drained of its salty brine. It lasted for months and could be sliced like cheese. Called *payusnaya*, this hard, pressed caviar is impossible to find today. Cheaper than soft caviar and more intense in flavor, the pressed cake was often the only kind a Russian worker could afford, although Greek shipping tycoon Aristotle Onassis ate it because he preferred it to soft caviar.

Even when pressed or soaked with salt, caviar spoils more easily than other foods. Its ephemeral nature was what limited the consumption of caviar for so many centuries, and what prevented the sturgeon from being completely wiped out. Once caviar could be pasteurized, adulterated with the preservative borax, and vacuum-sealed, it could be shipped safely anywhere in the world. And once caviar ceased to be a perishable local delicacy, the ancient sturgeon's days were numbered.

2

From the Pig's Trough
to the King's Table

The play, I remember, pleased not the million, 'twas
caviare to the general; but it was . . . an excellent play.

—SHAKESPEARE, HAMLET

*N*ot long after the Mongols conquered Muscovy in 1240, their
leader Batu Khan left his headquarters along the Volga and went with
his wife Yildiz to pay a visit to his new subjects at a nearby monastery.
It was a tense meeting. Having just burned Moscow to the ground, laid
waste to Kiev, and ravaged all of central Russia, the Asian warlord
wanted to show he could be a civilized ruler. The Russians inside the
Orthodox Christian monastery were no doubt eager to please their new
overlord, grandson of the formidable Genghis Khan, and they prepared
an elaborate feast that featured sterlet soup and a whole roasted sturgeon among its many courses. As a final show of respect, the monks

a mullet or bluefin tuna, although almost any Mediterranean fish will do. While the Italians and Turks might occasionally enjoy caviar or botargo, the food was deeply embedded in Greek culture. Georgacas decided that as a matter of national pride, he was obliged to prove the *OED* wrong.

He had other reasons to believe that Greeks were eating caviar centuries before the Italians or the Turks discovered the ambrosia. Ancient Greek civilization revolved around the sea. The Greeks were expert sailors, traders, and fishermen who used their skills to spread their culture throughout the Mediterranean. Salted fish was the mainstay of their seafaring diet, as well as big business. Because salt is a preservative, the fish cured by Greeks could be sold throughout the region. The demand for their sea products eventually propelled Greek sailors across the familiar Aegean, through the straits of the Dardanelles and the Bosporus, and into the wine-dark waters of the Black Sea. By the sixth century B.C., the Greeks had established fishing colonies in the rich river deltas of the Danube, Dneiper, Dneister, and Don, and the Sea of Azov—a region now shared by Romania and Ukraine. Those deltas teamed with sturgeon, just as the Volga delta does today.

Even before they colonized the northern Black Sea coast in the sixth century B.C., the Greeks would have encountered the sturgeon in the Mediterranean. They considered the sturgeon one of the "noble fish," probably because of its high cost. The fish's image appears in Egyptian temple carvings in Luxor, and on ancient coins found in Tunisia, suggesting the sturgeon's range once extended along the coast of North Africa. While the European sturgeon and the Adriatic sturgeon were the most common Mediterranean varieties, populations of beluga also lived in the Adriatic, spawning in the Po River near Venice.

The sturgeon may have been plentiful in the Mediterranean rivers in ancient times, but it was not an easy fish to catch. Human beings first mastered the basics of fishing around 10,000 B.C., yet sturgeon continued to present a special challenge. A baited hook was useless for catching the bottom-feeding sturgeon. Nets were often ineffective, too, because the sturgeon's sharp bony plates easily tore through the mesh, which was usually made of reeds or other primitive fibers. Some time around the second century A.D., Greek fishermen discovered they could snag the sturgeon with a hook that floated beneath the water's surface and was attached by a line to a tree or a grazing ox. The floating hook was the first reliable way of catching the big, bottom-feeding sturgeon.

Georgacas began his research like all classical scholars, by scouring the ancient Greek and Roman texts for references to caviar. The fishing method that Aelianus described was ample proof that the Black Sea Greeks were adept at catching sturgeon. But curiously, Aelianus said nothing about caviar. Georgacas continued to search for some mention of caviar in earlier texts, but much to his disappointment the linguistical evidence proved inconclusive.

Although the modern Greek word for caviar is *avyarion*, Georgacas could not determine exactly what the ancients called salted sturgeon roe. This is because he found only a single mention of the delicacy in all of classical Greek and Roman literature, and it was a secondhand reference at that. Something that sounds like caviar is discussed in a well-known list of recipes for salting fish compiled by Athenaeus in the second century A.D. Athenaeus attributed his information to an earlier writer named Dilphilos of Siphnos. Dilphilos, who lived a century before Athenaeus, had written a travelogue about a trip to Alexandria, the affluent and intellectual Greek city located in the Nile delta. Dilphilos was much impressed by the array of goods in the city market. According to Athenaeus' retelling, the sophisticated Alexandrines could choose from two kinds of caviar—the lightly salted kind we call fresh and the heavily preserved kind laden with salt.

Finding this reference should have been Georgacas' eureka moment. The problem is that Athenaeus doesn't actually use the word *caviar*, but a more generic phrase that Georgacas was forced to translate as "raw pickle." Since Dilphilos' original manuscript from the third century B.C. does not survive, there is no way of knowing whether he was really talking about caviar made from sturgeon roe or some other fish's roe.

Despite this setback, Georgacas continued to insist that the word for caviar originated in ancient Greece. In 1978, he published a book-length rebuttal to the *OED* entitled *Ichthyological Terms for the Sturgeon and Etymology of the International Terms for Botargo, Caviar and Congeners*. His evidence is tantalizingly circumstantial. Aristotle and Herodotus were both familiar with the sturgeon, but neither ever wrote anything specific about its roe. Georgacas attempted to explain this lapse by suggesting that when classical writers used the word for sturgeon, they really meant caviar.

The absence of any clear references to caviar in these ancient texts is puzzling. There is little doubt that the ancient Greeks were familiar with the sturgeon. They were skilled at using salt to preserve fish and they certainly had a taste for fish roe. It may be, however, that the early Greeks had trouble catching sturgeon on a regular basis. If that was the case, true sturgeon caviar would have been very rare, so rare that no classical writers ever had the chance to experience it. Based on early accounts that Georgacas discovered, sturgeon sold for fantastic sums, indicating that it was not a common dish. The fish was such a luxury that one writer claimed that a single bowl of sturgeon meat in the Athens market went for the same price as one hundred sheep and a bull.

The Romans say nothing about caviar, either, although they were full of praise for fresh sturgeon meat. Even in Roman times, sturgeon was a rare and expensive delicacy. Sturgeon was served only at special feasts and was often presented as part of an elaborate ritual. At the banquet marking Rome's defeat of Carthage, Pliny reports that a fanfare of trumpets announced the arrival of the platter bearing the sturgeon. The Roman emperor Severus was known to include flutes and drums along with the trumpets, and he had his sturgeon garlanded in roses. Since the Romans were also expert at curing fish with salt, they might have also eaten their sturgeon pickled. But even when sturgeon was preserved, it was still far beyond the means of the average Roman citizen. Writing in the first century B.C., Cicero noted that "this is a fish fit for only a few choice palates."

By the time Aelianus had observed Black Sea fishermen casting for sturgeon in the second century, Roman culture had become dominant in the Mediterranean, subsuming the Greek. In A.D. 301, the Roman emperor Diocletian requested an inventory of foods commonly eaten in Greek settlements. The resulting list made no mention of caviar. We have no way of knowing whether this was an oversight by a Roman bureaucrat, or an accurate reflection of the Greek diet.

Within a few decades, Rome's influence would fade. After the collapse of the empire, Europe settled into a long period of culinary darkness. "Fine cooking ceased with the fall of Rome," Georgacas reminds us. If caviar was indeed available in the ancient world, it seems certain that the knowledge of the delicacy was all but forgotten after the fall of Rome.

THE FIRST unambiguous references to caviar appear in medieval times. By the twelfth century, caviar was showing up in Constantinople, then the center of the Greek Orthodox church. In 1280, some four decades after Batu Khan had dined at the Volga monastery, the Russian Orthodox church formally sanctioned caviar and sturgeon as foods that could be consumed during religious fasts, when meat and rich delicacies were forbidden. The Russian name for caviar is the deceptively modest *ikra,* the word for spawn. Such a functional word says something about caviar's place in Russian culture.

Russia was still emerging as a nation in the thirteenth century, and its influence was limited to the ring of territory around Moscow. The Russians had not yet come close to conquering the sturgeon fisheries of the Caspian and Black Seas, although Orthodox Slavs were scattered throughout those regions. Most of the sturgeon that Russians consumed at that time would have come from the upper reaches of the Volga River, near the city of Kostroma. One monastery there still features frescos celebrating the mighty sturgeon.

In those days, the church governed even the most minute aspects of Russian life. Orthodox Christians were obligated to eschew meat for as many as two hundred days a year. This fasting regime had the effect of turning Russians into great consumers of fish, a preference that continues to this day. Sturgeon was a Russian favorite, partly because it is meaty and nutritious. Some 80 percent of sturgeon is edible, compared to 40 percent for most fish. Before refrigeration and motorized transportation made it possible to consume fresh sturgeon, Russians usually preserved the fish by salting or pickling. Even when the flesh was cured, sturgeon was still quite expensive. It was much cheaper to buy the roe. By sanctioning caviar as a fasting food, the church made it easier for the poor to comply with its religious demands.

The thirteenth century was a time of turmoil in Russia. The country had just suffered a humiliating defeat by Batu Khan, and the Muscovite princes continued to clash with the Mongols of the Golden Horde, who had settled along the southern steppe, from the Aral Sea to the Crimea. The Mongols' position astride the main water routes to the Black and Caspian Seas enabled them to control the region's rich fisheries and important trade routes. When Batu Khan established his capital, he chose a site just north of Astrakhan, an important crossroads of the Great Silk Road. The strategic position allowed the Mongols to profit from the caravan trade between China and Europe.

Chinese merchants had long traveled across the steppe into Europe, loaded with spices, tea, and furs. Marco Polo, who made the reverse journey overland in the late thirteenth century, transfixed his countrymen with tales of the exotic Asian lands. Soon merchant ships from Venice and Genoa began venturing east by sea, in search of the places Marco Polo described. Sailing through the Bosporus, equipped with a new invention, the compass, they headed toward the Crimea and the realm of the Golden Horde. The Mongols, who spoke a Turkic language, acted as middlemen, selling the Italians delicate silks from Persia, fine paper from China, and pure salt from the Volga delta. The Mongol traders convinced the Italians to take the occasional barrel of caviar from the sturgeon fishery in the Sea of Azov.

This was not caviar as we know it today. In order to survive the long journey across the seas, the sturgeon eggs had to be cured with large quantities of salt. Instead of possessing a gentle oceanic tang, this caviar probably tasted like a gulp of seawater. Despite the heavy salting, the eggs barely survived the long sea journey without turning sour or moldy. No wonder the Venetians did not immediately take to the Eastern delicacy. Caviar was sold by apothecaries, along with other suspect foods such as capers. A proverb of the time advised Italians that whoever "eateth of Cavialies (caviar), Eateth Salt, Dung and Flies."

Over time resistance to the strange food began to weaken, and by the fifteenth century, Venetian merchants were importing two shiploads of caviar a year from the Mongols. The writer Tobias Venner observed that caviar was even becoming a fad among Italians. "There is an Italian sauce called caviaro, which begins to be in use with us, such vain affectors are we of novelties," he wrote. But he advised caution. Caviar, he warned, "is prepared with the spawn of the sturgeon: the very name doth well express it, that it is good to beware of it." Caviaro, Venner knew, contained the Latin root for "be careful."

Galileo was among those fearless epicures who enjoyed caviar despite such warnings. In 1629, he sent a container of the delicacy to the Florentine convent where his daughter Virginia lived. She had taken her vows and become Suor Maria Celeste, but still welcomed gifts of exotic foods such as lemons and oranges from her father, and always shared her bounty with the other nuns. But this particular package was not a success at the convent, she complained in a letter to Galileo. "Suor Arcangela, when she saw the package of caviar that came from you the other day, felt cheated, convinced as she was that it must be the cheese from Holland that you usually send at this time of year." The suspicious dark jelly was thrown away. But Suor Maria Celeste was herself not completely averse to the delicacy. When Galileo sent her another container of caviar the following year, she mixed some of the roe with dried figs, nuts, and salt and sent it back to her father to eat as protection against the plague.

As a true Renaissance man, Galileo was as curious about new foods as he was about the workings of the universe. He was not alone in his culinary investigations. As Europe emerged from the confinement and superstition of the Dark Ages, society once again became interested in the fine cooking that had disappeared with Roman civilization. The numbers of people willing to sample the exotic eggs from the East began to grow.

Their curiosity happened to coincide with increased supplies of caviar. By the beginning of the Renaissance, advances in fishing technology, particularly the increased use of the anchor hook, made it possible to catch more sturgeon than ever before. By the time the Venetian merchants arrived in the Black Sea in the fourteenth century, the Mongols had become experts at using the floating hook. Because they could catch large numbers of sturgeon, they were able to offer the merchants ample quantities of caviar to take back to Italy.

FAR ACROSS Central Asia, where many of the nomadic steppe tribes originated, there is evidence that the ancient Chinese had discovered sturgeon fishing on their own.

Like the Greeks and Romans, they considered the sturgeon a very special fish. The sturgeon was the "king of fishes," and was supposedly able to transform itself into a dragon. The Chinese would have found plenty of sturgeon in the Amur and Yangtze Rivers. According to one Chinese account, people living near the Yangtze River in the tenth century were successful at catching sturgeon and enjoyed eating the roe. They had a much more elaborate method for preparing the eggs. Before pickling the eggs in brine, they steeped them first in tea.

The love of sturgeon was never universal, though. In the ninth century, the Caspian steppe was controlled by the Khazars, the storied tribe whose upper classes had converted to Judaism. A Turkic-speaking people, the Khazars were renowned for their commercial abilities, as well as their role as a bulwark against the Arab invasions. The Khazars presided over a vast and multiethnic empire, whose capital, Itil, was situated near present-day Astrakhan, and near where the Golden Horde later set up their capital. Although thousands of sturgeon coursed up the Volga past their capital each spring, the Jewish Khazars refused to eat either the meat or the roe. Because sturgeon have no scales, they are considered unclean under Jewish dietary law. Later, when Shiite Moslems came to dominate the southern rim of the Caspian Sea, in what is now Azerbaijan and northern Iran, they, too, would deem sturgeon an unclean fish.

WHILE STURGEON fishing was booming in the Mongol lands thanks to the anchor hook, the fish remained a rare delicacy in medieval Europe. The sturgeon was so valued that feudal fishermen were required to turn over all their catches to their lords, who roasted the meat. But the roe was discarded. Europeans still had no idea how to make caviar.

King Edward II of England was one of the first nobles to claim the sturgeon for his own larder. In the fourteenth century, he issued a proclamation stating that any sturgeon caught in English waters had to be turned over to him—unless it was hooked in the Thames. Then the Lord Mayor of London had rights to it. When these sturgeon were sold at the London fish market, they commanded a hefty price. In 1339, a single barrel of salted sturgeon cost the same as a dozen barrels of herring. The high price suggests that few sturgeon were landed in English waters.

Following the English example, both the Danish and Spanish kings also claimed the right to all sturgeon caught by their fishermen. In France, the archbishop was entitled only to the first sturgeon of the season from the Rhône River, which had a large sturgeon population. It became a tradition in medieval Arles to celebrate the event by parading the first male fish through the streets to the archbishop's house. The emphasis on celebrating the male sturgeon would seem to indicate that no special value was placed on the roe-bearing female. Describing the parade in Arles in 1439, an observer wrote that "the procession climbed from the port to the city . . . the tambourine players led the way, making a joyous din. Then came the fishermen carrying a monstrous fish on a litter." Once again, the writer says nothing about the eggs.

The Germans also adored sturgeon meat and fishermen were free to keep their catches. Sturgeon were caught in such numbers in the Elbe in the seventeenth century that one fishing town in Prussia adopted the image of a crowned sturgeon as its coat of arms. As catches increased, a local clergyman cautioned members of his congregation in 1675 that there would soon be none left unless fishermen adopted size limits, a foreshadowing of environmental disasters to come. As always, the warnings were ignored and the fishing continued unabated.

IN RUSSIA, where sturgeon had long been a popular dish, the fish was becoming even more widely available. As Mongol power waned in the fifteenth century, Russia pushed south along the Volga toward the Caspian Sea. In 1556, Ivan the Terrible swept down the Volga with his army, seizing the steppe north of the Caspian and driving the Mongols out of Astrakhan. Using stones from the palaces of the Golden Horde, Ivan built the first kremlin, or fort, in the Caspian port. The Russians finally assumed control of the rich Astrakhan sturgeon fishery. Ivan demanded a share of the Mongols' annual sturgeon catch as his tribute and insisted that the fish be delivered fresh to Moscow. Fishermen would pack the gasping sturgeon securely in straw and wrap its snout in vodka-soaked rags before embarking on the lengthy journey by cart from the Volga to Moscow.

Eager to colonize the steppe and fortify it against invasion, Ivan encouraged Russians to move south. Many of the arrivals were desperate people, such as runaway serfs looking to escape Russia's relentless feudal system. Others were religious dissidents unhappy with changes in the Russian Orthodox church. Like the nomads who came from the east, they drifted toward the rivers—the Volga, Ural, Don, and Terek. Many ended up as pirates and fishermen and became known as Cossacks.

While people tend to picture Cossacks on horseback, galloping across the plains with sabers slicing the air, the Cossacks of the steppe were also skilled fishermen. After the defeat of the Mongols, they came to dominate the sturgeon fishing industry in the Volga and the Don, gliding over the rivers in lightweight canoes made of bark. Although they were Orthodox Christians and spoke either Russian or Ukrainian, the Cossacks developed their own distinct identity. They were exempted from serfdom, but in exchange they were obliged to perform lifelong military service by guarding the Russian frontier.

The Cossacks did not always make the most reliable border guards. Instead of protecting the steppe, the Cossacks frequently attacked and pillaged ships on the Volga. Sometimes, the Cossack armies would act on their own, as they did in 1637 when they seized the Turkish fortress at Azov, an area known for its exceptionally good sturgeon fishing. But the tsar's regular army refused to come to their aid and the Cossacks were forced to retreat, relinquishing their fishing rights in the Sea of Azov.

After Alexei ascended to the Russian throne in 1645, he made an attempt to organize the loose bands of Cossacks into more formal, and more disciplined, military units. The Cossacks bristled at their new obligations. In the 1660s, a disgruntled Cossack officer named Stenka Razin led a major rebellion against Tsar Alexei. Razin was a notorious pirate, but he also had a popular reputation as a Robin Hood of the steppe. Today he is viewed as something of an early democrat, who challenged the tsar's authoritarian ways. When Moscow attempted to discipline him for his piracy, Razin formed an army of other disgruntled Cossacks and seized Astrakhan. Emboldened by their success, the

Cossacks began marching north, winning one engagement after another. For a time, it seemed Razin's army of Cossack pirates and fishermen might actually reach Moscow.

In the end, Razin was too ambitious. In 1671, the Cossack rebellion collapsed. Razin's followers fled into the high reeds of the Volga delta, where they survived by fishing for sturgeon. The village of Wolves' Island, which today supplies Evgeny Aptekar's caviar company with its sturgeon, was settled by Razin's renegade Cossacks. Razin himself was caught before he could reach the delta and hanged in front of a large crowd in Red Square.

With Razin gone, the Cossacks once again bowed to the authority of Moscow. They demonstrated their fidelity by presenting the tsar with a bowl of caviar, a symbolic gesture that mimicked the peasant tradition of offering bread and salt to honored guests. "Salted caviar," wrote historian W. P. Cresson, "packed in little wooden kegs, formed the most acceptable tribute which could be offered to the Russian court, and this delicate product purchased indemnity for many a Cossack misdeed."

Razin had intended to free the Cossacks from the obligations imposed by distant Moscow bureaucrats, but the reverse occurred. Four years after the Cossacks rebelled, Tsar Alexei issued an edict regulating the caviar trade and imposing a government tax on all sales.

By the time Peter the Great followed Alexei as tsar in 1682, sturgeon fishing had grown into a significant industry. Because Russians ate fish so often to comply with the religious fasts, the demand was huge, especially for salted fish. In an effort to win the Cossacks' loyalty and prevent future uprisings, Peter decided to allow them a number of special privileges. The Cossacks, who already dominated the fishing industry, were given exclusive rights to catch sturgeon. They were also assigned the job of collecting taxes on salt, an essential ingredient in the fishing industry. Peter, who was struggling to transform Russia into a modern European society, encouraged the Cossacks to use their new privileges to produce caviar for export.

But transporting the salted fish and caviar beyond Russia was still difficult. Caviar and other exports had to be hauled across the steppe by caravan, then floated down the Don River to the Black Sea, where it could be loaded onto ships bound for Greece, Venice, Germany, France, and England.

While few Europeans actually had an opportunity to try caviar, many had heard about it. Some assumed it was a mythical food like ambrosia and nectar. Others were baffled by its luxurious reputation. In the tale of Pantegruel, the French writer Rabelais mentions caviar several times, but always as an example of the ridiculous. Rabelais decribes how Pantegruel prepared for a long sea voyage by packing a trunk full of useless and inedible provisions. Caviar is one of them. Pantegruel never gets to eat the delicacy. When some starving monks approach Pantegruel to beg for something to eat, he obliges by giving them his supply of caviar. Judging by his satiric tone, Rabelais did not appreciate caviar's appeal.

Neither did Louis XV. Offered a taste by an emissary of Peter the Great, the French king was so repulsed that he spat the contents on the elegant carpet of the Versailles palace, something that even Batu Khan was too polite to do. A few years later, in 1741, Savary's *Dictionnaire du Commerce* nevertheless attempted to promote caviar with this backhanded praise: "It is beginning to be known in France where it is not despised at the best tables."

European tastes were changing. The day was coming when the scorned food of Russian Orthodox Christians would be seen as a defining mark of civilization and wealth.

3

.   .   .   ❧   .   .   .

Caviar's Industrial
Revolution

*Everyman and everywoman, reverently eating modern
ambrosia in the form of caviar, can identify as they
indulge in the mad extravagance of swallowing it—even
if they do not happen to like it—with what they see as the
last incarnation of the immortals.*

—MAGUELONNE TOUSSAINT-SAMAT,
A HISTORY OF FOOD

*B*efore caviar could achieve world renown as a delicacy, its natural
limitations first had to be overcome. The eggs were hard to obtain,
hard to transport, and hard to keep fresh. The international caviar trade
had begun only after the Mongols figured out how to catch large numbers of roe-bearing sturgeon. But commerce was constrained for centuries by the difficulty of conveying the perishable eggs over long

distances and maintaining them in edible condition. The Industrial Revolution would provide the solutions to both problems. It would also give rise to a class of moneyed consumers who craved new and foreign tastes. Over a few decades, caviar would be transformed from a food reviled by kings to one identified with them.

The man who accelerated caviar's transformation from a Russian peasant dish to a treat for the European upper class was a Greek sea captain and trader who had never tasted sturgeon eggs until he stumbled into Astrakhan in the 1780s. Ioannis Varvarkis had grown up on the small island of Psara in the eastern Aegean, when it was an outpost of the Ottoman Empire. He was a serious young man, with close-set eyes and a penetrating gaze that earned him the nickname "Little Hawk." As a youth, Varvarkis joined his father's shipping business, serving the nearby islands in their small corner of the Aegean. But in 1769, the events of the larger world intruded. Catherine the Great, who had long coveted the Turkish territory along the northern Black Sea coast, declared war on the Ottoman Empire, vowing to liberate all Christians inhabiting the territory from the Caucasus to the Balkans.

When the Orthodox Christian Greeks took up arms against their Ottoman overlords, Varvarkis was among them. Filled with patriotic fervor, he sold all his possessions to outfit one of his boats with cannons and soldiers and went to join the battle against the Turks. Varvarkis was given the rank of captain. But before he could see any action, the Turkish sultan sued for peace. Russia, which had long sought access to a warm water port, took the entire northern coast of the Black Sea in 1774 as its prize—gaining another rich sturgeon fishery in the bargain. Lost in the whirlwind of negotiations, however, was the fate of the Christians in the rest of the Ottoman Empire. The rebellious Greeks were left to settle scores with the Ottomans on their own.

Had Varvarkis gone back to his oppressed homeland, that would have been the last we heard of him. Instead he sailed to Istanbul, intending to sell his now useless warship. The Ottoman capital was an oddly naive destination, given the hostility there toward the Greek revolutionaries, and Varvarkis was soon in trouble with the authorities. His boat was seized and he had to flee the Turkish capital. Now both penniless and stateless, he made up his mind to seek compensation from Catherine, a plan he pursued with his usual quixotic single-mindedness. Since he was broke, this meant walking some 2,500 miles through Russia to lay out his grievances in St. Petersburg. Varvarkis not only succeeded in reaching the city, but after a chance encounter in a coffeehouse with Grigory Potemkin, Catherine's lover, he managed to obtain an audience with the tsarina. Catherine demonstrated her appreciation by handing him a purse of gold florins and an official document giving him the right to unlimited, tax-free fishing in the Caspian Sea.

While Varvarkis was undoubtedly grateful for the money, he hardly knew what to make of the royal fishing permit. He set out for Astrakhan anyway. But instead of setting up a fishing business, he used the florins to buy a distillery. His intention was to turn the sweet grapes of the steppe into wine. Before he had gotten very far in the enterprise, Varvarkis was befriended by an Astrakhan merchant named Piotor Semyonovich Sapozhnikov. He suggested that it would be more profitable to organize a fishing business, since Varvarkis already had Catherine's license and a seaman's knowledge of boats. At that time, many Russian fishermen still worked from small dinghies. Some still did not even use anchor hooks, relying instead on primitive baskets and harpoons to catch their prey. Varvarkis was able to build bigger and more sophisticated vessels that could penetrate the open sea. He single-handedly began to chart the northern Caspian. As his friend Sapozhnikov predicted, the fishing business flourished. Varvarkis' boats were bringing in sturgeon, white salmon, pike, and other valuable fish. Yet he still had not encountered the sea's most celebrated product.

One day, according to an early biographer, Varvarkis passed a peasant eating a black viscous substance with bread. He inquired about this strange inky food and the Russian peasant offered him a bite. Once Varvarkis tasted the briny delicacy, he recognized the true value of Catherine's gift. Back home in Greece, where fish roe was considered a delicacy, Varvarkis thought that caviar could fetch high prices. But he faced the same problem that had bedeviled Italian merchants centuries earlier: how to keep the perishable eggs from spoiling during the long trip across the steppe and sea.

Caviar was packed like most products of the time in wooden barrels. Often the wood was quite porous, which meant that air could penetrate the sealed kegs and contaminate the caviar, even when it was heavily salted. As an experienced merchant, Varvarkis knew how quickly spoilage could eat up his profits, so he set about searching for better means of packaging. From his Cossack fishermen, he learned about a special kind of linden tree growing in the nearby Caucasus Mountains. These lindens, or lime trees, they told him, produced smooth, impermeable staves, which did not react with the briny eggs like other woods, so the precious cargo stayed fresh longer. The wood was expensive, but that did not worry Varvarkis. He declared he would use only linden barrels for his caviar. By 1788, Varvarkis' caviar trade was so successful that he was employing three thousand Astrakhan workers to process and pack the sturgeon roe.

When Varvarkis started to export caviar on a large scale in the 1780s, he had to rely on plodding camel caravans and wooden sailing ships to carry the fragile eggs from Astrakhan to Greece. The barrels of heavily salted caviar were shipped up the Volga as far as today's

Volgograd, where they were transferred to caravans and hauled overland across the narrowest part of the Caucasian isthmus to the Don
River. Then they were floated back downstream to the Black Sea and
out the Bosporus to Istanbul. Despite his earlier trouble with the
Ottoman authorities, the area around Istanbul's Galata Bridge soon became Varvarkis' main caviar exchange. Middlemen from Greece, Italy,
and the Levant haggled over barrels of the newly popular delicacy.
Young, ethnic Greek boys came down from hills of Cappadocia to
work in the Istanbul caviar trade. The business flourished to a degree
that Varvarkis could never have imagined. In 1824, when he returned to
Greece to enjoy his homeland's new independence from the Ottoman
Empire, he was a millionaire several times over. He donated large
sums to build a covered market in Athens, a high school, a canal in
Astrakhan, and many other civic projects. Varvarkis died in Greece the
following year without seeing Astrakhan again.

Although Varvarkis revolutionized Astrakhan's caviar trade, the
only trace that remains of his caviar business there is the canal, built to
streamline the loading of linden barrels. Even that is a tenuous link.
The Soviets renamed it the First of May Canal after the revolution.
Only in 1991 did Astrakhan officials restore Varvarkis' name to the
canal he built, in a gesture of nostalgia for the city's glory days.

BY THE eighteenth century, Europe's merchants were eagerly charting
new markets. Russia was still a mysterious place, dangerous, barbaric,
suspicious of all foreigners and mistrustful of merchants in particular.
Attracted by the country's immense riches, European merchants were
determined to brave Russia's frigid winters, lack of roads, vast distances, corrupt officials, and cold-blooded bandits. Despotic as the

Russian Empire was, it offered Europeans an outlet for their finished goods such as woolens and pottery, and an opportunity to purchase boundless stores of raw materials. Merchants continued to push deep into Russia, seeking lumber for ship masts, hemp for rope, pig iron for furnaces, and silks, furs, and hides for Europe's expanding middle class. High on the list of must-visit places was Astrakhan, where the caravan routes of Central Asia intersected the northward-bound Volga shipping lines.

Among the first Europeans to arrive in the city was the German adventurer Adam Olearius. The Duke of Holstein, who ruled the area north of Hamburg, dispatched Olearius to investigate the prospects for trade between Russia and the German lands. Olearius sailed into Astrakhan in 1647 after a perilous voyage down the Volga, during which the crew fought off repeated attacks from swarms of Cossack pirates. In the more peaceful moments of the journey, Olearius marveled at the plenty that the Volga had to offer. The crewmembers would no sooner throw over a fishing line than they would pull in a large sturgeon. "These have very white, sweet, and delicious flesh," he enthused. "We were able not only to feed everyone aboard ship with this fish, but also to salt away a whole barrel of what was left over." Olearius was obviously fascinated by these big fish. He spent hours watching the crew work their lines and enjoyed many dinners of beluga, sterlet, and Russian sturgeon.

For all this, Olearius seems downright surprised to learn that Russians also considered the sturgeon's roe a great delicacy. "They have a very common food which they call *ikra,* which is made of the roe of large fish," he writes in a tone that suggests he has never heard of caviar before. Indeed, he never uses the German word for caviar in his description, although he notes the Italians were also fond of sturgeon roe and called it *caviaro*. "It is not a bad dish," he concludes. That is, "if one pours a bit of lemon juice over it, instead of vinegar, it gives a good appetite, and has a restorative effect."

Olearius was hardly the only foreign visitor to show more interest in the sturgeon's flesh than its roe. In 1703, a Frenchman named Cornelius Le Brun spent six weeks in the "Kingdom of Astrakhan" while on his way to Persia. Though he waxed enthusiastic about the salt ponds, the watermelons, the giant beluga and tasty sterlet—"the most delicious fish one can meet with, not only in Russia, but anywhere else"—either he never encountered caviar or he did not see fit to mention it. Over the next century, as a stream of merchants traveled to Astrakhan to buy silk, salt, and spices, it was often the same story. None deemed caviar worthy of more than a few lines, despite a more than amiable interest in sturgeon meat and the methods used to catch the enormous fish.

Surely this was not for a lack of caviar in Astrakhan. By 1770, when the Russian naturalist Samuel Gemelin surveyed the area, the Volga fisheries were supplying the delicacy throughout Russia. Caviar had ceased to be merely a religious food, eaten by devout peasants on fast days, and was becoming a popular dish among the well to do. John Perry, a British engineer who spent fourteen years building canals for Peter the Great, mostly in the Volga region, reported that he was frequently served caviar during his service in Russia, and grew as fond of the delicacy as any Russian. It was "admirable good; beyond what can be imagin'd" by anyone who had only tasted the heavily salted kind that was being imported into Europe, he wrote. Perry became convinced that Europeans would also develop a taste for the sturgeon's roe if only they could taste it fresh.

It was around this time that the English merchant Jonas Hanway arrived in Russia on another trade mission, as a representative of the

London-based Russia Company. Hanway left Moscow for Astrakhan in 1749, hoping to establish links with Persian silk dealers who operated in the Caspain city. It was there that Hanway tasted caviar for the first time. While he was just as ambivalent as Olearius, he felt duty-bound to evaluate the pros and cons of exporting the delicacy. Caviar might be profitably exported to England, he suggested in his account of his Russian experiences, which Dr. Samuel Johnson praised as a "Baedecker for commercial posterity." The Armenians in Astrakhan, Hanway noted, were already shipping excellent caviar to Orthodox Christians in the Levant. But he also feared that sending caviar up the Volga would be a risky venture because of the rampant piracy. Hanway's own caravan was plundered after he left Astrakhan, and most of his goods were lost. When he finally made it back to England after seven years in Russia, Hanway dropped all his plans for importing caviar and silk, and devoted himself instead to promoting the use of umbrellas in soggy London. If British merchants were in no hurry to import Russian caviar, at least they no longer despised it. Arriving in the Caspian in 1792 on a trade mission for the British East India Company, George Forster was delighted at being served a meal of beluga soup and caviar on the ship that carried him to Astrakhan. Unlike Hanway, whose Russian experiences are described with unwavering neutrality, Forster recounted his exotic dinner with gusto. A Greek merchant who sounds a lot like Varvarkis later invited Forster to be his guest in Astrakhan, and took him on a tour of the sturgeon fishery. Forster reported that Kalmyk shepherds were abandoning their flocks to fish for sturgeon, an indication of how important fishing had become in the steppe economy in the few years since Varvarkis' arrival.

· · ·

THE INTRODUCTION of icehouses in the eighteenth century was a big advance in the preservation of fish and caviar. Until then, salt had been the chief means of keeping perishable foods from spoiling. Certainly ice was readily available in the winter months in the northern countries, yet it seems that many people did not realize its potential for preserving food. The ancient Egyptian kings, who had snow carted from the mountains of Lebanon to their palaces, used the precious ice only to make cool drinks in the summertime. Chinese fishermen may have been the first to understand that perishables kept on ice would last much longer. Once frozen, dangerous organisms that cause food to spoil are kept in a state of suspended animation, remaining dormant until the meat or fish is returned to room temperature. In 1720, a Chinese fisherman sent a frozen sturgeon as a welcoming gift to Dr. John Bell, a Scottish physician who was visiting Beijing. It had been caught in the Amur River, which separates Russia and China, and transported hundreds of miles. The fish was rock solid when it arrived and perfectly fresh when it thawed. Bell was amazed and word of the Chinese technique spread throughout Europe.

Yet, even before the advantages were fully realized, freezing food was common in Russia. Game birds were typically displayed frozen solid at market stalls in the winter; indeed there was little merchants could do to keep them from freezing. As preservation became more of a science in Europe, blocks of ice were cut from ponds and lakes in the wintertime and carted to icehouses.

Just as the ice harvest was becoming an important industry, new machines were being developed that would create ice on demand. Inventors in France, Britain, and America were perfecting the first steam engines, which would revolutionize transportation and lead to the creation of refrigerators. By the late eighteenth century, ships powered by steam engines were making their maiden voyages. Steamships could travel faster and get their goods to market in better condition than the old wind-driven sailboats. The new fast ships could transport ice in less time, with less water loss. In 1820, the first steamship laden with a cargo of ice sailed down the Volga to Astrakhan. Inventors soon discovered that the same steam process could be used to run a compressor to cool water and create ice on demand. Within a few years, caviar merchants were able to wrap their caviar in a thick coat of ice and straw before sending their valuable product off on its uncertain journey.

Even as this new form of transportation brought the world closer together, steamships still took months to reach their destinations. That meant that the cargoes of caviar continued to require delicate handling. The blanket of ice had to be replaced repeatedly during the trip to survive the weeks at sea. The caviar was still salted heavily or pressed into a dry cake. The lightly salted malossol caviar that is today's standard could never endure such an ordeal. All the coddling made caviar a very expensive product by the time it arrived in Europe. But the high price did not drive people away.

To the contrary. Costliness became one of caviar's defining qualities, even one of its attractions. Caviar's ephemeral nature and exorbitant price gave the food a status that appealed to the burgeoning bourgeoisie of Europe. Having enriched themselves with the invention of industrial wonders such as the steam engine and the spinning jenny, they soon developed a hunger for exotic treats and faraway places. Caviar was a perfect balm for their yearnings. By the end of the nineteenth century, a time poetically recalled as the Belle Epoque, these newly moneyed merchants and manufacturers would do almost anything for a dollop on toast.

What made eating caviar all the more adventuresome was that it was eaten raw. Europeans believed that heating caviar, as Russians sometimes did, destroyed the delicate flavor of the eggs. All that was needed for bliss, the nineteenth-century French chef Antoine Beauvilliers advised his patrons, was a buttered slice of crusty bread, chopped shallots, and a dab of caviar.

TO EUROPEANS, caviar derived much of its allure from its association with the wealthy Russian aristocracy. As railroads made long-distance travel more common, Russian nobles were increasingly showing up in places such as Paris and Berlin, trailing sables and servants. Western Europeans were endlessly fascinated by their excesses. Upon arriving in Paris in 1840, the Grand Duke Alexis was said to be so appalled by the lack of fresh caviar that he dispatched a trio of servants to Astrakhan to fetch him some. Three months later they returned with two barrels swathed tenderly in ice.

At home in Russia, wealthy aristocrats thought nothing of having their sturgeon shipped live so they might enjoy their caviar at its freshest. The sturgeon traveled in tanks that were pulled by horse cart, and later rail, all the way from the Caspian to central Russia. The practice was bound up in the long-standing rituals of hospitality dear to wealthy Russians, which required that the host display a live, wriggling fish to his guests before turning it into soup. Russian railroads equipped their freight cars with water tanks expressly for the purpose of transporting live fish. The sturgeon fared better, though, when they were towed up the Volga in floating cages and then stocked in giant ponds on country estates.

In Russia, caviar was eaten all year long despite the challenges of keeping it fresh in warm weather. Devout Orthodox Christians had caviar on hand for the four great fast periods, which included the thirty-nine days before Christmas and the four long weeks of Lent. Caviar was also a special treat during Masylanitsa, or Butter Week, Russians' all-fat version of Mardi Gras, the last indulgence before the start of the pre-Easter fast. Along with stacks of butter-drenched blinis and buckets of sour cream, Russians took to ladling out as much caviar as they could afford. By the reign of Catherine the Great, caviar had shed its association with self-denial and was firmly associated with the Butter Week festivities. Caviar had crossed over from the realm of the sacred into the material world of the profane.

Having made caviar into a material indulgence, the Russian upper classes then devised the rituals for indulging. For well-off nobles, prosperous merchants, and state officials, it had been common since the time of Peter the Great to precede the main meal with a table of appetizers, called *zakouski*. These nearly always included a heaping bowl of caviar, from which guests took as much as they liked. In Gogol's comic masterpiece *Dead Souls*, published in 1842, the hero Chichikov encounters a typically sumptuous spread at the home of a corrupt police chief: "There appeared on the table beluga, sturgeon; salmon, pressed caviar, freshly salted caviar, herring, red sturgeon, cheeses, smoked tongues and *balyk*," or salted fish. The caviar, it is worth noting, was just one among many delicacies on the police chief's table, and notably, not even the most sought after. After assessing the temptations, Gogol's gluttonous characters rush for the table like racehorses let out of the gate. But instead of pouncing on the caviar, they devour the platter of fresh sturgeon, leaving nothing but the fish's tail. The Marquis de Custine, who found much to complain about in the Russia of 1839, grumbled that these groaning appetizer tables frequently encouraged such gluttony. Yet, the cantankerous Marquis managed to enjoy himself by heaping his plate full of freshly salted caviar, of a quality "such as is only eaten in this country."

· · ·

RUSSIANS PARTICULARLY deserve credit for that most sublime combination, blini and caviar, as perfect a culinary marriage as bacon and eggs or tomatoes and pasta. The best way to eat blini is to slather butter on the already buttery pancakes, drop a spoonful of caviar in the center, and roll the whole thing into a tube. Today, Russians will often substitute a layer of sour cream for butter, an even greater indulgence. But when they eat caviar with toast, it is always with a smear of butter. Outside of Russia, caviar is often served with what food writer Joseph Wechsberg called "a collection of nonsense" and what M.F.K. Fisher dismissed as "deceivers"—chopped onion, egg whites, lemon juice. In the Middle Ages, Russians favored even more elaborate garnishes. They ate caviar sprinkled with lemon juice, dotted with cranberries, spiced with saffron, or, as Batu Khan discovered, with warm apple preserves. It was common for Russians to press the liquid out from the eggs to create the nearly dry caviar called *payusnaya*, from the Russian word "to share." This was a staple of peasants and workingmen, who could cut off a slice and pack it into their lunch buckets the way a Frenchman might bring along a piece of pâté. By the nineteenth century, caviar was so abundant that it was liberally applied as a garnish itself. Elena Molokhovets, a popular nineteenth-century cookbook author, "dispensed caviar with a lavishness that we now find hard to believe," observed the editor of her reissued classic, *A Gift to Young Housewives*. Molokhovets suggested to her Russian readers that caviar could be lathered onto boiled pike to enhance its flavor, used in place of egg whites to strain the fat from bouillon, folded into sauerkraut, and mixed into sauces of all kinds.

In the course of its trajectory from a poor man's food to a rich man's snack, caviar enjoyed a brief populist following in Russia. Price lists surviving from Catherine's time indicate that the St. Petersburg markets sold caviar for roughly the same price as butter, putting it within a workingman's budget in the eighteenth century. Cossack soldiers carried kegs of pressed caviar with them when they marched on Paris with the Russian army in 1812, and some Russians claim that these rough frontiersmen were the ones who taught the French how to enjoy the delicacy. By the nineteenth century, caviar was a standard in Russian *traktiri*, the boisterous tavern restaurants where peasant singers entertained diners with traditional folk ballads. The caviar was usually set out in small wooden tubs on a common zakouski table, along with plates of anchovies, cold fish, cheese, and pickles. In the upper-crust establishments, which catered to nobles and merchants, the tubs naturally contained the finest malossol caviar, while pressed caviar was the standard in the more modest traktiri where ikons hung near the entryway and workingmen crossed themselves as they stepped over the threshold.

Because caviar was so deeply woven into daily Russia life, its consumption was less mannered than it is today. While the large-grained beluga roe was even then marketed as the highest grade, it was not unusual for different types of sturgeon roe to be mixed together, especially for payusnaya, or when the eggs were broken or underripe. Russians could choose from a wide array of local caviars. An 1890s traveler who wandered into Moscow's famous Eliseyev's gourmet shop, an immense room of swirling Art Nouveau pillars that was later renamed Gastronom No. 1 by the Soviets, was astounded by the array of caviars laid out on the dark wood counters. There was:

"Fine black sterlet caviar piled high in silver buckets, surrounded with rings of crushed ice. Dark sevruga caviar and large beluga roe tended to overflow the rims of their buckets. The fragrant pressed caviar, coming from the Saliansk fisheries, swelled in silver bowls. Further on, the dry sack caviar (whose roe could be cut in half with a sharp knife) stood erect on platters, keeping the shape of the sacks it was shipped in. Huge blocks of rare pressed caviar, Achevsk-Kuchugar, which had a special earthy flavor, towered over everything else on the table."

AS THE century drew to a close, the dark, glistening fish eggs that had sustained the ragged Cossacks on the steppe were moving into narrower, rarefied circles. Increasingly, caviar was becoming a food only affordable to the rich in Russia, but one that was still infused with a whiff of peasant tradition. By 1905, the year of the first Russian revolution, caviar prices were beyond the budgets of workingmen—a good enough reason for a revolution.

Caviar's inaccessibility was another example of the growing disparity between rich and poor in Russia. The upper classes could eat caviar as often as they liked. And because many believed that the tiny sturgeon eggs had great medicinal properties, they indulged daily. Young children, the sick, and those with poor eyesight were fed caviar regularly in the belief that it would build up their strength. Since caviar is high in protein and low in calories—74 to the ounce—it may well have done some good.

Caviar was not only an increasingly desirable delicacy in the nineteenth century, it was reputed to hasten sexual desire. The roe "excited the blood," a health manual from 1808 declared. While that claim has never been proven, it is known that the eggs slow the absorption of alcohol, allowing revelers to drink more vodka or champagne with their caviar, and perhaps eliminating the inhibitions that might otherwise get in the way of romance.

THE STEAM engine also made overland long-distance travel possible. Russia, which was notorious for its bad roads, understood that railroads would finally connect its vast outposts. When the railroad line from the Volga to the Don opened in 1856, the cumbersome caravan portage across the steppe was eliminated, speeding shipments of caviar to the Mediterranean countries, and awakening dormant markets in the northern reaches of Europe. In the first year of the railroad's operation, Astrakhan shipped a quarter of its caviar production to Europe. Caviar was now big business in Russia. Local merchant families, such as the Sapozhnikovs and the Khlebnikovs, set up export houses in the center of Astrakhan. Sapozhnikov, who had helped Varvarkis get into the fishing business, established his own caviar house in 1796. The family grew so rich selling sturgeon eggs to Europeans that they could indulge their passion for art. Their extensive collection included a lovely, glowing Madonna painted by da Vinci, which was later appropriated by the Soviets, along with the Sapozhnikov's caviar business. Their collection, built with caviar money, now hangs in the main galleries of the Hermitage in St. Petersburg.

But despite the booming Caspian fishing industry, Russia was losing ground to other caviar-producing countries. Foreign buyers were frustrated by Russia's knot of customs regulations. Despite the riches contained within the Caspian Sea, the Black Sea, and the Amur River, Russia was no longer the sole supplier of caviar to Europe at the end of the nineteenth century. Europeans had begun to look elsewhere for caviar.

JOHANNES DIECKMANN, like John Varvarkis, knew his barrels. But for Dieckmann, the barrels came first. He trained as a cooper in a suburb of Hamburg, and by 1842 was supplying many of the city's merchants with sturdy, watertight wooden shipping barrels. Hamburg had been a founding member of the medieval Hanseatic League, the chain of city-states that stretched from the Baltic to the North Sea. By the time Dieckmann took up barrel making, Hamburg was among the world's busiest ports, a key way station for all ships moving between Northern Russia and Flanders. After years spent around Hamburg's bustling docks, Dieckmann began to dream of doing something more than just fashioning staves into barrels. The answer lay at his feet, in the estuarine waters of the Elbe River. With his son-in-law Johannes C. F. Hansen, a Dane, he went into business salting herring and sturgeon meat that they bought in bulk from Elbe River fishermen and packed in their own barrels. In 1869, they set themselves up as Dieckmann & Hansen, "Bulk Fish Curers," in a brick warehouse overlooking the port.

It was a heady time to be a businessman in Hamburg. Although the entire city had burned to the ground in 1842, the tragedy hardly slowed its pell-mell expansion. Hamburg's population swelled from 130,000 to 700,000 in the second half of the nineteenth century. Soon, wooden cutters were giving way to huge, steel-hulled ships that steamed from St. Petersburg in a matter of days. The demand for salted fish, which had always been a favorite of the city's burghers and the Danes living a few miles north of Hamburg, grew proportionally with Hamburg's prosperity. Because salted fish was so inexpensive, it soon became the staple of the legions of workers who flooded the city seeking industrial jobs. Herring and the local sturgeon were among the cheapest foods available.

Expanding into the fish business had been a wise choice for Dieckmann the barrel maker. After several years of curing herring and the local sturgeon, Dieckmann and Hansen noticed the growing market for the Russian caviar in Germany. It must have seemed ironic that Germany was importing the very food that its own fishermen fed to their pigs. It occurred to the pair of fish curers that they could easily make their own caviar. After several experiments, they were soon producing German caviar as fine as the Russian osetra or sevruga, using the famous salt manufactured in the German city of Luneberg.

The taste for caviar was quickly moving west, from the Orthodox Christian Slavs, across the seas to Italy, and up the continent to the industrial powerhouses of northern Europe. In 1887, Dieckmann & Hansen built their own plant on the Altona docks, south of central Hamburg, enabling them to transfer the sturgeon quickly from the fishermen's boats to the processing tables, in order to obtain the freshest caviar. That year, the city opened an ornate, glass-and-steel Art Nouveau wholesale fish market on the same dockside, a Crystal Palace for fish. Caviar from the Elbe River was now the most valuable product in Dieckmann & Hansen's line.

Throughout Europe, eating caviar had become a full-fledged craze among the new rich of the Belle Epoque, along with champagne, oysters, and other exotica. It is often forgotten that out of the misery of the Industrial Revolution, there also came a sizable class of urban people with money to spend on restaurant meals, entertainments, and other luxuries. The novel concept of leisure time had taken hold among the well to do, who discovered the pleasures of lingering in cafés, playing tennis, and swimming at the seaside. People in Europe and America were held spellbound by such exquisitely useless things as Fabergé eggs, by new inventions such as gaslight, and by the idea of speed, in the form of bicycle races and trans-Atlantic steamships. Suddenly it seemed perfectly reasonable for a wealthy Russian from St. Petersburg to vacation on the French Riviera, or for an American from the Midwest to spend a few months wandering around Paris. The same year that Dieckmann & Hansen built their new processing plant to supply the growing demand for caviar, James Gorden Bennett Jr. started a Paris edition of his father's New York *Herald* to report on the comings and goings of privileged American expatriates living the good life on the continent. It was no coincidence that the Ritz Hotel opened its doors in Paris a few years later, in 1898. Its famous bar would become a hangout for expatriates, Hemingway among them, and caviar with champagne would become one of the signatures of its menu. Two decades later the lost generation's most glittering hosts, Sara and Gerald Murphy, would indulge in caviar-and-champagne parties with Hemingway and the Fitzgeralds in Antibes, serving caviar that was flown in fresh from the Caspian to the Riviera. By then caviar was so common among the smart set that F. Scott Fitzgerald complained to Murphy that serving it was "the height of affection." Such dismissive judgments did not stop Annie Oakley, in Irving Berlin's musical biography, from trilling, "I wanna wedding . . . with champagne and caviar. I wanna wedding like the Vanderbilts have."

Many other firms were rushing to get into the caviar business besides Dieckmann & Hansen, but the Hamburg house continued to dominate the European market. By 1891, caviar had become so profitable that they decided to concentrate exclusively on the delicacy, leaving it to others to pack salt herring for the working classes. Dieckmann & Hansen opened offices in Paris, London, and Stockholm to satisfy demand from all over Europe. The caviar trade had made the former barrel maker very wealthy, as it had done for Varvarkis a century earlier.

But the industries that turned Hamburg into a prosperous city and gave it a taste for caviar were now taking their toll on the Elbe sturgeon. The river was a convenient dump for factory and human waste. In 1876, only seven years after Dieckmann & Hansen first started selling German caviar, sturgeon catches took a sharp dip. Fishermen caught 3,500 sturgeon in the Elbe in 1888, but only half that number in 1900. Overfishing was to blame as much as pollution. The river was spent. But caviar was now Dieckmann & Hansen's only business. Suffering from what they called a lack of "raw material," they dispatched their sons to America in 1876 to investigate the possibility of making caviar from Delaware River sturgeon. Caviar was unknown in America, just as it had been in Germany only a few years earlier. Unaware of the huge hunger for sturgeon eggs, American fishermen continued to throw the roe to their pigs as their German counterparts had once done. But after a small push from Dieckmann & Hansen, American fishermen would ensure that caviar would still be available for the new middle class.

4

. . . ❧ . . .

The American
Caviar Rush

Forth upon the Gitche Gumee,
On the shining Big-Sea-Water,
With his fishing-line of cedar,
Of the twisted bark of cedar,
Forth to catch the sturgeon, Nahma,
Mishe-Nahma, King of Fishes,
In his birch canoe exulting
All alone went Hiawatha.

—HENRY WADSWORTH LONGFELLOW, "HIAWATHA"

$\mathcal{T}$he sturgeon is a most American fish. Bunyonesque in size, it tra-
verses vast distances as relentlessly as a pioneer in a covered wagon.

The colonists who arrived in the seventeenth century found enormous crowds of sturgeon elbowing their way up America's coastal

rivers, greater in numbers and variety than in the Caspian Sea. The Delaware River was so jammed with procreating sturgeon in the spring that Philadelphia ferry passengers were treated to acrobatic displays of leaping fish, and occasionally had to scurry to avoid one nose-bombing the deck. William Penn fretted that one might easily jump into a fisherman's skiff and capsize the boat. In the Great Lakes, spawning sturgeon massed in shallow coves and could be easily hoisted onto boats with gaff-hooks. But nobody bothered except the Indians. For more than 250 years, the European settlers of America wanted little to do with the wandering sturgeon.

When the sons of Johannes Dieckmann and Johannes Hansen arrived in America after the Civil War, they were astounded by the quantity of sturgeon on the East Coast. But the caviar craze sweeping Europe had left Americans cold. Fishermen might occasionally catch a sturgeon and sell the carcass for fertilizer to make a dollar or two, but more often they tossed the whole fish, roe and all, onto the offal heap.

Shad, a smaller anadromous fish that migrated upriver every spring alongside the sturgeon, was the money fish in nineteenth-century America. Sturgeon only got in the way of the shad. The sturgeon's sharp scutes tore up the cotton shad nets, which fishermen and their wives had spent all winter knitting and patching. If a sturgeon was foolish enough to run into a shad net, most fishermen felt the prudent thing to do was bash in its brains to prevent it from ever repeating the crime.

The idea that the sturgeon was a pest to be destroyed must have flabbergasted Indian fishermen. For thousands of years, the nomadic tribes that roamed near North American coasts had celebrated the arrival of the sturgeon with an orgy of fishing. Toward the end of March, the Leni Lenape Indians would head down to the marshes along the Delaware River and the Chesapeake. There, among the salt marsh grass and the cattails, they set up their camps, built fish weirs out of reeds and brush, and awaited the great rush of migrating shad, herring, and sturgeon. The river yielded an abundance that is unimaginable today. Shad, which was easily caught, dried, and transported, was the Lenape's mainstay. But once the main catch was packed into woven baskets, the Indians could at last devote their time to chasing their favorite prey, the sturgeon. Armed with antler-tipped harpoons, the Lenape skimmed the water in their supple bark canoes, eager to do battle with the great Mishe-Nahma—the mythical sturgeon of Longfellow's poem.

Landing a twenty-pound shad requires no great courage. Shad swim headlong into the mesh of a gill net, become stuck, and are easily hauled up into a canoe. But skill and daring are needed to snare a two-hundred-pound Atlantic sturgeon from a small boat. Like the Cossacks, American Indians developed weirs to block the sturgeon's course. Then the real work began. Some Lenape would attempt to lasso the sturgeon using ropes made of twisted grapevines. Others would pierce its leathery skin with a harpoon fashioned from wood and horn, and attached to a rope. As often as not, the sturgeon would bolt to the bottom, leading the fisherman on a wild ride, if not pulling him down into the water. Any fishermen who succeeded in catching a sturgeon was "counted a cockarouse, or brave fellow," reported Robert Beverley, an eighteenth-century chronicler who witnessed the spectacle in Virginia.

The spring fishing season was an idyllic time for the Lenape, the historian Herb C. Kraft discovered. He spent years poring over the remains of a Lenape settlement on the Delaware near Trenton, sifting through the layers of soil to piece together the tribe's habits. "Living together and feasting on fish and roe, watching for the return of marsh birds and the emergence of new plants provided the Indians with leisure time to renew acquaintances, arrange marriages, barter for goods and services," Kraft wrote.

American Indians could choose from ten different kinds of sturgeon and paddlefish, from monsters big enough to sink a canoe, to fish small enough to be carried home by the tail. Some of these American sturgeon live only in fresh water, while others rarely leave the sea. The white sturgeon, found along the Pacific Coast, is nearly the size of the beluga, while the East Coast's shortnose and the Mississippi's shovelnose never reach lengths of more than three feet. The lake sturgeon, which resides exclusively in the fresh water of the Great Lakes and the Mississippi, produces exquisite caviar. Its Mississippi cousin, the paddlefish, probably gives the driest, least succulent eggs. Most enigmatic of all is the green sturgeon, which glows a khaki green. Though rarely sighted in its Pacific waters these days, both its flesh and roe were once thought to be poisonous.

The white sturgeon is the most aggressive of any sturgeon. It will swallow a baited hook and put up as much of a fight as a marlin. Because it is such a challenge to catch, California permits a limited season of white sturgeon fishing. Northwest Coast Indians prefer to drive the white sturgeon into a bag net where it can be safely harpooned. When those methods fail, young men from the Yurok tribe in Northern California like to show off by diving into the water and trying to ride the sturgeon to shore like a wild bronco. The secret, according to Jane Rundquist, an anthropologist who studied the tribe, is to pull the fish's head back as far as possible, forcing it to the surface. Few tribesmen actually succeed at this feat, but those who fail to land the sturgeon barehanded at least have the consolation of displaying their well-earned scars from the fish's rough scutes.

Less risky techniques often worked just as well for American Indians in the past. Paddling their canoes in close formation, they would probe the river bottom with long poles until they sensed a sturgeon. The extraordinary sight was described in 1864 by Sir Arthur Birch, the colonial secretary in British Columbia, in a letter to his brother:

"All the Indians now fishing and it is great fun to watch them spearing Sturgeon which here run 500 & 600 lbs. The Indians drift down with the stream perhaps 30 canoes abreast with their long poles with spears attached kept within about a foot of the bottom of the River. When they feel a fish lying they raise the spear and thrust it at the fish seldom missing."

AMERICAN NATIVES may have considered the sturgeon a gourmet meal, but the early European settlers eyed the fish warily, even as they devoured Chesapeake oysters, worked the New England cod banks, enjoyed enormous amounts of shad, and happily consumed other native foods. It is not clear why the colonists found sturgeon so distasteful. Back home in England, the sturgeon was revered as a royal fish. Yet because it was so expensive and rare, few ordinary Englishmen had actually encountered one before sailing across the Atlantic. The abundance of sturgeon in America was one of the attractions frequently mentioned in seventeenth-century advertisements intended to lure potential colonists. After traveling down the James River for the first time, an English explorer praised the location as a "deep and bold channel so stored with sturgeon and other sweet fish as no man's for time hath ever possessed the like." But when the colonists actually came face to face with the storied sturgeon in the wilds of America, and saw its enormous, rooting snout and rough armored plates, they seem to have lost any desire to make a meal of it.

Given the emphasis on the sturgeon in official notices, it seems strange that the Jamestown colonists arrived in the Virginia wilderness with neither fishing nets nor supplies of salt. During the first year in America, they made no attempt to fish at all. But with all their corn exhausted in 1607, hunger got the better of the colonial gentlemen. At the insistence of Captain John Smith, they waded into the river with frying pans and swords in the hope of knocking out or spearing a meal. They somehow managed to catch a few sturgeon in shallow water using this method, and it was these meaty fish that kept them from starving.

"Wee had more sturgeon than could be devoured by dogge and man," Smith recounted happily afterward. To concoct an edible dish, Smith's party dried and pounded the sturgeon meat, then mixed it with caviar, sorrel, and other herbs. Encouraged by their modest success at fishing, the London Company, which had dispatched them to America, requested that the colonists send a few barrels of caviar home to be sold in the Baltics. By the time those barrels arrived on the London dock in 1609, the stench of decay was evident. In Jamestown, conditions deteriorated. Fed up with their patrons and preoccupied with their own survival, the colonists refused to spend any more time developing a caviar business. As soon as the famine passed, so did their taste for sturgeon.

The Jamestown experience set the tone for other colonists. The European settlers were repulsed by the sturgeon's strong, oily smell, which clung to the Indians who gorged themselves on its meat. Sturgeon, for them, was a food for more primitive people. The newcomers felt the same way about salmon and lobster, two sea creatures that were equally beloved by Indians. As these Europeans struggled to make their way in the wild land, it seemed that eating such a grotesque bottom-feeding fish as the sturgeon would be the equivalent of sinking into barbarism. Their resistance to the meaty fish baffled the explorer Henry Hudson. "There are plenty of sturgeon which the Christians do not make use of, but the Indians eat them greedily," he wrote in a report to the East India Company in 1609.

In time, the American colonists found a use for sturgeon flesh: feeding slaves. Sturgeon meat was cheap and filling, and nobody else seemed to want it. The sugar plantations that occupied almost all the arable land in the Caribbean had large labor forces that needed to be fed. The plantation owners were always struggling to keep their costs down. Indeed, that was one of the main justifications for slavery in the first place, and they were continually on the lookout for low-cost, high-protein foods. Slaves in the West Indies needed to consume large amounts of salt to endure the crushing work of chopping cane in the broiling tropical sun. Salt cod, and then salt shad, became staples of the plantation diet. Sturgeon fishermen thought there was room in the market for their product, too. In 1753, a New Jersey merchant named Edward Broadfield began processing sturgeon for the Caribbean trade. The meat was packed in barrels and transported by ox team to New York and Philadelphia before being shipped to the plantations. Jonathan Richmond set up a rival sturgeon business in Trenton in 1770, which he advertised in the Pennsylvania Gazette:

CHOICE PICKLED STURGEON, cured in the Baltick manner, by JONATHAN RICHMOND, at Trenton Falls; WHO, by his experience these seven years in the business, and not trusting to hired servants or slaves, who often spoil, by not putting up the proper part of the fish, as many so curing neglect. By observing the following directions, to preserve the fish, draw the cork or bung of the keg, and pour out the pickle in a clean basin or pan, then knock up the hoops, and take out the head that is branded, and take what fish you want out, then harden on the hoops, and put the cork in as before; then pour in the liquor into the keg, if not enough to cover the fish, add a little of the vinegar to it, and take a coarse double cloth, and spread it over the head, then put the head on the cloth, and a stone or weight over the head, to keep it close from the air, and it will keep good in the warmest climate, and warrant it good.

Jonathan Richmond struggled with the same problem that had vexed the ancient Greeks, the medieval Italians, and Ioannis Varvarkis: how to keep the sturgeon from going bad in a warm climate. Fishermen on the Kennebec River in Maine also tried pickling sturgeon, but found it spoiled too easily and gave up the business. Perhaps if there had been a bigger domestic market for sturgeon, as there was for cod and shad, those early merchants wouldn't have been forced to rely on the Caribbean slave markets and might have been able to sell sturgeon closer to home, thus incurring lower transportation costs. But almost two centuries after the Jamestown colonists turned up their noses at sturgeon, virtually no middle-class people in America ate the fish. Sturgeon was a food for the great unwashed—Indians, servants, and slaves.

Despite the distaste for sturgeon, the fish remained an object of curiosity. On the Delaware River, the shad fishermen reported seeing thousands of Atlantic and shortnose sturgeon heading toward Philadelphia and the spawning grounds beyond. They were compelled to pull in their nets to prevent the crazed sturgeon from tearing them apart. One day in the early part of the nineteenth century, while the steamboat *Sally* was heading north from Philadelphia, witnesses standing near a porthole saw "a large sturgeon in jumping made such a leap that it passed clear through one of these windows and landed in the vessel, where it was killed."

In the 1840s, a small notice in a Philadelphia newspaper reported that a Russian immigrant had settled on Ridley Creek, a Delaware tributary a few miles below Philadelphia, and was offering fishermen a dollar for each live sturgeon they brought him. What is notable is that he kept the sturgeon in a river pen, much as the Russian sturgeon fishermen do today, so the roe could be taken at its peak from a live fish. This Russian, whose name is not recorded, sold the meat in New York and made oil from the heads. Unlike his predecessors in the sturgeon business, he did not throw away the roe. It was salted, packed in tin cans, and exported to France, Germany, and Russia. The anonymous Russian had started America's first successful caviar business.

A RUSSIAN may have figured out how to prepare good caviar from American sturgeon, but Germans made an industry out of it.

Bendix Blohm, the first of these German caviar dealers, could not have been more ill prepared for the role. Born in Holstein, the region north of Hamburg, he immigrated to America in 1852, intending to start a business exporting pickled sturgeon back to Germany. He set out without knowing the first thing about making caviar.

Blohm, who was already forty-one, wasted no time in heading for New York's Hudson River. He had no doubt heard that American fishermen thought so little of the sturgeon that they tossed them on the trash heap. In reality, Blohm's information was already out of date. By the 1850s, the influx of poor immigrants from Europe had created a new market for cheap sturgeon meat. Immigrants were accustomed to eating a wider range of foods than the squeamish Americans of English descent. Smoked halibut had been the immigrants' favorite fish, but when halibut prices shot up, they had no qualms about switching to sturgeon. Some maintained that sturgeon even tasted better than halibut. In 1857, a New York smokehouse began processing sturgeon, which street peddlers sold door-to-door in immigrant neighborhoods. Hudson River fishermen nicknamed the cheap sturgeon meat "Albany beef."

The development of a profitable domestic market for sturgeon meat finally gave fishermen an incentive to process their catches. Boiling down the head and other waste for oil was one means of maximizing profits. Sturgeon yielded an oil that was less smoky than sperm oil from whales and lasted longer. Isinglass gelatin could also be made from the sturgeon's swim bladder. Before the discovery of isinglass in the early nineteenth century, gelatin had been derived from boiling beef bones, a time-consuming and expensive process. The availability of cheap sturgeon gelatin fueled a middle-class fad for jellied concoctions, made with fruit or meat.

Fishermen now began to think about doing something with the roe other than using it for bait. In 1849, a Boston entrepreneur named N. K. Lombard attempted to set up a caviar business in Woolwich on Maine's Kennebec River. He bought about 160 tons of sturgeon—roughly a thousand fish—and extracted the meat, oil, and roe. The meat and oil sold well, but the caviar was a disaster. Lombard had apparently undersalted it and the entire batch spoiled. The following year Lombard did not spare the salt. Another disaster. He abandoned the business in 1851.

When Bendix Blohm began fishing on the Hudson the following year, he was just as clueless as Lombard about preparing the roe. The sturgeon that Blohm managed to catch were sent directly to New York City to be turned into Albany beef. Fishing on the Hudson proved much less profitable than Blohm expected. From the city of Troy, south to Manhattan, the Hudson is really an extension of the sea, an estuary with powerful tides that wash up from New York harbor. The mildly salty estuarine waters are ideal for sturgeon but terrible for fishermen, and there are only a few hours during the day when the water slackens enough to allow a seine net to be let out. Blohm fished this way for a decade, catching just enough sturgeon to survive, but never producing any caviar. When the country went into an economic slump following the Civil War, Blohm decided to take his boat and nets to Penns Grove, New Jersey, and the calmer waters of the Delaware.

Penns Grove is an old-fashioned small town located on the western shore of New Jersey where the state bulges into the Delaware. It has straight shady streets and sprawling Victorian houses. Because the Delaware coast is so marshy, most towns in the area are located a few miles inland on the higher ground. But Penns Grove developed in one of the few places where the fast land extends right to the Delaware, making it a convenient port. Steamers from Philadelphia docked right at the foot of West Main Street, depositing families eager to spend a few weeks away from the city.

Whatever its other attractions, Penns Grove's main business was fishing. When the shad and herring started running in March, the men would cast off in their dories and not come home until the fish was piled up to the sails. The local people still viewed sturgeon with the same disdain as most American fishermen, despite the growing market for Albany beef among the inhabitants of New York tenements, but Blohm was delighted with the situation. He was the only fisherman working the rich sturgeon grounds south of Penns Grove. The fish coursed up the Delaware in huge numbers, far more than in the Hudson, and in the calm waters, the advancing horde could be virtually skimmed off the bottom with seine nets.

Blohm still knew nothing about making caviar. But determined to expand his business, he invited a couple of Germans from New York to come down and teach him the process. Blohm rented an old sawmill where they could work, and by the spring of 1870, they were shipping caviar by the barrel back to Hamburg.

With his new foolproof recipe and his German connections, Blohm began to turn caviar into an American commodity. Men all over the country were eager to try new enterprises now that the ravages of the

Civil War were finally over. Blohm hired six Penns Grove fishermen to fish exclusively for sturgeon, paying them a generous twenty-five to thirty-five dollars a month.

On the opposite bank of the Delaware, the bustle of the times could be gauged by the plumes of black smoke wafted over Philadelphia from its many factories. The city took pride in being the workshop of the world. Philadelphia was now the second-biggest city in America. Men who had been ordinary soldiers in the Civil War were making their fortunes by turning out locomotives, men's hats, and carpets, and they hungered for emblems of their newfound status. In the past, socially prominent Philadelphians had disdained extravagant shows of wealth, but new entrepreneurs had different tastes. The Caldwell jewelry store found it hard to keep up with orders for diamonds. An exotic food such as caviar appealed to this ambitious business set.

As his caviar business grew, Blohm dug a pond near the river so he could hold live sturgeon until the roe was ripe and could be packed for its trip across the ocean. Transatlantic steamships now ran regularly from Philadelphia to the Continent. The idea that a wealthy family in Hamburg could enjoy sturgeon roe packed in New Jersey didn't seem as fantastical as it had just a few years earlier. Blohm could also send the sturgeon meat up to New York on the Pennsylvania Railroad. The telegraph lines that had been installed in the 1850s made it possible to wire orders in the morning and have the goods on the train the same day. Instead of pickling the sturgeon meat as he had sometimes done in the past, Blohm decided there was a stronger market for smoked fish. Blohm's caviar business, which had seemed like an eccentric gamble before the war, now seemed to be part of America's growing optimism as the centennial celebrations of 1876 approached. Increasingly Philadelphia's new middle class found the time to ride the ferry across the Delaware to spend a summer day in Penns Grove. Thomas Eakins, one of the greatest painters of the era, scoured many Jersey fishing towns for subjects. He painted a series of canvases depicting men working the shallow-bottomed shad boats and hauling in large seine nets. The equipment used to catch shad was virtually identical to that used for sturgeon. Eventually, Penns Grove's shad men couldn't help noticing Bendix Blohm's success. Pretty soon, they stopped throwing away the sturgeon trapped in their nets. The American Caviar Rush had begun.

LIKE THE Gold Rush out in California, the Caviar Rush was short and intense and made relatively few people rich. The Caviar Rush also produced its own boomtown, a jumble of crudely built wooden structures on the New Jersey side of the Delaware, at the point where it stops being a river and starts to become a brackish bay, just a few miles south of Penns Grove. Fishermen were soon calling the town Caviar.

During its brief existence, Caviar was the Astrakhan of America. The little New Jersey boomtown supplied more of the world's caviar during the 1880s than any place on earth. It had a hotel, post office, restaurant, icehouse, and its own rail line, which sent fifteen train cars packed with caviar up to New York every day. Nearly all of it was transferred to steamers bound for Europe. Some of New Jersey's caviar even went to Russia. Caviar's advantage over Penns Grove was that it was some twenty miles closer to the head of the bay. The land at Caviar spilled right down to the water, as it did in Penns Grove, so fishermen could easily pull up to the docks and unload their catches. Recalling the town's bustle a few decades later, a fisherman named George Pyle penned a nostalgic ballad to Caviar:

I saw great fleets of fishing skiffs.
Come down before the gale,
Like a great flock of sea gulls,
So snow-white was each sail.

Today, the town of Caviar is no longer visible. The opportunistic salt marsh grass has run amok, carpeting the rotting foundations of the processing sheds and dormitories with a high cover, which stretches in every direction, all the way to the milk-bottle tower of the Salem nuclear power plant hovering on the horizon. Not a single one of the dozens of buildings remains. The tracks of the railroad have been asphalted over. Even the town's name has been eclipsed, replaced by the generic Bayside. Only the Delaware remains as it was, a broad, implacable, greenish expanse.

The sole evidence of Caviar's bustling port is a few wooden pilings poking their wrinkled necks out of the water near the mouth of Stow Creek, and some black-and-white photographs filed in the local historical society. They show a regiment of wharves projecting from the shore, each one thronged with people. In one image, a group of bowler-hatted men hover at the edge of a pier, waiting to greet a skiff loaded with sturgeon. Nearby, a workman stands next to a hoist as he prepares to lift a huge fish out of the boat. Behind him in the distance are the shanties where fishermen lived during the season. Fishing nets are draped like hammocks to dry on the piers. Some belong to Wyatt Miller, a descendant of slaves, who made enough money repairing nets to open a restaurant in Caviar. In one of the open-air processing sheds, the sturgeon are stacked like logs. A workman in high boots rips open a fish's belly to reveal a bulging clump of eggs. In another picture, three men tentatively massage the sturgeon eggs over a sieve. A few steps behind them, women in high-necked blouses and ankle-length skirts smile in delight as the eggs are transformed into caviar.

In 1895, Boyd's Cumberland County directory listed twenty-two caviar and sturgeon wholesalers with offices in the town. During the fishing season, Caviar's population swelled from a few dozen to four hundred people. Fishermen bedded down in dormitories, ready to jump into their boats whenever the tides commanded. These were usually twenty-six-foot skiffs equipped with both sails and oars, but some fishermen had the misfortune to work from houseboats. These were foul-smelling barges with a single cabin where fishermen slept, ate, gutted fish, and made caviar.

ONE OF the men looking for work during the Caviar Rush was Charles A. Dolbow, a Penns Grove fisherman descended from Swedes who settled on the Jersey side of the Delaware during the time of William Penn. The Dolbows made their livings as farmers and fishermen in Penns Grove.

After the war ended, Charles Dolbow was lucky enough to find a job with Bendix Blohm and his new caviar enterprise, as captain on a sturgeon boat. He would have much preferred to work for himself, but like many of the town's fishermen, he lacked money and connections, not to mention experience at making caviar. If he hoped to start his own operation, Dolbow would need to save enough money to buy a set of boats and nets.

Not long after Dolbow went to work for Blohm, two more Germans from Hamburg arrived on the Delaware coast. They were the sons of Dieckmann & Hansen. Peter Hansen and John Dieckmann had left Hamburg with instructions to sign up caviar suppliers, but they quickly discovered that other than Bendix Blohm, no one knew the first thing about making the delicacy. The pair traveled along the East Coast, handing out nets and sieves to fishermen and teaching them the fine points of salting sturgeon roe. Charles Dolbow eagerly signed on with Dieckmann & Hansen, and in exchange the Hamburg firm lent him five hundred dollars to purchase the equipment he needed to start his own business. In 1876, Dolbow was able to leave his job with Blohm and establish his own fishing camp in Caviar. He shipped thirteen hundred sturgeon to New York his first year, and invested some of the profits in a schooner full of ice from Boston. The ice, which arrived the following spring, would fill a refrigerated storehouse for caviar and sturgeon meat. In a matter of a few years, Charles Dolbow and his son Harry would become Dieckmann & Hansen's most important supplier in America. The two Penns Grove fishermen were so successful that by the 1880s, there was a good chance that a dish of caviar appearing on a German table had originated in New Jersey and was packed by a Dolbow.

Other German caviar merchants followed Dieckmann & Hansen to America. P. Feddersen, a Berlin dealer, found his way to the tiny island of Solomons on the Chesapeake in southern Maryland, where he contracted with a prominent oyster fishermen named Joseph C. Lore. Feddersen provided Lore with barrels, strict instructions about salting, and a good supply of Germany's renowned Luneberg salt. Along the Atlantic seaboard, sleepy fishing ports went to work to satisfy Europe's caviar hunger: Chester, Pennsylvania; Port Penn, Delaware; Savannah, Georgia. A decade after Dieckmann & Hansen arrived in America, there were more than nine hundred watermen trawling for sturgeon along the Atlantic coast.

Most of the American caviar was sent to Europe, but sometimes second-rate batches were sold domestically. A few New York bars began handing out free caviar sandwiches, in the hope that the salty snack would increase drink orders. The Denver and Rio Grande Railroad offered caviar in its dining car, for the same price as a plate of olives and celery, two other novel delicacies. Most of the caviar was processed with a salt ratio of 9 to 10 percent, double today's standard, in an effort to prevent spoilage. The Dolbows also offered a better grade with 5 percent salt, but only for the European trade.

The Delaware was where America's caviar industry began, and it was Delaware fishermen who dominated fishing up and down the East Coast. Because the sturgeon started spawning earlier in the warm, southern rivers, the northerners shipped their boats by rail to Georgia around February to meet the first runs of sturgeon. Working their way north river by river, the Delaware fishermen followed the sturgeon until they reached the town of Caviar. They started in the Savannah River, put their skiffs on a flatbed train for Virginia, moved on to the James River, hopscotching up the coast from the Potomac River, to the Patuxent, Chesapeake, and Delaware, where the season lasted until the end of June.

Chasing the sturgeon north, a fisherman could earn good money, more than if he stayed home to wait for the shad run. It was tough work, though. Sturgeon nets weighed two hundred pounds even when empty, and quite a bit more after they were pulled up wet and loaded with fish. Fishermen spent nearly the whole day on the river when the sturgeon were running. A single female brought two dollars at the wharf. That was a hefty sum when a workingman's weekly salary might be ten dollars. By 1897, the price for a female sturgeon swollen with eggs had jumped to thirty dollars.

Not every sturgeon was of equal value. American fishermen soon learned to rank sturgeon much as Russians do today, saving their highest regard for egg-laden "cows." Still, most fishermen had no qualms about salting the roe from "runners," female fish caught before their eggs were hard and ripe, even though the caviar was second-rate. It could be sold as sandwich caviar. As for the male "bucks" and the female "slunkers," which had already given up their burden of eggs, they were good only for meat. The juvenile "mammoses" were nearly worthless. After fishermen had paid their expenses, they could take home five hundred dollars, enough to allow them to spend the rest of the year sitting around, telling stories and mending nets.

For ambitious fishermen like Charles Dolbow, who processed the fish himself, the profits were even higher. He arranged to sell everything separately, the caviar, meat, isinglass, and oil. Caviar naturally commanded the most money. German dealers were paying nine dollars for a 135-pound keg of caviar in 1885, but fifteen years later the cost shot up to a hundred dollars a keg. Fishermen had never seen such prices for any other fish. In 1908, a professor at the University of Pennsylvania, Walter Tower, published a short history of the sturgeon fishery. "Nowhere else in the whole annals of commercial fisheries," he concluded, "is there a parallel to this case of sturgeon, rising as it did in less than a quarter of a century from a fish despised and ruthlessly destroyed . . . to the highest rank of commercial value." Most fishermen expected the prices to keep rising.

With all that money being made off the sturgeon, fishermen failed to notice that they were catching fewer of them. In the 1870s, fishermen caught an average of sixty-five sturgeon each time they hauled their heavy nets out of the water. A decade later, the average had fallen to thirty. At first it didn't matter if there were fewer sturgeon struggling in the gill net, because the price for a cow was doubling every year. The Delaware, always the most fruitful of the East Coast rivers, saw its total catch drop by half between 1890 and 1897, from 5 million pounds down to 2.5 million, yet fishermen's incomes remained stable, or even increased.

By then Dieckmann & Hansen was firmly established in America. Ferdinand Hansen, a grandnephew of the company's founders, had arrived in 1886 to run the firm's New York office and oversee operations in Penns Grove and Caviar. Although Hansen was just seventeen, he had enough experience in the caviar trade to recognize what the falling catches meant. It had taken barely thirty years to pick the Elbe clean of sturgeon. In 1899, exactly twenty-nine years after Bendix Blohm made his first batch of caviar in Penns Grove, Delaware fishermen averaged only eight sturgeon in a net. Dealers scrambled to find enough American caviar to satisfy Europe's appetite. Some fishermen made crude attempts to pass off other fish roes as sturgeon caviar. The Berlin wholesaler P. Feddersen wrote to his Chesapeake supplier Joseph Lore in June 1899 to vent his frustration, and to beg for the real thing:

The season, "is pretty well done . . . There is a big lot (of) Chesapeake caviar in the market. Where does it come from? One man wrote me he had 25 kegs and another party had 150 kegs in N.Y. I went there, but I like to buy caviar made out (of) sturgeon roe, but not dirt—shad roe—put up. I tell you there is some bad stuff in the market."

THE SEASON of 1900 marked the thirty-year anniversary of the American caviar industry. After three decades of relentless fishing along the East Coast, vast numbers of spawning sturgeon had been taken out of the reproductive pool. The fish that should have been spawning for the first time in 1900 had never been born. Their eggs had long ago been eaten. That year, sturgeon stocks crashed in every river along the East Coast. In the James, the Chesapeake, the Delaware, fishermen pulled up empty nets. Some years later, Charles Dolbow's son

Harry, who had taken over the business and changed his family name to Dalbow, would recall bitterly that "caviar never got a decent, respectable price until the failure of 1900." European dealers closed their American operations. Others moved west, to the Great Lakes and the Pacific coast. Dieckmann & Hansen did not give up their American operation entirely, but the firm's attentions were now focused on the rich Russian fishing grounds. In 1895, they started making caviar on Siberia's Amur River, and then moved to Astrakhan in 1902. The supplies from Russia more than made up for the decline in American production. Harry Dalbow continued to fish the Delaware, and Ferdinand Hansen continued to buy from him. But everyone sensed it was the end of something. The start of the twentieth century marked a watershed for the Volga as well as the Delaware: Astrakhan produced 29,800 tons of sturgeon in 1900, a record that would never again be surpassed.

HARRY DALBOW wasn't ready to believe that caviar was over. In 1891, he had formed a partnership with one of his relatives, Joseph "Yaller" Dolbow. They started with a pair of sailboats moored at Caviar, but were confident enough in the future to invest in the new gasoline-powered engines. Eventually they built a fleet of twenty boats.

Many fishermen came to believe that the sturgeon fishery needed regulation to survive, and made attempts to police the bloody free-for-all. In 1904, fishermen from Caviar, Chester, and Port Penn gathered in the Davis Hotel in Philadelphia to form the Sturgeon Fisherman's Protective Society. The first item on the agenda was a proposal to throw back any sturgeon measuring less than four feet. Such young fish could not possibly have ripe eggs. But some fishermen contended the effort was pointless; most of the fish would be dead or injured before they could be separated from the nets. Ferdinand Hansen pursued another tack. He appeared before the legislatures of New Jersey, Pennsylvania, and Delaware and tried to convince them to fix a season for sturgeon fishing. By cutting off fishing on May 15, he suggested, a portion of the sturgeon population would be spared and given a chance to spawn. His plan was rejected, and years later, he complained that the lawmakers sided with the fishermen, who "preferred to kill the goose that laid the golden eggs." In a way, the crash of 1900 acted as a brake on fishing, thinning the ranks at Caviar. Even his partner Yaller Dolbow gave up fishing in 1901. But Harry had been raised on sturgeon, and like the fish he stubbornly returned to the river he had always known.

Although Harry earned two thousand dollars from sturgeon fishing in some years, the money was never enough to make him rich. Every year after the fishing ended, he would take odd jobs on Salem County vegetable farms, the gardens of the Garden State. South Jersey's vegetable industry was in its heyday. Growers sent truckloads of tomatoes, beans, and asparagus to the area's booming canning factories such as Campbell's Soup in Camden. In the fall of 1906, Harry was helping out on a neighbor's farm on the assembly line where the tomatoes were being packed into tin cans and sealed using a new vacuum process. As Harry tamped down the lids he had a small epiphany. Why couldn't caviar be packed in small, airtight containers and sealed shut? He did not have to go far to test his idea. South Jersey was a hotbed of innovation in the new science of food preservation. The French chef Nicolas Appert had invented the first reliable canning and bottling methods in 1809, and South Jersey farmers built on his discoveries. In 1847, they produced the first canned tomatoes for commercial sale in Jamesburg. The acceptance of canned foods expanded during the Civil War, when Union troops were fed on canned pork and beans, canned sardines, and canned succotash. The American-Can Company became one of the largest employers in South Jersey. Harry decided to ask the company to design a machine that could pack caviar just like tomatoes.

The marriage of canning and caviar could not have happened at a more propitious time. America's ancient sturgeon populations, so abundant at the nation's birth two hundred years earlier, were vanishing in every river. The Atlantic sturgeon had been reduced to a few scattered populations of fish by 1900. Catches of white sturgeon in the Sacramento River peaked in 1885, and California banned sturgeon fishing altogether in 1901. Although the white sturgeon in the Columbia River was not fished commercially until 1888, the stocks there were exhausted in twelve years flat. Lake Erie, which had yielded 5 million pounds of sturgeon in 1885, sent a mere 200,000 pounds to market ten years later. Fishermen resorted to making caviar from the roe of the Mississippi paddlefish. Dry and grainy as it was, they passed it off as Russian caviar.

The [Indians] who had the sturgeon to themselves for so long, found their survival threatened by insatiable demand for caviar. "A good many whitemen are yet fishing now near Harrison River, openly stealing our fish, our only food. They want to see us starving, we cannot bear it," four Chilliwack chiefs from British Columbia complained in an 1894 petition to the Canadian government. Unless something was done soon, they warned, Indian fishermen would surely resort to violence to destroy the commercial sturgeon lines draped across the rivers. By 1902, the sturgeon on the Harrison River were hardly worth the commercial fishermen's time. What remained was left to the Indians. But the prospects for these original Americans were almost as bad as the sturgeon's.

Greedy fishermen were not alone in killing off the sturgeon. Pollution was taking its toll. The Delaware River, which had been clean enough in the early nineteenth century for ships to fill their water casks in midchannel, was now a cesspool, so slick with oil from the Philadelphia refineries that it was known to combust into flame. The building boom that followed the surge of immigrants had also damaged the river. Silt from construction, new roads, and farms poured into the Delaware and the Chesapeake, forming a cushion of silt over the hard rocky surfaces where sturgeon liked to spawn. Out west, the runoff from sawmills around the Great Lakes reduced the oxygen levels, suffocating both the rivers and the sturgeon.

As fishermen scoured America's rivers and lakes for the remaining sturgeon, it was becoming increasingly difficult to fill the standard 135-pound keg. Those wooden barrels had hardly changed from the ones Varvarkis had used in Catherine the Great's time, and looked old and crude in an age of gasoline-powered engines and airplanes. Harry Dalbow's canning operation offered a sleek and modern successor: the little glass jar. With American-Can's help, he not only mechanized the packing of caviar, he put the delicacy into individual glass jars that could be sold directly to consumers. The jars were intentionally small, two and four ounces. By packing the caviar in smaller containers, Harry was able to make his limited supplies of caviar go further. He could also charge a lot more, too, when people were buying caviar by the ounce instead of the keg. The canning machine turned out to be a profitable form of rationing the remaining American caviar.

Dieckmann & Hansen recognized that Dalbow's idea would change the way people thought about caviar. No longer would it be ladled out of giant barrels. Caviar would be sold like precious gems in the finest shops. The vacuum-sealed jars also had the advantage of extending caviar's freshness. Caviar could now be pasteurized, giving it a shelf life of a year or more, and the pungent smell of decomposing eggs would become mostly a memory.

IN 1912, Harry sailed to Europe on the *Lusitania* to instruct Dieckmann & Hansen's staff in the secrets of canning. He spent several months in Astrakhan, teaching workers at the packing house how to use the canning equipment. Soon after he arrived home, his partner, Ferdinand Hansen, opened America's first retail caviar shop on the ground floor of the Waldorf-Astoria Hotel in New York. Hansen, who had previously used the trade name "Russian Caviar," decided that the product needed a more romantic sounding name for its label than the family names his ancestors had used. He wanted something exotic, something Russian, something that evoked wealth. The obvious name was Romanoff Caviar, after the Russian royal family. With the American rivers exhausted, Hansen expected that most of the caviar in the tiny jars would soon be Russian, anyway. He was right. Unable to find enough caviar to fill a sufficient number of one-ounce jars, Harry Dalbow shut his cannery and sold his boats in 1925. Just a half century after Americans began to make caviar, the sturgeon were gone.

5

Caviar for
the Masses

*That is caviar, she explained to him, and this is vodka,
the drink of the people, but I think you will find the two
are admirably suited to each other.*

—C. S. FORESTER, COMMODORE HORNBLOWER

*W*hen the Bolsheviks came to power in 1917, Russia was the last
place on earth where the sturgeon still existed in large numbers. In
America and Europe the fish had been wiped out by greedy dealers, im-
provident fishermen, and the insatiable public demand for caviar. That
situation gave the Communists a valuable monopoly over the caviar
trade, and they were determined the new Soviet state should control it.

The nationalization of the Russian caviar industry began with
bloodshed. In 1919, the Communist government announced that it was
assuming ownership of the Caspian fishery. The region had produced

more than two-thirds of Russia's caviar before the revolution, and so it was the logical place for the State to start its takeover. At the time, however, the Bolsheviks were still in the midst of a civil war with the anti-Communist forces. The fighting in Astrakhan was especially bloody. By 1919, the city's factory workers and fishermen were so fed up with food shortages and Communist rule that they declared a general strike. The workers' action enraged the Soviet regime, which responded with a fury even more extreme than usual. The Communist forces rounded up everybody, not just striking workers but so-called bourgeois elements as well. Dispensing with the formality of trials, execution squads simply imposed death sentences on everyone who had been arrested. Some prisoners were pushed into the Volga with bricks tied to their ankles. Others were shot. To speed things up, group executions were carried out right on the barges in the middle of the Volga, and for the first time the river of sturgeon glistened with a slick of human blood.

The carnage marked the end of Astrakhan's glory days. Everything in Astrakhan had always revolved around fish, and fish had made Astrakhan rich. At the time of the revolution, more fish were taken from the Caspian than from the Baltic and Pacific fisheries combined. When the caviar craze hit Europe in the nineteenth century, Astrakhan became richer still. Caviar production in the Caspian, which had been a mere four tons annually in 1860, had soared to well over three thousand tons a year by 1900.

The poet Khlebnikov might grumble about the smell of fish, but the caviar business had been responsible for turning Astrakhan into a cultured oasis on the empty steppe. At the turn of the century, the city hummed with theaters, an amusement park, a European-style hotel, a Victorian, red-brick natural history museum, and gourmet food stores selling everything from English tea to Jaffa oranges. Rich merchants built sumptuous houses in the new Style Moderne. The Nobel brothers, who made a fortune drilling for oil a few miles south, in Baku, opened an office in Astrakhan. The city was known around the world not just for caviar and crude oil, but for its local hat. Made from a newborn lamb's tightly curled fur, the brimless, peaked cap is still called an Astrakhan, whether it's produced in southern Russia or an enterprise zone in China. Astrakhan's position at the crossroads of Asia and Europe gave the city a strongly cosmopolitan flavor in the beginning of the twentieth century. There were sizable settlements of Tatars, Kazaks, Kalmyks, Persians, Armenians, Azeris, Georgians, and Jews, as well as clusters of Hindus and Zoroastrians from India. Each of these groups had its own area of specialty, silks for the Persians, watermelons for the Azeris. For the Russians and their Cossack cousins, it was always caviar.

In 1902, Dieckmann & Hansen opened an office in Astrakhan with high expectations. Having already witnessed the quick depletion of stocks in the Elbe and the Delaware, the Hamburg firm was eager to find a stable source of caviar. The huge concentration of sturgeon in the Caspian seemed to promise a steady supply for years to come. The firm would not have to worry about educating the Russian fishermen either, as they had done in America. The Russians were the experts at catching sturgeon and making fine caviar.

The Hamburg company's strength was its expertise in packing and shipping. Their experience in America had taught them that the best way to prevent spoilage was to divide the caviar into small batches, rather than putting all their eggs into one huge barrel. When Dieckmann & Hansen arrived in Astrakhan at the turn of the century, they introduced the tin cans they had been using in America. These tins, which held roughly two pounds of eggs, replaced the wooden barrels that had been used to hold caviar since the days of the Mongol traders.

The simple tins work astonishingly well. First the caviar is gently ladled into an open container, then the cover is slowly fitted over it until all the air is squeezed out. After a near vacuum is created, a rubber band is fitted over the seam as a shield against the elements. For further protection, Dieckmann & Hansen would wrap the cans in cheesecloth bags, three to a bag. Then they were stacked inside a shipping barrel with generous amounts of ice. If the caviar went by ship, the barrels were usually stored below the waterline, where the air was coolest, since refrigerated ships were not common at the beginning of the twentieth century. The same packing regime was followed even in the winter, when the Volga was iced over and the only way to get the caviar out of Astrakhan was on a single-track railroad that crept north to the port in St. Petersburg. Even after Harry Dalbow came up with his method for packing caviar in glass jars, the firm still used the tins to supply its wholesale dealers.

Before the revolution, Russians consumed most of the caviar produced from the Caspian and foreign sales remained relatively puny. In 1913, on the eve of Russia's disastrous entrance into Europe's Great War, Astrakhan fishermen landed more than 28,000 metric tons of sturgeon in the Caspian and extracted some 3,000 tons of caviar. All but a fraction of this immense catch ended up on Russian tables. Dieckmann & Hansen was the largest foreign producer, yet it exported a mere 100 tons of caviar a year. Despite caviar's status in Europe, caviar was still primarily a Russian food.

As the Russian appetite for caviar grew, Astrakhan's producers began looking beyond the Volga and Ural deltas. In 1893, the enterprising Lianozov brothers managed to obtain a fishing concession from the Persian government, giving them the right to trawl for sturgeon in the southern part of the Caspian. The area off the Persian coast had not been heavily fished for sturgeon in the past, partly because the water there is much deeper and more treacherous than it is in the northern Caspian. There was also the issue of local tradition. The inhabitants of the southern Caspian coast were all Shia Muslims, a mix of Persians and Azeris. Many of them considered the sturgeon and its roe an unclean food. Some local fishermen refused to touch a sturgeon. The Lianozov brothers had to bring in crews of Russian fishermen to work the boats. But even when Russian fishermen and Russian techniques were transplanted to Persian soil, the end result remained inferior to the mix made in Russia. One reason was that the roe was taken from immature sturgeon in the open sea, rather than spawners in the river. But the lack of a caviar-consuming culture may have also affected the quality. The inferior Persian production usually sold at a significant discount in Russia.

Thanks to Lianozov's expansion into Persian waters, the overall Caspian sturgeon catch continued to increase. But there were signs that the sea was being taxed beyond its limit. Paul Reinbrecht, who was posted to Astrakhan in 1902 to manage Dieckmann & Hansen's new plant, recognized the troubling signs right away. Fishermen had started to voice the now-familiar complaint that it was taking more effort to catch the same number of fish. Reinbrecht sent a dispatch to the Hamburg office predicting that the sturgeon catches in the Caspian would soon begin to fall drastically, following the same pattern that Dieckmann & Hansen had witnessed in Germany and America.

The home office was shaken by such a dire forecast. The Volga delta had always been celebrated for its abundance of fish. Sturgeon were so plentiful there that almost no one bothered taking a boat into the Caspian Sea to catch them; it was too easy to drop a net in the river and wait for a fish to swim into it. But now everyone agreed that the crowds of sturgeon swimming upriver were growing thinner. In 1901, the fishing companies petitioned the Russian government for permission to fish at sea to compensate for the falling river catches. The request was granted, but they didn't have to go far to make up their losses. The area just beyond the mouth of the Volga teamed with young sturgeon, who fed on the nutrients brought south by the river. Millions of juvenile sturgeon spent their youth frolicking in the warm shallow waters of the northern Caspian, where they fed on a smorgasbord of mollusks and worms. Catching a sturgeon there was as easy as shooting a buffalo on the open prairie. Even if fewer of these immature fish had eggs in their bellies, their flesh could still be sold for meat.

During the season, large boats dropped anchor for months at a time and set up fixed nets on poles. When the fish swam into the nets, their gills snagged on the openings. All the fishermen had to do was haul up the catch several times a day. These standing nets caught a lot more than just sturgeon. Although fishermen had rarely troubled themselves with lesser fish such as perch, roach, or herring, the demand for them had increased as the sturgeon catches fell. It was a typical fishing pattern. Once the prime species is fished out, fishermen work their way down the ladder of desirable species. The small bony fishes were rapidly becoming a staple of the Russian diet, especially among poor workers living in the squalid slums of Moscow and St. Petersburg. So great was the demand for cheap sources of protein that some sturgeon fishermen started to go after the humble *kilka*, a fish the size of an anchovy.

JUST WHEN it seemed that the Russians would do to the Caspian sturgeon what the Germans and Americans had done to their stocks, a temporary reprieve came in the form of war and revolution.

The Astrakhan fishing records from the early twentieth century reflect the dramatic events occurring thousands of miles away. The century started with bright promise and a record catch of nearly 30,000 tons of sturgeon in the northern Caspian. Catches remained reasonably good even after the first distant rumblings of World War I in 1914. But once the German forces advanced on the Marne a year later, catches began to fall, slowly at first, then more sharply. In 1917, when the war had brought down the decrepit Romanov dynasty, fishermen brought in only 8,500 tons. With the new Bolshevik government mired in civil war, just 2,100 tons of sturgeon were caught in 1920, barely enough to make 300 tons of caviar.

For most of a decade, the people who would have normally been pursuing the sturgeon were busy pursuing something else. Russian fishermen stopped fishing after 1914 and went off to battle the Germans. Four years later, they abandoned their nets again to fight the Communists or the Whites—depending on their ideological bent—in Russia's civil war. The foreign caviar companies had all fled Astrakhan at the beginning of the hostilities. The Germans were too busy digging trenches and battling the French to think about nibbling sturgeon eggs. Many of Russia's wealthy caviar merchants had also left after the revolution. By the time Lenin and the Bolsheviks had defeated the last of their challengers in 1921, the few remaining caviar merchants were desperately scrambling to get out of the country.

The pause in fishing saved Russia's sturgeon. Those six or seven years of human turmoil gave the troubled fish the peace and quiet it needed to recover its numbers. After Russia's crisis subsided, the Caspian fishermen naturally drifted back to their old routines. Catches slowly started to rise again. The Communists had formally nationalized the fishery after 1919, but because they were anxious to increase food supplies they let the fishermen continue as private businessmen. But the fishermen knew their days of independence were numbered. The Communists were determined to collectivize the fishermen, just as they had done with the peasants and in 1925 finally managed to organize the first fishing collective. In a matter of a few years, every fisherman would become a state employee.

The Communists understood as early as 1920 that caviar could be a profitable business. That year, two Armenian brothers by the name of Petrossian struck a deal with the Foreign Trade Ministry to ship regular supplies of Astrakhan caviar to Paris. Encouraged by the results, the Communists reached out a few months later to the prerevolutionary caviar house of Dieckmann & Hansen and offered to provide them with regular supplies of the Germans' favorite delicacy. The trade agreements were a sign that the West's initial hostility to the Communists had waned. While their ideology wasn't exactly to Europe's taste, caviar was, and their dealers were willing to pay hard currency to get it.

Cash was what the struggling Soviet government needed more than anything else. German marks, French francs, and British pounds were required to buy tractors, trucks, locomotives, machine parts, and all the other equipment necessary to turn Russia into an industrialized nation. The money from caviar, the Soviets soon discovered, could purchase these essential commodities. As it increased control over the caviar trade, the government made it illegal for individuals to export the bourgeois snack privately. There was actually a historical precedent for giving the state control over the caviar industry. Tsar Alexei had issued virtually the same order after triumphing over Stenka Razin and the Cossack rebels in the 17th century.

The caviar business proved so lucrative for the Soviets that they began to eye fishing grounds outside their own borders. In 1925, they seized control of the Lianozov's caviar operation, oblivious to the fact that it was located in Persian territory. This did not sit well with the Persian monarch, Reza Shah Pahlavi. Worried about the precedent, as well as the Soviet Union's growing monopoly of the caviar trade, he evicted the Communists from the Lianozov property and announced that the fishery would be leased to the highest bidder. Unfortunately for Persia, the winning bidder turned out to be a group of anti-Communist

Russian exiles. The Soviet Union made it clear they would never toler-ate their archenemies as competitors in the Caspian. They mounted a campaign of open threats and diplomatic intrigue. Eventually, the pres-sure from Moscow proved too much and the shah caved in, agreeing to split the ownership of the fishery between Persia and the Communists. According to the 1927 contract, Tehran was supposed to receive half the proceeds from the joint venture. Yet somehow most of the profits and all the caviar ended up in Russia.

The Soviet Union was now the undisputed boss of the Caspian. With the production from the Black Sea and its other sturgeon fisheries, Moscow controlled 90 percent of the world's caviar supply. The Communists ran their caviar monopoly like every other monopoly in the world. They dictated all the terms. Through a state agency called Prodintorg, the Soviets decided how much caviar would be produced each year, what the price would be, and who could buy it. The Russians even set prices for Iranian caviar. Although there were many small caviar houses around the world, the Soviets preferred to deal with a few giant wholesalers. In Germany, it was Dieckmann & Hansen. In France, it was Petrossian. For a while, most of the caviar that went to America passed through Romanoff Caviar or through the Swiss com-panies Porimex in Zurich and Caviar House in Geneva. The Soviet Union guarded its caviar production the way De Beers protected its di-amond mines. For many years, no foreigners were allowed anywhere near the caviar fisheries.

In building their new cartel, the Communists were great standard-izers. They built modern fish processing factories equipped with auto-mated canning machines. They created three export grades for their caviar and gave each its own color-coded label—blue for beluga, yel-low for osetra, and red for sevruga. Whatever flaws the Soviet system had, its management of caviar exports was a model of efficiency compared to the collection of companies that control the Caspian now. Western caviar dealers speak of the Soviet cartel with nostalgic fondness. "The Soviets would always tell us, 'This is how much caviar we have and this is how much money we want.' It was easy, so easy to plan," said one dealer, stressed by the uncertainty of the 1990s.

Through their strict control of production, the Communists ensured that caviar remained a luxury product. Although they could have sold much more caviar in the West, they kept exports steady at about 10 percent of production to guard against a potential price-deflating glut. Given the small amount of exported caviar, there should have been plenty for the home market. But, like so many Soviet products, caviar was always hard to find.

The better the Soviets got at supplying caviar to the West, the worse they were at distributing it domestically. While a wide cross-section of people had eaten caviar during the tsarist era, under the Communists the traditional Russian zakouski gradually became a food for the elite. There was probably less caviar to go around, since sturgeon catches did not approach the prerevolutionary totals again until 1935. Somehow, though, Communist bosses always seemed to have access to secret supplies of caviar, which they would produce for special meetings, birthday parties, and foreign visitors. The government also used caviar as a form of payment. Kremlin employees would often receive a jar of caviar in their New Year's food parcel, which was itself a way of mitigating the shortages that prevailed the rest of the year. Other Russians who wanted caviar had to make do with vacuum-packed tins of gloppy salmon roe from the Soviets' Pacific fisheries. When real caviar did make it to the stores, it was always priced well below its market value.

Tons of domestic caviar disappeared down the subterranean corridors of the black market during the latter years of Soviet rule. Caviar became an underground currency, a luxurious way of greasing palms and extracting favors. Caviar might be used to acquire tickets to a sold-out concert at the Bolshoi Theater, or to win favor from a professor at exam time. The one place where caviar might be available was in the theater's snack bar. When intermission was called during a performance at the Bolshoi or Taganka theaters, crowds would rush out to find stacks of open-faced caviar sandwiches. Prepared hours before and left unrefrigerated, the eggs would often be dried out and chewy, but still edible. For many Russians, it was the only way they knew caviar.

CAVIAR HAD helped bring the Soviet Union the hard currency it needed to import Western technology. But both Lenin and Stalin knew that money alone could not transform Russia into an industrialized nation capable of holding its own against the West. More than cash, Russia needed electrical power.

That power would be found in the rushing waters of the Volga River. The Volga travels farther and carries more water than any other river in Europe, transporting the melted snows of the Arctic across the hot steppe and down into the Caspian Sea. Although three hundred rivers drain into the sea, some 80 percent of the sea's volume comes from the Volga alone—a staggering amount of moving water. Countries all over the world had obtained cheap electricity by blocking the flow of their less powerful rivers, so why shouldn't Russia do the same to the Volga?

Dams had become the technological frontier in the 1920s, after the end of World War I. With peace, the electric grid systems introduced at the beginning of the century could be expanded, fueling a second industrial age. Electricity usage shot up in the United States and Russia, and the demand for cheap sources of power increased. The Soviets keenly understood that electricity was essential to a modern country, and eyed the West's network of electric lines enviously. The idea of bringing electricity to every village in Russia had gripped the imagination of the country after the revolution. "Communism equals Soviet power plus electrification," was one of Lenin's most quoted dictums.

There was a less appealing aspect to this equation. By damming the Volga for electricity, a large proportion of Caspian fish would be cut off from their spawning grounds. Sturgeon, which traveled farthest upriver to lay their eggs, would be hurt most. But other fish, such as white salmon, herring, pike, and perch—fish that formed a large part of the Russian diet—would also be unable to reach some of their spawning places. Concerned about damaging such an important food source, the Soviet Union's leading scientists, the members of the Academy of Sciences, sent a letter in 1933 warning that the Volga dam would create an environmental catastrophe. But electrical power was one of the Soviet Union's fundamental obsessions, and Stalin pressed ahead.

Fortunately, the damming of a river as long as the Volga could not be accomplished in one stroke. More than a dozen separate dams were built along the northern part of the river and its tributaries. The Volga's flowing waters were gradually being turned into a series of placid lagoons that could be filled and drained at will to supply electric power to factories, provide water for irrigating the arid steppe, control flooding, and aid navigation. Stalin, who dragged Russia by force into the industrial age, envisioned hundreds of steel foundries, paper mills, and chemical plants clustered around the power-producing dams. Russia would cease to be a backward nation of peasant farmers and would at last harness its natural resources to become an industrial giant.

The start of World War II brought dam construction to a halt, another reprieve for the sturgeon. Because the first dams were situated upriver, not far from Moscow, they had little immediate impact on the fish's reproduction. There were still plenty of spawning places below the dams. For Stalin and his engineers, the real prize lay much farther south, at the confluence of the Volga and Akhtuba Rivers, near what was then called Stalingrad and is now called Volgograd. But before the main dam could be built, the Soviet Union would have to weather the devastating trials of World War II, which would leave Stalingrad a smoldering ruin.

The Battle of Stalingrad was a turning point in the war against the Nazis. Though it reduced the city to rubble and claimed over a million Soviet lives, the Russian victory prevented the German forces from reaching the Caspian oil fields and obtaining the supplies of crude they needed to carry on the war. As a reward for the city's heroic resistance, Stalin promised to build Europe's biggest dam on its shores. When the Soviet Politburo gave the go-ahead, the newspaper *Pravda* devoted its entire front page to the story.

Stalin's dam is indeed a colossus. The massive, concrete span seems to go on forever across the three miles of river, like a never-ending, flat-roofed Greek temple. The wall at the main portal is decorated with Socialist Realist murals depicting muscled workers in full stride, their arms piercing the sky to urge others forward. The construction of the dam was almost as heroic as the defense of Stalingrad. It took six years to build and required the efforts of fifty thousand workers. When the turbines were turned on in 1961, they produced enough electricity to light up virtually the whole of western Russia. By that time, though, the Caspian sturgeon were heading toward extinction.

PROFESSOR Igor Burtsev, one of Russia's most respected sturgeon specialists, emanated a grayish cast, like a sturgeon that has been out of water too long. After the Soviet collapse in 1991, the oceanographic research institute where he worked in Moscow could no longer afford to keep the lights on during the day. The gloom seemed to accentuate the grayness of his homemade sweater, silvery crew-cut, and broken eyeglasses held together with rubber bands.

Despite his institute's poverty, Burtsev had been responsible for two groundbreaking advances in sturgeon aquaculture. Along with other scientists at VNIRO, the Russian Federal Research Institute for Fisheries and Oceanography, he had developed a completely new species of sturgeon, called bester, a cross between the giant beluga and the tiny sterlet. The bester resembles the beluga in size, but like the little sterlet, it matures early and produces large, pearly, mild-tasting eggs. Since the bester can turn out a crop of eggs every two years, it is the perfect species for aquaculture farms to raise for caviar.

Most sturgeon farms have to kill their precious fish to get the eggs. Burtsev thought this was a big waste of fish, especially when the wild sturgeon population was in decline. He was sure there must be a way to keep the sturgeon alive after removing the eggs. After many years of trial and error, he perfected a method of siphoning the roe from live sturgeon. He called it "milking," although the operation is really the fish equivalent of a cesarean section. In the future, Burtsev is convinced that all caviar will be obtained by milking sturgeon. "It's simply not rational to kill these endangered animals," Burtsev argued. As proof of his superior method, Burtsev likes to serve his guests a plateful of open-faced sandwiches spread with bester eggs. The mother fish, he tells them proudly, is still happily swimming in his laboratory tank.

Burtsev's commitment to his labor-intensive sturgeon milking may have something to do with the spectacle he witnessed shortly after the main wall of the Volgograd dam was completed in 1959. He was working in the regional fishery institute at the time and had watched the dam take shape. Eager to inspect the latest marvel of Soviet engineering, he took a stroll across the dam's roof, which would later become a road-way. It was a fine day in late spring, a few weeks after the fish migrations had started. When Burtsev gazed down below at the surface of the water, he was shocked to see a mass of sturgeon bunched up at the base of the dam. He estimates that 600,000 migrating sturgeon were caught in the immense snarl. Frustrated in their attempts to return to their birthplace, and temperamentally incapable of turning back, most ended up dead, floating belly up in the slow waters that lapped at the base of the dam.

BY THE time the dam was finished, everyone agreed the sturgeon's future looked dire. Engineers had installed an elevator that was supposed to lift the migrating fish up and over the dam, but it was never capable of sending more than a few upriver at a time. As far as the sturgeon are concerned, Europe's longest river now ends at Volgograd. The dam reduced the Volga to a quarter of its original length. Dams also blocked many other rivers around the Caspian. Only the Ural River, once the exclusive domain of the Cossacks, continued to flow freely. The impact of the new dams was immediate. Catches dropped by 25 percent between 1950 and 1960. Scientists such as Burtsev feared most for the beluga, the oldest and most primitive of the sturgeon, and the one least likely to adapt to the new conditions. While the other varieties had lost perhaps half their breeding grounds, the beluga had been cut off from 90 percent of its traditional spawning places. It was habitat loss on a massive, frightening scale.

When people think about the animals that have been threatened with extinction—elephants in Africa, buffalo in America—the tendency is to attribute the situation to overconsumption. The herds of elephants and buffalo have been depleted by hunters, just as the sturgeon have exhausted by fishermen. But in the twentieth century, overconsumption became only part of the problem. As human civilization has advanced and expanded, all sorts of animals have been crowded out of their natural habitats.

The Soviet dams not only reduced the size of the sturgeon's environment; they diminished the quality of their watery realm. Because the Volga now filtered through a dozen dams on its way south, the river was abnormally clear when it arrived in the Caspian. Much of the rich nutrients are left behind. In such transparent waters, inch-long baby sturgeon become easy prey, while the plankton and mollusks they feed on fail to grow properly. The clearer water was hardly cleaner water. Just as the Soviets had dreamed, the dam had made it possible to build dozens of new factories along Volgograd's riverfront. Lacking any sort of environmental controls, they sent streams of toxic waste, including PCBs, heavy metals, and oil products, into the Volga with abandon. By the 1980s, every single sturgeon egg tested by scientists was found to have abnormalities preventing many from becoming live sturgeon

If sturgeon couldn't reproduce on their own, then the Communists would do it for them. In 1959, after the wall of the Volgograd dam had been set in place, the Soviet Union opened its first fish hatchery to breed sturgeon and stock the Caspian. The process for culturing sturgeon had been developed in the mid-nineteenth century by a Russian scientist named Fyodor Ovsyannikov. But there was never any economic incentive to go to all the trouble of breeding fingerlings in tanks. After 1959, however, when the Soviets realized their caviar business was in danger, they decided to try Ovsyannikov's methods. Hatcheries were built along the rivers where sturgeon had once spawned, including the Volga, Don, Dneiper, and Amur. By the mid-1960s, fish biologists were funneling millions of sturgeon fingerlings back into same rivers. With all the money being put into hatcheries, the Soviet Union realized it also needed to manage the fish in the delta, where the fingerlings grew into adults. Fishing was banned in the sea in 1962, one year after the Volgograd dam opened and sixty years after declining catches had sent fishermen into the open waters of the Caspian. The juvenile sturgeon would once again be allowed to frolic unmolested.

The determination of Soviet fish biologists paid off. The sturgeon population stabilized. The hatchery program was one of the Soviet Union's greatest achievements. No other country had ever succeeded before in keeping its sturgeon population from crashing. But Russia, with the machinery of its authoritarian system, was able to impose strict controls on fishing. The memories of mass executions and prison camps were still fresh in Astrakhan and no one dared break the rules.

Soon, catches actually started to rise. By the 1980s, fishermen were bringing in more sturgeon than any time since the days of the Romanovs. In 1980, Caspian fishermen netted 26,600 tons of sturgeon, only a few tons short of the record set in 1900. During the 1980s, when everything in the Soviet Union seemed to be collapsing, the sturgeon catches reached record levels.

Despite all the affronts to the Caspian environment, the sturgeon had displayed amazing resilience over the previous decades. Three times during the twentieth century the sturgeon was on the verge of extinction and three times its doom was forestalled. First it was the Russian Revolution that saved the sturgeon from rapacious overfishing. Then, during the Soviets' all-out struggle to repel the Nazis, the fish was granted a second respite. The ancient sturgeon was saved for yet a third time by the laboratory, when the Soviet Union introduced an intensive hatchery breeding program.

The sturgeon was not indestructible, however. Between the day that the Bolsheviks stormed the Winter Palace in 1917, and the day that Boris Yeltsin prevented the storming of the Russian White House in

1991, the beluga's average lifespan was reduced from close to a full century to a mere twenty years. By then, most of its replacements were being birthed in hatchery labs rather than the river.

The Russians had misread the meaning of the fish's repeated comebacks. They interpreted its survival as proof that nature could take whatever they did to it. They believed that the giant sturgeon, like the immense Soviet empire itself, would go on forever.

Part Two

· · · ⚜ · ·

Ten Years That Shook
the Caviar World

6

.   .   .   ✺   .   .   .

On the
Poacher's Trail

In her mind's eye she saw the picture of a wild, slit-eyed
people who, armed with harpoons, dragged long, fat
sturgeons onto moss-grown riverbanks. The men were clad
in furs and had wide cheekbones and dark skins. And they
killed the sturgeons, shouting "Utsh"—end.

—KURBAN SAID, THE GIRL FROM THE GOLDEN HORN

*C*ommunism had been hard enough on the sturgeon, but capitalism
would prove far worse.

By the time I arrived in Astrakhan in the spring of 2000, the state-
run caviar monopoly had been thoroughly dismantled. In a sense, history had been reversed. Just as the Bolsheviks had seized Astrakhan's
private caviar houses after the revolution, new private Russian companies seized the state's caviar operations after 1991. The fishing boats,

sturgeon nets, hatcheries, and canning factories were divided up among a handful of shrewd entrepreneurs, who became Astrakhan's new caviar barons. Moscow no longer dictated how much caviar would be produced or what it would sell for. The caviar trade had become an extremely lucrative and competitive business. It had also become an extremely corrupt one.

In theory, only licensed entrepreneurs were permitted to catch sturgeon and trade in caviar. But in practice, thousands of poachers swarmed the tangled banks of the Volga and other rivers, determined to catch as many sturgeon as they could. They called themselves *brakanieri,* a variation of the English word buccaneer. And like the original buccaneers, they lived by pillaging the waters.

The buccaneers would alter the caviar trade more profoundly than any development since the steam engine. They fished for sturgeon in the middle of the night, made caviar in their kitchens, and sold it to middlemen for less money than the Cossacks had received in the nineteenth century. Never before had caviar been so cheap or so plentiful. Within a short time, these poachers would become main suppliers of the world's caviar, as well as the main threat to the sturgeon's survival.

The buccaneers were merely the first link in a very long chain that stretched from the ramshackle Volga villages to the gourmet shops of Europe and America. Before the poachers' illegal caviar could be served up in crystal bowls with triangles of warm toast, it first had to be smuggled out of the delta.

SASHA WAS the first buccaneer I met in the Volga delta. He was just coming home from a night of checking his hook lines when I bumped into him on the dirt lane that leads from the river to the cluster of small wooden houses in the village of Sergeyevka. He was empty handed, although it was a warm May morning at the height of the sturgeon run. He told me he had come home without a catch the day before, too. This was not unusual, he insisted when I remarked on his bad luck. "Poaching is like gambling," he explained. "One day you strike it rich."

Even on the days when Sasha did hit the jackpot, the payout was rather small. Sasha, like all poachers, was a bit player in the international caviar trade. When he found a cow on his snast line, he would rush back home with the fish still quivering in his arms and quickly process the caviar in his yard. When the eggs and salt had set, Sasha might have ten pounds of caviar, worth thousands of dollars in the West. But like all poachers in Sergeyevka, Sasha was obliged to turn his valuable contraband over to his *krisha*. The word means "roof" in Russian and is slang for the people who run protection rackets. After collecting caviar from all the village poachers, Sasha's krisha would have delivered the haul to a bigger krisha.

In Moscow, my friends spoke of Caspian buccaneers in the same tones that Americans reserve for drug dealers. But those criminals know something of the ways of the world, and Sasha seemed to know only the ways of his village. As an ethnic Kazak, Sasha had the same broad, round face and Asian features as the Mongol horsemen who charged across the steppe with Batu Khan, but none of their proud, savage bearing. He had a habit of staring glumly at his feet when we talked, watching fat ants push up from the sandy ground and scurry over his flip-flops. Though he was all of twenty-five, he was already missing his share of teeth and had a drinker's budding paunch. His wife had left him a few years earlier, and after that he decided to move back to his parents' house.

I had expected it would be difficult to find someone in the poaching business. But it turned out to be easy to meet a poacher in Sergeyevka. Every man in the village kept a snast line in the water, just to earn some extra money. On average, they each caught three or four sturgeon a week and got by on the caviar they sold. Everyone knew that it was illegal to fish without a license, but when I mentioned this, they shrugged and asked what else they should do to feed their families. They would also complain that it was getting harder to make a living from sturgeon because more and more buccaneers were working the river. And when I suggested that there were also fewer fish heading upstream, they would vigorously deny this possibility.

Sasha had started poaching professionally when he was in his late teens. By the time he was old enough to hold a job, there were none to be had in the Volga delta. Russia was a land in ruins in 1991, when the Soviet Union collapsed. Up and down the Volga, the factories sputtered to a stop. Sasha's father had worked all his life as a fisherman with the government collective in Sergeyevka. When that collective fell apart, both became buccaneers. Sasha started with one snast line that had more than a hundred hooks strung along its length. Later he added more lines and more hooks. As he became established, he also acquired the rights to his own section of river.

Sasha's days fell into a routine. He woke late in the morning, puttered for a while with his car, or drank with friends. Around ten P.M. each evening, if there was no sign of the fisheries police, Sasha would head down to the river. He rowed out to his spot, taking care not to splash his oars too loudly. The fisheries police had caught him a few times already. They could usually be bribed, but Sasha hated to waste the money. When they were in a bad mood, they would seize his snast lines, which were expensive to replace. Generally though, his krisha made sure that the police didn't bother him too much.

Sasha rowed slowly, looking for a particular, bent-over willow tree that he used to mark the place where he kept his snast. The line bobbed just below the surface, making it difficult to see. Pulling his boat even with the tree, he would reach underwater until he felt the line. He could tell right away whether there was a fish because of the extra weight. Moving along the line, hand over hand, he pulled himself and the boat through the water, until he came to the hook holding the sturgeon.

I asked Sasha whether he would use the caviar if the sturgeon were already dead. He smiled indulgently at me, as if I had asked him whether he threw away wrinkled dollar bills. The rule about making caviar from live sturgeon was nothing but an old wives' tale, he said.

No poacher would ever waste a single egg of sturgeon roe, Sasha said. A few days before we met, he had found a large female Russian sturgeon fluttering in the current on his snast hook. He wrapped the fish in a towel and carried it home. But when he cut her open on his kitchen table, he was disappointed to find a mere two pounds of roe in her shriveled ovaries. Usually a fish's entire belly cavity is bursting with eggs; a sixty-pound Russian sturgeon might yield ten or twenty pounds of osetra caviar. The lack of eggs in the fish's belly could have been an indication of poor health or, worse, a genetic abnormality caused by the stew of toxic chemicals in the Volga. Sasha said he mixed the two pounds of roe with salt anyway and took the caviar to his krisha, who gave him a thousand rubles, then about thirty dollars, almost enough to get him through the month.

Sasha was growing tired of handing his caviar over to someone else. He knew a few poachers who had stood up to their krisha. They delivered their caviar directly to dealers in Ikryanoye, a small city about twenty miles north of Sergeyevka. Sasha had heard that there was a caviar market right in the center of Ikryanoye. He knew he could get a much better price for his caviar if he delivered it himself, maybe twice as much as he was being paid by his krisha. Sasha's problem was that he had no way to get to Ikryanoye.

Not long after Sasha told me about this plan, I found him hunched over the engine of an orange Moskvich that had come to rest in the sparse grass next to his house. Sasha said he was trying to get the car working so he could bring his caviar to Ikryanoye. He had talked with some of his neighbors about the plan and they promised to give him their caviar to sell in Ikryanoye. But Sasha's ambitions went beyond just running the caviar up to the market. "I have contacts in Ikryanoye," he explained. "I want to get a license to buy fish. It is possible to do that. You just have to pay taxes. I won't be fishing anymore. I'll be buying fish from other people. I just have to fix my car first."

I was surprised to hear Sasha plan his future around sturgeon. Since he first began poaching, each season had been worse than the previous one. So much poaching was being done at sea that the number of sturgeon making it upriver to Sergeyevka had been greatly reduced. Even after adding hundreds of hooks to his snast lines, he was still collecting only about three fish a week by the spring of 2000. And on average only one of those was a female. "This has been a bad year," Sasha conceded, "but there have been lots of bad years. I don't believe what the government says about the sturgeon going extinct." Many poachers make the identical argument. Having been lied to for years by the Soviets, many Russians automatically doubted everything their government told them.

"No, I don't believe we are killing the sturgeon," Sasha said again, with increased conviction. "The Caspian Sea is vast. Maybe the sturgeon will go to Kalmykia or Kazakstan. But it is impossible to exhaust the sturgeon."

With that, he let the hood of his Moskvich slam shut, and set out on foot for the riverbank to see whether any sturgeon had snagged themselves on his lines.

· · ·

IKRYANOYE WAS still slumbering when our taxi driver deposited us near the town's outdoor market early one Sunday morning in late May. Mira and I made our way past the padlocked stalls just as my watch said six A.M. A few stray dogs sniffed among the empty tables, and a single vendor was laying out fan-shaped arrangements of dewy scallions and crunchy, pickle-sized cucumbers, but otherwise the market was still in its dormant state. On the narrow causeway into town, I had seen dozens of small boats tied to trees, which were submerged up to their lower branches by the regular spring flooding. Even the fishermen must have been sleeping. As we continued through the market, we spotted a large weathered placard hanging near the entrance. THE SALE OF FISH IS CAT-EGORICALLY FORBIDDEN!!! it proclaimed in big red letters. From years of living in Russia, I knew the warning could mean only one thing: we must be getting close to the black market for caviar.

Sasha had told me that the trading starts early, but he hadn't been very precise about where it took place. As we left the market, we were drawn toward a cluster of ten-story apartment blocks. Like so many Soviet-era towers, the buildings looked as if they had been air-dropped at random onto the site. I imagined that the moment the workers laid the last brick, they must have run off to the next project, because no one had bothered to landscape the area around the towers or, for that matter, to level the raw dirt around the perimeter. Rounding the corner, we came to a courtyard of buff-colored earth, with moguls as large as the steppe's. The skeletal remains of a swing set stood at one end. Overhead gas pipes, held up at intervals by metal stilts, marked the playground's boundaries. Several poor peasant women were standing in the dirt yard, close to the street, as if they were waiting for a bus. Each woman clutched an empty plastic shopping bag emblazoned with the names of Western shops such as Benetton and Next. "What are you waiting for?" Mira asked. "Fish," answered a Kalmyk woman with a head of lavish, country-western curls, before stepping away from us. We decided to wait, too.

Every time a car went by, I could hear the faint involuntary flicker of shopping bags. After an hour or so, the women cocked their heads like birds listening to a far-off call. Two men on a red motorbike drove past the lot. The motorbike circled through the empty market, and whipped past the lot again. On the third trip around, the motorbike slowed to a cautious stop. Instantly, the women rushed at the riders, waving their bags like battle standards as they surrounded the two men. I was straining to see what was happening when the Kalmyk woman fell back from the crowd, grasping her leg in pain. Someone had kicked her. Before she could recover herself, a Russian woman hurried away, clutching her swollen bag to her chest. The high bidder, she had just acquired a side of sturgeon meat from the two poachers. One of the women explained that she planned to salt it for balyk and sell it at the fish market in Astrakhan. The remaining women scattered around the lot to resume their desultory waiting.

Mira and I approached the motorbike. Its riders were teenage boys, not men as I had first thought. The younger of the two, a red-haired youth of sixteen, was grinning with delight. After a night of fishing, his face and hair were caked with river slime. But in his pocket were eighty rubles, equal to four dollars. I asked if they had any caviar to sell. "The krisha took it," Red explained. The boys' krisha had also taken some of the meat, leaving them with about half the stellate sturgeon they had caught. They had brought only four kilos—eight and a half pounds—to the Ikryanoye market because the penalties for selling sturgeon are much stiffer after five kilos. Their krisha didn't fully douse their natural suspicion of the police.

While our conversation circled around the subject of poaching, several men gathered to listen. "How much caviar do you want? Ten kilos? Twenty?" a man in wraparound sunglasses hissed over my shoulder. Dressed in a loose track suit and still wearing house slippers, he looked as if he had tumbled out of bed and gone straight to the market. His aggressive sales pitch made us uneasy. But when he motioned us to follow him, we complied. He walked a few steps ahead of us as we crossed the rutted playground. Was it safe to buy caviar from this dealer? What would I do with ten kilos of caviar? I wondered what would happen when I slid all those cans through the X-ray scanner at the Astrakhan airport. And even if I somehow succeeded in taking it to Moscow, and even if I gave it all away to friends, I would still be complicit in the dirty business that was killing the sturgeon.

Just as we reached the gloomy vestibule of his apartment building, the dealer seemed to hesitate. Had I misunderstood his offer? Perhaps he was suspicious of our motives. Then it occurred to me that he really didn't have as much caviar as he had boasted. We stood at the entrance for a few moments, awkwardly kicking at the buff earth. He waved good-bye as he entered the building, suggesting that we come back later.

THE FALL of the Soviet empire did more than close history's door on Communism; it also sealed the end of Russia's three-hundred-year-old caviar cartel.

Since 1675, the year that Tsar Alexei first forbade the Cossacks from selling their caviar directly to foreigners, the Russian state had maintained strict control over its caviar exports. When the Bolsheviks came to power, the state went beyond merely regulating foreign sales. They assumed total control of the caviar business from start to finish, from deciding how much caviar to produce to how much to charge. The attention that the Soviets paid to the caviar industry was out of all proportion to its place in the economy. Oil brought in far more hard currency, yet there was no cultural pride in pumping this other black gold across the steppe. The Soviets guarded their caviar industry with the same zeal as their space program. Everything to do with caviar production was managed by top fisheries officials in Moscow, thousands of miles from where the sturgeon roamed.

With the collapse of the Soviet Union in 1991, the Caspian lost its autocratic caretaker. Where before Russia and Iran had cooperatively shared its bounty, now there were five nations around its perimeter, all in fierce competition with one another. Russia and Iran remained the big players, but Kazakhstan, Azerbaijan, and Turkmenistan became strong competitors. These three new countries could market as much of their own caviar as they wanted, at whatever price they wanted. Even Russia did not speak with one voice any longer when it came to caviar. Its Caspian coastline was subdivided among three federal republics, Kalmykia, Daghestan, and the Russian Republic.

Though these republics were similar to states in America, they were not always obedient partners of the central government in Moscow. Relations were especially strained between Buddhist Kalmykia and Moslem Daghestan, which had never felt completely part of Russian society. Notoriously corrupt, those republics became the center of the underground caviar industry. The federal fisheries police would regularly arrest poachers, only to have the local judges throw the cases out of court. In 1995, the fisheries police were stopped at gunpoint by the local Daghestan police. They had just seized an entire trawler-load of contraband sturgeon, but the Daghestan police insisted that the poachers be allowed to keep their haul. Worse was yet to come. In November 1996, a bomb went off in a ten-story apartment house in Kaspisk, a small town along Daghestan's Caspian coast, where members of the fisheries police were based. Sixty-eight people, including women and children as well as guardsmen, died in the explosion. Although Kaspisk residents long ago gave up hope that the authorities might find the culprit, everyone in town believes the bombing was a direct result of the highly profitable caviar trade.

WHILE THESE new states bickered, the poachers kept fishing and the sturgeon's numbers kept falling. The consequence of this abuse is that Russia is no longer the world's largest producer of caviar. That title now goes to Iran.

Oddly enough, eating caviar was one of the few Western habits that Ayatollah Khomeni tried to encourage after the Iranian revolution. The ruling mullahs were looking for ways to improve Iran's economy and thought that the fishing industry would benefit if Iranians could enjoy its products. The Sunni Muslims in Turkey had no prohibition on caviar, why should the Iranian Shiites? The mullahs convened a committee of Iranian scientists to study the sturgeon's anatomy. After a year of research, they were pleased to discover that the fish did indeed have a small cluster of scales tucked between the dorsal and caudal fins. "There are plenty of scales," Mohammed Pourkazemi, chief biologist of Shilat, the state trading company, assured me with a conspiratorial laugh, when we met. Ayatollah Khomeini declared caviar *halal*, or clean, in 1981, but Pourkazemi concedes that many Iranians still won't touch it.

That hasn't hurt Iran's caviar industry. While Russia was dismantling its state-run caviar industry, Iran was methodically building up an efficient network of hatcheries and processing plants based on the Soviet model. The Iranians replace every sturgeon they take from the Caspian, releasing about 24 million hatchlings a year. The number of fish caught each year varies, but the amount of fish caught and the amount of fish returned to the sea are supposed to be in balance.

Most connoisseurs claim that Iranian caviar is better than Russian. But this is a recent development. In the past, roe from sturgeon in the shallow waters of the northern Caspian was considered superior. In theory, the caviar should be just as good no matter where it originates in the Caspian. The sturgeon swim in the same general area and eat roughly the same food, and the varieties of sturgeon in the north and south of the Caspian are almost identical. Other than the differences in water temperatures, the only factor that truly distinguishes Iranian and Russian caviar today is the quality of processing. Iranian packing plants are newer than Russia's. But the real reason for the difference is that poachers make a large proportion of Russian caviar, and their crude methods render poor-quality caviar.

A decade ago, few would have imagined that Russia's caviar industry would shrink to such ignoble proportions. In 1990, Russia's section of the Caspian produced three times as much caviar as Iran's—770 tons to Iran's 286 tons. But by 1996, Russia's output was down to 82 tons, while Iran was packing 135 tons. The turn of events is astonishing, not just because caviar is an expression of Russian culture, but because the rich, shallow, northern waters of the Caspian are the world's most perfect sturgeon nursery, far better than the deeper regions along the coast of Iran. Two-thirds of the sea's sturgeon population congregate at the mouth of the Volga. How can Russia have more sturgeon but produce so much less caviar?

It depends how you add up the numbers. The international environmental group TRAFFIC, which began a campaign in 1996 to save the sturgeon, contends that Russia's official figures only account for a small portion of the real catch, perhaps as little as 10 percent of the actual haul. Poachers, they say, collect the other 90 percent. Based on TRAFFIC's estimates for 1998, that would mean the underground poachers turned out somewhere around 360 tons of caviar, far in excess of the paltry 40 tons that Russia's legal caviar companies packed. Russia's total caviar product that year was more like 400 tons.

The uncontrolled poaching only explains part of the decline. By 1991, Russian hatcheries had run out of steam—and money. Hatcheries, like all sorts of Soviet factories, could no longer pay their workers. They had no money to buy fish meal for the young sturgeon fry or pay the cost of heating the water in their fish tanks. The number of baby sturgeon released into the Volga quickly dropped off, falling by a third just between 1990 and 1994. Since very few sturgeon were being born the old-fashioned way, hatcheries had become the main way of replenishing the sturgeon population in the Caspian during the Soviet era. But in the new capitalist environment, the hatcheries couldn't keep up. At the exact moment that poachers were wildly creaming off the adults, fewer baby sturgeon were being put into the sea to replace them.

Nature's cycle was seriously off kilter. The number of buccaneers working the Volga and the Caspian was growing, but the number of fish available for them to catch was shrinking. In order to keep up their catches, the buccaneers had to go after increasingly younger and smaller fish. It was exactly what had happened to fishermen who worked the Elbe and the Delaware Rivers. First they started catching fewer fish in their nets, then the fish became smaller, until finally there weren't enough left to bother with fishing. If the hatcheries remain dormant and the poaching keeps up at the same pace, the Caspian sturgeon could soon go the way of the sturgeon of North America and Europe.

IN RUSSIA, the boundaries between what is legal and what is illegal are always blurred. It is little wonder that one of Dostoyevsky's most chilling characters is the omnipotent Grand Inquisitor, who appears in a dreamy section of *The Brothers Karamazov*. He alone arbitrates what is permitted and what is not. We knew it was illegal for Sasha to fish for sturgeon in the Volga. It was illegal to take caviar out of Russia without a permit. It was illegal for the two boys in Ikryanoye to sell their sturgeon at the Ikryanoye market. But it was not illegal to sell sturgeon at the Astrakhan fish market.

The fish market is located about a mile from the center of town, in a large vaulted building of Soviet vintage. Inside the immense space, rows of tables ran the length of the building. Each table was manned by its own vendors, who presided over identical pyramids of various smoked and salted sturgeon. Some pieces were the color of old varnish, some were yellow as butter. Solid bricks of beluga meat stood alongside lacquered slabs of Russian sturgeon and delicate stellate balyk that curled at the edges. The vendors maintained a constant vigil against the flies by shaking pieces of newspaper over the unwrapped, unrefrigerated balyk. Somewhere, far in the back of the room, vendors also sold herring, pike, dried vobla, and other Volga fish, but the overwhelming impression was that the entire contents of the Caspian had been brought to Astrakhan and laid out for sale in the fish market. Seeing this bounty of sturgeon openly displayed, I couldn't understand why ordering sturgeon shashlik in a restaurant had been such an ordeal.

As I went down the aisles accepting samples from the eager vendors, I noticed a man prowling the market with a proprietary air. He noticed me, as well.

"Caviar?" he inquired by way of a greeting.

"Maybe," I answered, neither wanting to commit, nor scare him away.

It quickly became evident that no discussions of any subtlety were possible inside the market, so we agreed to meet at a nearby café. He gave his name as Volodya, a nickname for Vladimir. His small, hunched appearance, his greasy black hair, pocked skin, and twinkling, gold-toothed smile, were offset by his ringing cell phone, which gave him an air of success.

We sat down at an outdoor café beside the Volga and ordered Cokes. It was a lovely spring day. There was a mild breeze coming off the water, and the warmth of the sun wrapped us in a cocoon of well-being. Sitting under the café's red-and-white-striped awning almost made us feel that we were in a resort town. We watched a Russian fisheries patrol boat make a wide, ostentatious U-turn alongside the café; it was in no more of a hurry than a pleasure boat. Volodya would interrupt our riverside idyll occasionally to bark into his phone. He had come a long way since 1991, when he was living in a communal apartment without plumbing. In the late 1980s, while he was still in his thirties, he had been allowed to retire from his job at a chemical plant after being exposed to a spray of toxic fumes. What had been a decent disability pension in 1991 was reduced to scrap paper within a year of the Soviet collapse. So, like a lot of ambitious people in Astrakhan, he started buying caviar from the Russkaya Ikra factory and shuttling it up to Moscow. After the factory was privatized, he bought caviar wherever he could find it. Volodya made enough money in those first years to buy a modern two-bedroom apartment for the family, a second apartment for his twenty-four-year-old son, and a secondhand Toyota Corolla. He was also putting his daughter through law school. Now he had reached the point where he could sit comfortably at a trendy café and order a round of Cokes with a wave of his hand.

As his business grew, Volodya prudently obtained a license to sell sturgeon meat. It had cost a lot, he said, but was worth it. He was now the owner of several of the balyk stalls we had seen in the market. Apparently some of the restaurants in town had not bothered to get licenses, he told us, and now these papers were hard to come by. That's why they had to sell sturgeon shashlik on the sly. Volodya still dabbled in his illicit caviar business on the side, but with diminishing enthusiasm.

There was no profit in caviar anymore, Volodya complained. The price kept going down, but the risks of doing business kept growing. "People think Astrakhan is the source of caviar, but there's nothing left here," he complained. "You have to go to Daghestan now. The prices there are ridiculous. They sell the caviar for nothing. It doesn't make any sense. And the caviar is not good quality." Anyway, he said, the caviar being turned out by Russian poachers in the delta had become inedible. "The poachers don't understand they have barely an hour after the fish dies to remove the eggs. They don't understand they have to use clean water—not Volga water."

Volodya leaned back in his chair, his face contorted with disgust. This year's catch was the worst in his memory. "I'm already looking around for something else. I have some business with Iran," he said, brightening again. What kind of business? "I'm selling them lumber." Where was he getting lumber on the treeless steppe? "From Siberia, of course," he laughed. Before the revolution, Astrakhan had been a major crossroads for goods coming from the east. The city had grown rich by routing the raw materials of Siberia and the luxuries of Asia all over Europe. Trade was Astrakhan's future, not caviar, Volodya declared. "If no measures are taken," he predicted sagely, "we'll see the sturgeon only in pictures." After a while his phone rang again. "Business," he explained, excusing himself.

BEFORE THE Soviet Union dissolved, before buccaneers discovered they could make a living mixing sturgeon roe in their kitchens, before Daghestani poachers started dredging the Caspian for every last remaining fish, half the caviar made in Russia was packed at the sprawling Russkaya Ikra plant in a corner of Astrakhan. Western caviar dealers always spoke of Russkaya Ikra in reverent tones. It was the magic fountain from which so much caviar had sprung for so long. Until the final years of the Soviet Union, few outsiders had ever seen the place. Foreigners were rarely allowed inside its gates, not even such important customers as Petrossian or Dieckmann & Hansen, until the 1980s, when the factory was known as the Caspian Caviar and Balyk Processing Factory. Although the Soviet plant had been put in private hands in the early 1990s, I felt a tingle of excitement that I was about to take a tour of the storied inner sanctum of the Russian caviar industry.

Russkaya Ikra was located on the edge of Astrakhan, a few miles from the wooden packing sheds that had lined the Volga in the nineteenth century. It was set along the canal named in honor of Ioannis Varvakis. During the fishing season, ships carrying live sturgeon in tanks would cruise up the Volga to unload their precious cargo at the plant's dock. Russkaya Ikra, which simply means "Russian caviar," also salted, smoked, canned, and packed tons of Volga fish every week.

Because Russkaya Ikra exported its product to hard currency markets, it had been one of Russia's better-off factories. The entrance to the sprawling complex was neatly landscaped with flowerbeds and shade trees. But as our taxi pulled up to the front gate, I noticed that a sullen quiet pervaded the complex. No one stopped us as we entered the silent administration building and climbed to the second floor in search of the director, Vyatcheslav Mironov. We found Mironov alone and brooding at a desk the size of tugboat. One of his four phones rang: "It's a bad year," he told the caller. "We've taken only fourteen hundred kilos. Yesterday they got five or six sturgeon, only two or three with caviar. We can't get more till the water goes down. I don't know what you're going to do about the lack of fish, but as for me, I've started growing eggplants and tomatoes."

Mironov had only recently become the director of Russkaya Ikra, and in a way that epitomized Russia's new market-driven economy. He was working as an ikryanchik on the packing floor when the government began privatizing state companies by distributing shares among the employees. Mironov had the foresight to recognize the world was changing. He began buying shares from co-workers who preferred to have cash upfront rather than bet on Russia's uncertain economic future. Pretty soon Mironov, along with a few silent investors, was the owner of the largest caviar packing plant in the world. As a demonstration of his new status as a businessman, Mironov had acquired several thick gold neck chains, which he wore with a T-shirt that set off his Popeye-the-Sailor arms.

It was clear from the moment we walked in the door that Mironov did not want to bother with us. When we had telephoned to arrange a meeting, Mironov had cordially promised to show me where Russkaya Ikra made its caviar. But there was no roe to pack on the day we arrived, and Mironov told us that he had sent Russkaya Ikra's entire workforce home. He promised again to give a tour of the processing lines if we came back in a few days. But when we returned as planned, there still was not enough roe to justify turning on the machines.

This time, he asked his assistant, Nikolai Shirmanov, to show us around. This was probably for the best. Mironov had trouble answering the few simple questions I had managed to pose, but Nikolai could reel off Russkaya Ikra's stats like a game show contestant. "I've worked here since 1982," he explained with a shrug. "I was the director."

After Russkaya Ikra was privatized, Nikolai was bumped down to plant manager. It was now his job to run the oversized factory as efficiently as possible. Sometimes, he had to keep sturgeon alive in tanks for a month before there were enough fish to run the processing lines. In 1987, while he was still director, the lines ran constantly from early spring to late summer, turning out fourteen hundred tons—tons, not kilos!—of caviar annually. Russkaya Ikra is lucky to make six tons a year now.

"There used to be one very thrifty owner here who followed very strict measures. They thought about the future," Nikolai reminisced. "The poachers only think about today. Did you know that 100 percent of the caviar sold in Moscow is from poachers?" He didn't try to hide his nostalgia for the Soviet Union, for the days before crafty ikryanchiks became factory directors. "Sturgeon were the pride of the country," he sighed. "But now we care more about oil. The U.S. couldn't save the buffalo and we can't save the sturgeon."

We walked over to the processing building. Nikolai showed us the room where ikryanchiks like Mironov had sieved, washed, and salted the eggs. This was where the vast majority of Russian caviar had once been prepared, yet it was no bigger than an American kitchen. We followed Nikolai into the much larger packing room. It used to be filled with tables where workers filled caviar jars by hand. But now it was largely empty except for a sparkling, stainless-steel packing machine. The contraption had automated the artisanal process of canning caviar. It filled the little glass jars with measured amounts of caviar, capped them, and sent them trundling down a conveyor belt to a big heated box where they would be steamed and pasteurized. Russkaya Ikra had just bought the equipment from Mondini, an Italian firm specializing in canning equipment, in the hope of cutting its labor costs. So far, Russkaya Ikra had hardly used it.

Stacked up next to the machine were boxes of new jars, in one-, two-, and four-ounce sizes, and boxes of red, yellow, and blue caps. They were waiting to be filled. I noticed there were none of the traditional blue kilogram tins. Russkaya Ikra, Nikolai told us, had discontinued them. There wasn't enough caviar to produce a whole line of them.

. . .

BEFORE LEAVING Astrakhan, we made one more trip to the fish market. Volodya had mentioned there was a store next to the main hall where you could buy caviar legally. It was the only such shop in all of Astrakhan. It turned out that we had passed by several times without noticing the place—a small, metal building that looked as if it had been converted from a shipping container. Through the greasy glass of the display case, Mira and I glimpsed a forlorn side of fresh sturgeon and a few tins of osetra caviar. The meager array reminded me of how Soviet food stores used to look. We asked for a taste and the clerk obliged by wiping a metal spoon on a filthy towel. Taking a tin from the case, he struggled to break the vacuum seal. When it wouldn't budge, he raised the tin to his lips like a trumpet and blew a burst of air. The lid popped open. He scooped out a small bit with the aluminum spoon, an act that would have appalled connoisseurs who know that metal causes the caviar to oxidize. The caviar was a bit mushy, the kind Russians call *zhirovaya*. It had obviously been taken well before the sturgeon was ready to spawn. But it still tasted pretty good to us and at forty dollars a kilogram it was still a bargain. I knew that people were paying half that price in Ikryanoye, but this had the virtue of being legal.

We didn't realize why until we paid our bill and the clerk handed us a certificate of purchase. It turned out that the fisheries police had seized our caviar. That explained why it was *zhirovaya*. It had been made by poachers who didn't have the means to ranch their catches until the sturgeon's eggs were ripe. I was also surprised to see a familiar name on the certificate. It was stamped with the seal of Karon, Evgeny Aptekar's company. He had been given the right to sell everything the police confiscated.

Even with the Karon stamp, I expected that we would have to do some explaining at the airport. Mira and I packed our caviar in our carry-on bags, along with some bricks of balyk, so it wouldn't appear that we were trying to hide anything. We approached the control point tentatively, patting the Karon receipts for comfort. But before we knew what was happening, the police shooed us through. Our tickets were checked, our passports were inspected, and we walked into the waiting lounge carrying our booty. No one had so much as opened our bags, never mind asked for Karon's certificate. If we wanted, we could have bought a dozen kilos in Ikryanoye and carried it all to Moscow. From there we could have taken it almost anywhere.

7

Branding
Caviar

There is more simplicity in the man who eats caviar on
impulse than in the man who eats grape-nuts on principal.

—G. K. CHESTERTON

*F*or the better part of the twentieth century, only two companies mattered when it came to caviar: Dieckmann & Hansen and Petrossian. These two superpowers dominated the world trade during the seven decades of the Soviet Union's existence, carving up the globe as neatly as Washington and Moscow.

The two great caviar houses were as different as the great Cold War adversaries. Dieckmann & Hansen had been a presence on the Hamburg docks since the first half of the nineteenth century. Petrossian was a French upstart that didn't open its elegant Paris shop until after the Russian Revolution. Dieckmann & Hansen was managed by steady,

German burghers who turned caviar into a serious industry. Petrossian was run by Frenchified Armenians who enthusiastically cultivated caviar's mystique. By the end of the century, Dieckmann & Hansen had become a wholesaler, selling caviar by the ton to airlines and cruise ships. Petrossian remained, as always, an elite retail brand that was dispensed by the tin. Dieckmann & Hansen probably sold more caviar, but Petrossian was more famous. Even people who had never eaten caviar had heard of Petrossian. Its celebrated name was the most important advantage that Petrossian had over Dieckmann & Hansen.

Their rivalry can be traced back to the year 1920, when they each obtained the right to distribute the Soviet Union's caviar. It was a good time to be selling the exotic eggs. Europe was beginning to mend from the devastation of World War I and people were seeking to start afresh, to discard the starched collars and frills of the prewar era for more straightforward things. The Modernist influence had brought a stream-lined aesthetic to painting, literature, music, architecture, and fashion. Artists reduced their compositions to their flattest, most abstract essentials. Writers pruned texts of lofty, Victorian verbiage. Le Corbusier and Mies van der Rohe pushed toward a purer architecture of straight lines and basic geometries. Caviar, a food of unadorned simplicity, was perfect for the modern palate.

The renewed longing for caviar occurred just when Lenin's new Bolshevik government was desperate to find a source of hard currency. Dieckmann & Hansen was the obvious choice to help the inexperienced Communists market their valuable caviar abroad. The firm had fled Russia in 1914 when Tsar Nicholas declared war on Germany, abandoning its fishing boats and packing machines on the Volga quays. Now that the war was over, Dieckmann & Hansen was eager to return to the caviar business. The terms had changed, of course. When the Soviets welcomed Dieckmann & Hansen back in 1920, it was as a buyer, not a producer. Having no choice in the matter, Dieckmann & Hansen accepted the Soviet offer to become the sole distributor for Russian caviar in Germany.

The Petrossian family also discovered caviar in 1920, but it came to the business by a far more circuitous route. Until the revolution, the family made their living cultivating silkworms on a farm near Tblisi. The Petrossians had only recently migrated to Georgia from a poor mountain village in the neighboring region of Armenia, but they had done well for themselves. Like other merchants working amid the ethnic babel of the Caucasus, the Petrossians adopted the Russian language for business, as well as many Russian customs. The two eldest sons, Melkoum and Mouchegh, were eventually sent to Moscow to study law and architecture, where they remained until the Bolsheviks stormed the Winter Palace in St. Petersburg.

When the rest of the Petrossian family fled to Paris with the first wave of nobles and merchants, the two brothers were stuck in Moscow. It was dangerous to leave the city without official permission, and even more dangerous to travel through a Russia consumed by revolutions, riots, and civil war. Eventually, they found a way out of the city and made their way south, passing through their native Caucasus Mountains, until they reached the frontier with Persia. Their ultimate destination was Paris, but first they had to spend several months in Teheran waiting to obtain passports and travel documents. By the time Melkoum and Mouchegh were reunited with their family in 1920, the Petrossian clan was casting around for a way to make a living.

While the brothers were discussing their futures with their family, the conversation turned to the heaping bowls of caviar that had once graced the family table in Tblisi. It occurred to them that they might make some money selling the delicacy in Paris. The pair decided to pay a visit to the new Soviet Embassy and ask for a meeting with the foreign trade representative. This was easier said than done. The trade official refused to see them. But the brothers weren't ones to give up easily. They continued to petition the embassy until they were at last granted a meeting and allowed to make their proposal. Despite the embassy's initial reluctance to let them in the door, the Soviets were now willing to do business. The Petrossians were told they could have as much caviar as they wanted—so long as they paid first in cash. The brothers returned to the embassy with a briefcase filled with enough franc notes to cover two tons of lightly salted caviar.

The money represented everything the Petrossians had managed to take out of Russia. And here they were sending it back. The deal with the embassy seemed too good to be true. Months passed, and the brothers heard nothing from the Soviet Embassy. Frantic telegrams were sent to Moscow. Finally, eight months after the Petrossians turned over their savings, their first shipment of caviar arrived by train in Paris, still snug in its linden barrels.

The Petrossian brothers' timing was perfect. Cesar Ritz eagerly took a ton for his fashionable hotel on the Place Vendôme. Encouraged by their initial success, Melkoum and Mouchegh plunged into their new business. They rented a corner shop near the Quai d'Orsay, on the Boulevard de Latour-Maubourg, and painted the interior the same blue as the large Russian caviar tins. They hired a former colonel in the tsar's army named Vorotunceff to wait on customers, who included many homesick Russian exiles. But the Petrossians knew they would have to broaden their market if they were to succeed, so they began making the rounds of food shows where they would hand out samples. According to family lore, the Caucasian delicacy wasn't an easy sell in Paris; the Petrossians even had to keep a spittoon nearby for those who didn't immediately take a liking to it. But the brothers' business grew and expanded beyond the confines of their small Paris shop. The Soviet government granted the firm exclusive distribution rights in France, the same arrangement that it had made with Dieckmann & Hansen in Germany. The relationship was so good that the Soviets later made Petrossian the sole distributor for its Pacific crab, a franchise that would be worth millions. Petrossian would later expand its operation to the United States, putting it in direct competition with Dieckmann & Hansen's American division, Romanoff Caviar.

As the Petrossian reputation grew, the brothers often repeated and embellished the story of their firm's serendipitous beginnings, until the event grew into something more heroic than the mere founding of a business. In their story, as recounted today in the company's official history and catalogues, it was Melkoum and Mouchegh who "first introduced Paris to the magic of caviar."

MYTHS ARE one of the key ingredients in caviar. Stripped of its shroud of legend and tradition, caviar would just be fish eggs. Most caviar dealers are loath to admit it, but when caviar is properly made and eaten fresh, the different brands are as much alike as two kinds of baking soda. Yet, I can hardly remember a time when I did not associate the name Petrossian with caviar. The sound of the word itself, with its double *s* hissing like a Caucasian wind, calls up an image of a village in those high, jagged mountains, a place where meals are served on velvet-soft carpets, with warm flatbread, scented tea, and a cool bowl of fresh caviar.

The person who knows the story of the illustrious caviar house best is Armen Petrossian, one of Mouchegh's sons. He had taken over the family business in the late 1980s from his older sister, Tamara Kotcharian, who had followed her father and Uncle Melkoum into the caviar trade. (There was also another brother, Christian, who ran the

American operation for a while.) Tamara, Christian, and Armen have a double pedigree in caviar; sixteen years after their father opened his Paris shop, he married a Mailoff girl. The Mailoffs were also refugees from the revolution, but before fleeing to Paris, they had operated an armada of sturgeon boats in Baku. The children of this merger grew up across the street from the family store on Latour-Marbourg, all of them eating caviar from the time they were babies. I was eager to meet Armen and have him show me where the Petrossian caviar house originated. After several rounds of faxes, he invited me to have dinner with him at the restaurant he had recently opened over the family shop.

There was no mistaking Armen Petrossian as I approached a small group of people standing at the restaurant's bar. He might have been transported directly from nineteenth-century Astrakhan. His mustache was waxed and curled to sharp points, and he wore a jaunty bowtie. Despite his ample girth, he managed to convey a silver-haired elegance. If Petrossian was a throwback to another era, the restaurant designed by his brother Karen represented up-to-the-minute minimalism. The walls and carpets were a pale gray—sturgeon gray—while the chairs and trim were all lacquered a gleaming black—caviar black. The Paris restaurant was a sign of Petrossian's resurgence as a force in the caviar business after a long, hard decade of being shunted to the sidelines.

Before I left for Paris, I had gone to see Petrossian's American director Eve Vega at the firm's New York restaurant, which had occupied the ground floor of the elegant Alwyn building near Central Park South since the mid-1980s. Vega was as unfussily down-to-earth as Petrossian was swank, and spoke with a familiar New York accent. While we sat around scooping dollops of fresh beluga, osetra, and sevruga onto warm toast, she confided to me that the firm had nearly gone under with the Soviet Union, when a flood of cheap caviar was unleashed on the market. "A Wild West mentality prevailed," Vega said. "All this cheap stuff was coming in, in suitcases, avoiding customs. They sold it cheaper than we did. I had chefs telling me to lower our prices. I lost a lot of accounts." Pausing for a moment, she suggested that I forgo the warm toast that the waiter had left by my elbow. "Use the back of your hand," she instructed, licking a clump of eggs from the top of her fist.

When the Soviet Union was around to set prices, caviar was exempt from the gravitational pull of supply and demand. But once the Communists were out of the picture, the roe became just another furiously traded commodity. The early 1990s were a time when anyone with enough cash, daring, and a willingness to deal with the Caspian buccaneers could start a caviar house. Prices tumbled as Russian émigrés, fish dealers, and gourmet food companies shuttled in more and more caviar. In Europe, the official statistics show imports declining slightly during the same period. But that is because suitcase smugglers were bringing in so much caviar that many retailers and restaurants didn't even bother buying the legal stuff. Between 1991 and 1997, the official amount of caviar imported into the United States tripled from thirty-two to ninety-five tons annually, although the real increase was probably far greater.

It is safe to say that during the 1990s the United States became the single largest consumer of caviar outside of Russia, surpassing the Germans, the French, and the Japanese. Caviar had always been available in America, usually in specialty shops and fancy restaurants, but around late 1994 it suddenly burst into view in the most quotidian places—in department stores, train stations, airports, suburban supermarkets, on the Internet. It was the Internet, more than the other venues, which made caviar accessible to anyone, anywhere. To buy caviar on a whim, you no longer had to live in a place that was big and sophisticated enough to have a gourmet food store. With a click of the mouse, you could call up the Web page of one of the new caviar distributors, order as much as you wanted, and have it overnighted on a pack of dry ice to your front door.

When caviar became mainstream, it also became cheap. By 1995, Macy's was selling a kilogram of osetra for $310, even while Petrossian was still bent on getting more than $1,000. Americans could well afford to indulge. At the exact moment when caviar prices were tumbling to record lows, Americans were making record salaries. By the mid-1990s, the booming stock market had plumped up portfolios of many middle-class investors. Caviar trickled down from Wall Street brokers and dot-com millionaires to the ranks of college professors and company managers. Not only did middle-class people have money to splurge on the luxury of sturgeon eggs, their palates had been primed for its sensuous, salty-sweet flavor. Having become more adventuresome in their tastes, people all over America were buying extra virgin olive oil in supermarkets and drinking espresso at highway rest stops. Caviar was a logical frontier for the food conscious masses. Affluence had the same effect on Americans as it did on the newly wealthy industrialists in nineteenth-century Germany: it made them crave the exotic.

The democratization of caviar took Armen Petrossian by surprise, he told me as we sat down at one of the pale gray tables in his restaurant. In the beginning, he had hoped to ride out the market turbulence by doing what Petrossian had always done, which was to sell its caviar in an atmosphere of exclusivity and luxury. The strategy failed, and by the mid-1990s he was forced to lower prices to stay competitive. He promoted a new label, Dom Petroff, as a way of selling second-grade caviar without compromising the Petrossian name. "It was a very difficult time," he recalled. "A lot of people were saying, 'Why are you charging so much? Why don't you buy the poached caviar?' . . . The new market was driving me crazy." What Petrossian didn't say, but was becoming clear to me, was that people were buying the cheap caviar because, to them, it tasted pretty much like the expensive stuff.

Armen Petrossian could see that caviar was becoming a mass-market food. The challenge was to find a way to make the Petrossian experience unique. It was no longer enough merely to sell caviar. Petrossian was at heart a shopkeeper, who still lived next to the store, and yet he knew that Petrossian's strength lay in the power of its name to evoke a special kind of opulence—an opulence with a pedigree. Rather than retrench, Petrossian decided to expand. The office over his father's shop would become a restaurant and would use the Petrossian name. But unlike in the family's New York restaurant, sturgeon roe would not be the main focus. Just as his father and uncle had built their business by redefining a well-known luxury, so would he. In 1999, he hired one of France's top chefs, Philippe Conticini, and together they began working on the menu for the new restaurant.

Petrossian was now perusing Conticini's menu and trying to decide what I should eat. Conticini had been famous for his desserts before he took charge at Petrossian—the French press describes him a "virtuoso of sugar"—and Petrossian boasted of the sweets that lay in store for us. But first we were obliged to have dinner, he reminded me. Petrossian explained that the menu was designed so that "you can have caviar or no caviar." I would start with "no caviar," he said. "No caviar?" I asked. "You will have the swordfish," Petrossian announced.

Our plates arrived papered with transparent leaves of smoked swordfish, so delicate and buttery that they nearly evaporated the moment they touched my tongue. Petrossian had the waiter bring us a very good red wine and an elegant, giraffe-necked bottle of water, then began to tell me the history of Petrossian. The French, he began, had known nothing about caviar before his father and uncle arrived in Paris. Petrossian was repeating the same claim I had seen on the Petrossian Web page. "French people didn't like caviar at first," he continued. "They were suspicious of eating something from the inside of a fish . . . But after eighty years, because of Petrossian, caviar has become a French tradition. That is an extraordinary thing."

Petrossian leaned back for a moment, taking pleasure in his family's accomplishment. Around him, the restaurant was populated by the kind of very thin, very tan women of a certain age who are found in great numbers in Paris, each one with a Hermès famous Kelly bag at her feet. I knew Petrossian's claims were greatly exaggerated and wanted to challenge them, but in a way that wouldn't sound too aggressive, especially since there were three more courses to go.

"What about Rabelais? He mentions caviar," I ventured. "And wasn't caviar the rage in France during the Belle Epoque?"

"Maybe French fishermen ate it," was all Petrossian would concede.

I could see that I had already put him on the defensive. "Petrossian not only brought the idea of caviar as a delicacy to France, but as a luxury," he added vigorously. "That's why we are so well known. We are the only caviar that has a trademarked name. We are recognized as synonymous with caviar . . . The shop is an institution. People come to visit it like a museum."

As if to punctuate his words, Petrossian announced that we would now eat caviar with blini. In my mind, I saw half-moons of thin, folded pancakes, and inside, a dollop of black eggs forming a bullseye against the white of the crème fresh. But when the waiter appeared, he was carrying a plate with a large brown oblong form perched in the middle. It turned out to be a soft-boiled egg that had been entombed in a shell of deep-fried blini. Miniature crab cakes stood at its feet like sentries. The top of the oblong ball was crowned with a ring of tiny black grains that turned out to be osetra. I was eager to taste the caviar. But the moment I grazed the caviar with my fork, the blini broke and a lava of runny yolk sent them sliding onto the plate. I picked up a few individual eggs between the tines of the fork. The blini, if it could be called that, was as rich and delicious as the swordfish. Conticini enjoyed merging ingredients, textures, and tastes in unexpected ways. The next course was even more elaborately composed, a wedge of fried rouget balanced precariously atop a stewed tomato, which itself sat in perfect equilibrium atop an egg roll, but it was clear now that caviar would have only a minor role in the meal.

I tried to steer the conversation back to caviar, particularly the anarchy that was threatening the Caspian sturgeon. "There are no rules anymore, except who is stronger," Petrossian told me. He missed the Soviet days, when everything was more orderly. But he was no longer worried about the sturgeon's survival. The international community, he believed, was now acting to protect the stocks. Petrossian, meanwhile, was preserving the tradition of making caviar, he said, with a secret recipe. "The fish is not the most important thing," he explained, "the maturation is." I had never heard any caviar dealers speak of maturation before. I had eaten caviar out of an ikryanchik's bowl and it had tasted heavenly. It is true that as the salt penetrates the casings of the eggs, the taste deepens, but by two months the caviar has usually reached its peak. After a year, it is on the decline.

Petrossian persisted. "You must let caviar mature, two months to one year. The merchandise should be aged, controlled like salmon or vodka. The maturation is what makes Petrossian caviar unique." I mentioned that Dieckmann & Hansen didn't keep their caviar so long. "The Germans," he sniffed, "think of caviar as an industry. The French think of it as a delicacy."

Later, after I said good-bye to Petrossian, I stopped in front of sthe Petrossian shop, which was closed, to look in the windows. The street-lights cast a glow over the tins inside. The front window was decorated with a variety of Russian folk art—painted wood eggs and samovars. Petrossian was right. The shop was just like a museum. And then, epiphany struck. I had just spent three hours with Petrossian in the ele-gant restaurant that bore his family's great name, eating a sumptuous four-course meal and dining on ethereal desserts, yet I had consumed barely a dozen grains of caviar.

In the same instant, I realized that this was the future. Petrossian may not have introduced caviar to the French, as they liked to claim, but the firm had certainly helped shape the way we thought about caviar. The Petrossian name evoked a more luminous time when Diaghilev's Ballets Russes and the Lost Generation of expatriates were all living it up in Paris, nursing their exile with caviar and cocktails. Petrossian was so effectively associated with the mystique of caviar that the actual sub-stance was less crucial to the experience. It was like Magritte's painting of a tobacco pipe that proclaimed it wasn't a pipe. The Petrossian name represented the idea of caviar, just as the painting represented the idea of a pipe. This was a very useful quality at a moment when fewer and fewer sturgeon were coursing up the Volga to deposit their eggs. Of course, you could still order a plateful of caviar at Petrossian's restau-rant, but the dish was no longer the main attraction. You didn't have to eat any caviar at the Petrossian restaurant to feel you were participating in an aristocratic indulgence. Somehow, Petrossian had managed to pry the essence of luxury from the atom of caviar, serving everything asso-ciated with the delicacy except the delicacy itself. That was a lot more amazing than selling cheap caviar.

•   •   •

THE PETROSSIANS weren't the only ones to perpetuate the aura of caviar. Throughout the twentieth century, writers, artists, and restaurateurs larded the delicacy with myth, turning it into a touchstone of culinary nirvana.

Ludwig Bemelmans, the creator of the Madeline books, devoted an entire chapter of his memoirs to his caviar experiences. Though Bemelmans is primarily known for his whimsical drawings, rhyming couplets, and spunky Parisian schoolgirl, he once dreamed of a more pragmatic career in the hotel business. As a young man, he spent long days serving an apprenticeship as a busboy in the kitchen of the Ritz Hotel in New York. It was there that he developed the habit of helping himself to a few generous spoonfuls of caviar, which he would devour after hours with his fellow busboys in a dark corner of the empty ballroom. "Those were the best caviar days I can remember," he wrote. From then on, caviar would always be a guilty pleasure for Bemelmans.

M.F.K. Fisher, who turned her epicurean memoirs into a literary form, was similarly transformed by her youthful encounter with caviar. It happened when she was just twenty-three and traveling around Europe with her parents. After a hard day of sightseeing in Paris, the three decided to treat themselves to an indulgent lunch at the Café de la Paix. Fisher ordered a portion of caviar. They liked it so much, they ordered another, and then another, until the waiter simply bestowed the entire tin on their table. "That was a fine introduction," she concluded, "to what I hope is a reasonably long life of such occasional bliss."

Henri Soulé, proprietor of Le Pavillon restaurant, one of the few impeccable French restaurants operating in New York, in the 1950s, played an important role in preserving caviar's high reputation in the dark days of the Cold War. Whenever anyone ordered caviar, he insisted that it should be served with the maximum of theatricality. The caviar was wheeled out on a silver cart, flanked by an honor guard of waiters, who presented the dish as if it were a holy sacrament. One waiter would place a crystal bowl heaped with eggs on the table with a small bow, while the others discreetly introduced a retinue of warm toast, chilled Latvian vodka, and shredded egg whites. The restaurant's reputation for good caviar got around, and its devotees flocked to Soulé's tables. He personally selected the caviar served in his restaurant and made a point of opening a fresh tin for such favored guests as the Duke of Windsor.

Though the duke's fellow Englishmen were late in embracing caviar, once they did, it became an obsession. When Winston Churchill dispatched Lord Beaverbrook to discuss the war with Stalin in 1941, he instructed him to return with an agreement and twenty-five pounds of good caviar. In the pages of *Brideshead Revisited,* Evelyn Waugh's bittersweet look back at the England that existed before World War I, there are many descriptions of food, but few so sensuous as his account of a meal of caviar and blini, when "the cream and hot butter mingled and overflowed separating each glaucose bead of caviar from its fellows, capping it in white and gold."

Everyone had his own opinion about the best way of eating caviar. Aristotle Onassis demanded pressed caviar when he took his meals at the Hotel de Paris in Monte Carlo. Christian Dior liked to drape a lightly fried egg over his sturgeon roe. On a visit to San Francisco in the 1930s, Somerset Maugham took his caviar with a two-fisted ensemble of champagne and martinis spiked with absinthe. Pablo Picasso loomed large in the art world, but was convinced that the tiny pinprick sevruga eggs ruled the caviar world. Ian Fleming preferred the nuttier osetra and so, we may assume, did James Bond. Edward Ruscha, an American pop artist, liked to make a subliminal connection between his family name and Russia's most famous export by slathering caviar on his canvases. Too bad he never charmed the Russians the way Charlie Chaplin did with his little tramp character. Although the Soviets did not believe in paying for copyright permission, they made an exception for the beloved film star when they printed a thousand-word excerpt from his autobiography in *Izvestia*. Chaplin's royalty payment was nine pounds of caviar, roughly a teaspoon per word.

BY THE time the shock waves of Moscow's collapse reached Hamburg, Dieckmann & Hansen was no longer a family-run caviar house. It had puttered along in its cautious way between the two world wars, occupying itself mainly with the German market. During the allied bombing of Hamburg in 1943, the firm's warehouse and its entire stock of caviar were reduced to cinders. When peace came, Germany was in ruins. Germans had neither the time nor money for trifles like caviar, and it took Dieckmann & Hansen great effort to rebuild its business. The firm survived, but in diminished form. In its new, postwar configuration, the old German house was reduced to a subsidiary of a large corporation, the Romanoff Caviar Company. Now it was the American child, which Ferdinand Hansen had started as a one-store operation in the early 1900s, that was calling the shots in the caviar business. The Cold War's tensions obliged the companies to turn to Iran for supplies, instead of selling Russian caviar as Dieckmann & Hansen had always done. Romanoff made some effort to maintain the Dieckmann & Hansen traditions, however. They handed the management of the German operation over to a distant relation of the original Hansens, Horst Gödecken. But in 1962, the family had all but lost interest in the company, and Gödecken hired a young woman named Susanne Schwerdtfeger as his apprentice.

Although Susanne Schwerdtfeger was not related by blood, Dieckmann & Hansen became her adopted family. She worked her way up to general manager, then bought a share of the company in 1993, on the eve of the house's 125th anniversary. Schwerdtfeger had come to Dieckmann & Hansen barely out of her teens, a pretty girl with short-cropped blond hair, apple cheeks, and a willingness to do all sorts of jobs. She began working on the receiving docks, doing customs clearance. She often went to Leningrad to inspect the caviar before it was sent to Hamburg. She would open the barrels and pull out bunches of straw matting until she located the tins, packed in threes in linen bags. She had to count them to make sure the shipment was complete. As her knowledge of caviar increased, she was asked to handle certain accounts and market the caviar to new customers.

Under the management of Gödecken and Schwerdtfeger, Dieckmann & Hansen regained some of its former prestige. The booming economy in the 1960s meant Germans could again afford to put caviar on their tables. That made Dieckmann & Hansen a desirable company. In 1969, a Texas rice grower call Riviana Foods acquired both Dieckmann & Hansen and Romanoff. Riviana was then gobbled up by the Colgate-Palmolive Corporation in 1976. The toothpaste company only wanted the German part of the business, so it split the company in two. Romanoff was sold to Iroquois Brands. Even though Dieckmann & Hansen remained part of the conglomerate, the split restored some of its independence. The interests of the two firms had diverged; Romanoff was now exclusively a retail brand. Gödecken and Schwerdtfeger thought the company would be stronger by itself. The decision to become an independent company turned out to be a blessing after 1977, when Iran cut off supplies to the American company. But independence from Romanoff would leave Dieckmann & Hansen without a label on store shelves.

By the time I met Schwerdtfeger in her office on the Hamburg waterfront, the old fish houses around the Dieckmann & Hansen offices had been converted to offices, loft apartments, and trendy restaurants. You could, however, still see the tangle of cranes and red-brick Victorian warehouses across the inlet at Hamburg's free port. The border with Denmark was only a few miles away, and from there the Elbe meandered on to the North Sea. In the days when the river was crowded with sturgeon, they swam past Dieckmann & Hansen's door as they migrated to and from the sea.

Over the years, Schwerdtfeger had learned almost everything there was to know about caviar. She knew that summer was not a good time for caviar to arrive, that most of it would just sit around until the Christmas season. She knew that the autumn catch from Iran was nice, but not from Russia. You had to watch out that the Iranian caviar wasn't too early, because so much of it was caught at sea before the females were ripe. From her husband, John Taylor, who had once worked in the Iranian oilfields, Schwerdtfeger learned that the region's mountain people pressed caviar into a loaf and ate it by the slice with bread and a glass of milk. She kept in her head a list of the Russian rivers where the sturgeon could still spawn and those that had silted over. Schwerdtfeger didn't get to visit Astrakhan until 1987, when Gorbachev's perestroika made such things possible, but she knew from talking to her suppliers that the reason the quality of the caviar dropped off in the 1960s was that the Russians had started drilling for oil in the Caspian Sea. When the environmental group TRAFFIC began investigating the poaching problem in Russia in 1996, Susanne Schwerdtfeger was the obvious person to guide their researchers through the murky world of the caviar trade. Exhausted by the upheavals in the caviar business, Schwerdtfeger had recently made the difficult decision to close Dieckmann & Hansen, ending the reign of the world's oldest caviar house. She thought her experience no longer mattered in the new, more cutthroat business.

It had taken a year or two for Dieckmann & Hansen to feel the full effect of the new, post-Soviet order. Gradually, her old reliable suppliers began to vanish and Schwerdtfeger had to scramble to find new ones. "We entered the '90s as an experienced packer," she told me. That meant that Dieckmann & Hansen imported large kilogram tins of caviar into Hamburg's free port and divided the contents into one- and two-ounce jars at its packing house. The firms that bought the small jars would sometimes affix their own label, then sell the caviar at a significant markup. For a long time, Dieckmann & Hansen also dominated the airline and cruise ship trade. Those clients didn't care about labels, since they served the caviar in a restaurant setting. It was nothing for Dieckmann & Hansen to sell a ton to an airline in a single transaction. Yet, the firm's reputation as a wholesaler was also its weakness. It meant that the average person never saw the Dieckmann & Hansen name on a jar of caviar.

As poachers smuggled more of the delicacy out of Russia, dozens of new dealers started competing with Dieckmann & Hansen for the cruise ship and airline trade. Those dealers were willing and able to sell caviar at a fraction of the old prices. Schwerdtfeger wasn't as fussy as Petrossian about maintaining caviar's mystique, and tried to buy cheap caviar from whomever she could—Romanians who caught sturgeon in the Danube, Chinese who fished in the Amur River, Turks who trawled the Black Sea, even Poles, although she knew they had no sturgeon industry at all and were buying it from Russian poachers. The problem, she found, was that "you couldn't trust their caviar."

It was getting toward evening as we talked in her office, surrounded by boxes of documents, photographs, and memorabilia from Dieckmann & Hansen's glory days. The sky over the Elbe had faded to a pale evening orange, and her words began to take on the form of a postmortem. By 1997, she recalled, "caviar was selling for half of its old price, and you still couldn't move it all. There was too much caviar on the market. I had people coming in here with suitcases full of the stuff. Usually it was sour or yeasty. . . . I wouldn't buy it, but I know a lot of others did."

While Schwerdtfeger was scrambling to find suppliers and keep Dieckmann & Hansen in business, the report that she helped TRAFFIC to write was being vigorously discussed in international environmental circles. TRAFFIC's research had made it plain that the Caspian sturgeon were veering toward extinction. Between the frenzy of poaching and the failure of hatcheries, almost no new sturgeon were being born. Prodded by scientists and the TRAFFIC researchers, the international agency that monitored trade in endangered species began to talk about putting the fish on its list of threatened species. Some scientists felt extreme measures were needed and advocated a complete ban on the caviar trade, similar to the prohibitions against ivory sales. But most thought a ban was too extreme. The international trade agency, which is known as CITES—the Convention on International Trade in Endangered Species—decided to take a middle position. It imposed export quotas in the hope of controlling illegal fishing, which made it much harder for poachers to get their caviar out of Russia. The old established dealers such as Petrossian and Dieckmann & Hansen welcomed the restrictions in the belief that they would steady the market. But because the regulations limited legal supplies, it was also harder for those dealers to get the caviar they needed.

In early 1999, Schwerdtfeger and most of the top caviar dealers began to focus on the forthcoming millennium celebrations. For a caviar dealer, New Year's Eve is what Easter is to florists. Schwerdtfeger was thrilled to find early in the year that she could buy ten tons of caviar from Kazakhstan. But because of the tangle of new regulations, she wanted to make sure it was legal. She called the European Union's health ministry to check on Kazakhstan's standing, and it confirmed that Kazakhstan was approved to sell caviar. A few days later, she signed a contract and transferred $620,000 into the account of her Kazakh supplier. A few days later, European officials announced a total ban on Kazakh caviar, not because the eggs were poached, but because the processing plants there didn't meet European health standards. Dieckmann & Hansen was barred from bringing the caviar it had just paid for onto European territory. "When we protested, they were like rubber walls," Schwerdtfeger complained bitterly.

In the end, Dieckmann & Hansen got its money back. The Kazakhs were only too happy to sell the caviar elsewhere, especially since prices were going up all the time. By then, most of the legal caviar had been claimed. It was the biggest bash of the century and Dieckmann & Hansen had no caviar to sell. Schwerdtfeger felt she was getting too old for such a roller-coaster business. She had been hoping to sell the company and retire, but after the millennium debacle Dieckmann & Hansen seemed as worthless as a punctured balloon.

The problem went beyond Dieckmann & Hansen losing the millennium trade. The caviar industry had become so fragmented that Dieckmann & Hansen was just one of many dealers. While the average consumer of caviar was likely to associate the Petrossian name with the delicate sturgeon eggs, the name Dieckmann & Hansen meant nothing to most people. Schwerdtfeger was worried about the firm's lack of brand recognition, and by the 1990s she was thinking about starting a retail line of Dieckmann & Hansen caviar. "At first it seemed there was no necessity to have a brand. My predecessor didn't see a reason and I didn't either," Schwerdtfeger said. She realized later how wrong her thinking was. "I was always so conservative," she explained. "I didn't want to widen the business. I always wanted to see what was going on. Dieckmann & Hansen was highly profitable. It was under good control. We thought there were other things more important than a lot of advertising. We mainly sold to wholesalers." Still, she knew that profits would be higher for retail. "After '91, we had this idea. We started to develop a logo. In Japan, we had a strong market for Dieckmann & Hansen." They planned to introduce the new brand there.

Unfortunately, it was already too late. Dieckmann & Hansen couldn't match the competition, Schwerdtfeger said. She dug into one of the boxes surrounding her desk and picked out the silver booklet that the house had published for its 125th anniversary. "The ever-growing number of satisfied customers is proof . . . of the success of first-class leadership and dedicated teamwork," the history concluded. Four years later, the oldest caviar company in the world had ceased to exist.

IN AMERICA, the Dieckmann & Hansen line didn't quite die out; it mutated into a new form.

In 1980, Romanoff Caviar was sold to Iroquois Brands, a large food manufacturer with a diverse line of products. The American side of the Dieckmann & Hansen family hoped that the new owner would reinvigorate their new division with an infusion of cash. Instead, Iroquois decided to take Romanoff downmarket.

The founder of the American caviar industry was gradually reduced to a purveyor of low-grade lumpfish roe. Food coloring was added to make the pale lumpfish eggs resemble sturgeon caviar, but the gloppy concoction was as much like the real thing as oatmeal. Romanoff's decline troubled Arnold Hansen-Sturm, the last member of the Dieckmann & Hansen clan to run the label. Hansen-Sturm had stayed on as the head of Romanoff after Colgate took over the company in 1976, but when the company was sold again four years later, he decided to start his own house. He called it the Hansen Caviar Company, after one of the early Dieckmann & Hansen ventures in the

United States, and settled into a small warehouse across from the railroad tracks in Bergenfield, New Jersey. Hansen-Sturm was convinced there was a niche for good-quality caviar in America and he wanted the Hansen name on it. More than anything, Hansen-Sturm was determined to preserve the family legacy.

Schwerdtfeger had given me Hansen-Sturm's telephone number, but when I called I had the feeling that he wasn't eager to talk about Hansen Caviar. He put me off by saying that he was busy negotiating a deal for a huge quantity of Caspian caviar. Those negotiations went on for months before he reluctantly agreed to let me visit him in Bergenfield. On the morning that we were supposed to meet, he called to cancel again, but I had already left for New Jersey. When I appeared at the door, Hansen-Sturm had little choice but to let me in.

Hansen-Sturm took me into his office to show me his collection of Dieckmann & Hansen memorabilia. His prize was an old tin marked "Sandwich Caviar," the name for the cheap American sturgeon roe that had been briefly popular at the end of the nineteenth century. The walls of the office were adorned with old anatomical prints of sturgeons, photographs of Russian tonyas, and glossy studio shots of Hansen caviar jars. Looking down sternly on all of it were his grandparents' oil portraits.

Hansen-Sturm told me that while there are still several Dieckmann and Hansen relatives around, he is the only member of the clan still involved with caviar. His daughter dabbled briefly in the business, and he was disappointed when she decided not to stay with his company. When I met Hansen-Sturm, he was close to retirement age. The stress of the business was evidently taking its toll. The daily sight of his ancestors' portraits on the walls helped keep him focused on the task of preserving the Dieckmann & Hansen line.

Hansen-Sturm was only the third family member to run Romanoff.

The company was started by his great-uncle Ferdinand Hansen, who had come to America for Dieckmann & Hansen in 1886 to teach Delaware River fishermen how to make caviar. Ferdinand, who was descended from the Hamburg company's founders, ended up staying in America even after the sturgeon were exhausted. Ferdinand built Romanoff into the best-known caviar name in America. For his label, he chose a picture of a Russian Cossack and the Hapsburg eagle, signaling the marriage of the Russian delicacy and German marketing skill.

After World War II, he selected a nephew, Gunter Sturm, to run the company. In gratitude, Gunter appended Hansen to his family name, thus maintaining the line that went back to 1869. When Gunter retired, his son Arnold Hansen-Sturm became the third and last family member to run Romanoff. Some of the Hansens were upset when Hansen-Sturm announced he was selling the company to Riviana Foods in 1969, but there was little they could do to stop him.

As part of the arrangement, Hansen-Sturm continued to oversee Romanoff's production. But he soon found there was a downside to being part of a large corporate environment. Romanoff's relations with Iran's caviar house, Shilat, deteriorated, and in 1977 the company made a fateful decision not to renew its trading contract. Romanoff's preemptive action signaled a new strategy for the company. Romanoff had effectively withdrawn from the high-end caviar market. It now planned to use its prestigious label to sell what it called "affordable caviars," meaning lumpfish roe from Iceland and salmon eggs from the Pacific Northwest. Hansen-Sturm's role in fashioning this corporate strategy is unclear, but he ultimately fell victim to the market turmoil that followed the Iranian revolution. In 1980, when Colgate decided to dump its Romanoff line by selling it to Iroquois Brands, Hansen-Sturm lost his position at Romanoff.

While Hansen-Sturm might not have enjoyed watching Romanoff turn into a second-rate caviar company, he was changed by the experience of working for a large conglomerate. He now believed that the definition of caviar could be stretched beyond sturgeon eggs. In America, any kind of fish roe can be called caviar as long as it is qualified by the name of the fish, such as paddlefish or salmon. Not long after starting Hansen Caviar Company, Hansen-Sturm began to look for other products that could reasonably be sold as caviar. He traveled to the Mississippi River to teach fisherman how to make caviar from the paddlefish roe. While paddlefish roe is far superior to lumpfish roe, Hansen-Sturm knew that it did not compare in taste and texture—not to mention price—with sturgeon caviar. Like Ferdinand, Hansen-Sturm dreamed of selling real American caviar. The American sturgeon roe that most resembles the Caspian varieties comes from the Pacific white sturgeon. The only problem for Hansen-Sturm was that wild white sturgeon is struggling for survival and selling its caviar is illegal.

A BANK TELLER in the Columbia River town of Dollars Corner in Washington state was the first person to realize something odd was going on. Sorting through the receipts from the local Value Motel one day in 1990, the teller noticed that some of the bills were streaked with a telltale red dye. Only a couple of days earlier, a neighboring bank in town had been held up by two gunmen. The teller there had the presence of mind to insert an exploding dye pack in with the loot. Now the money was starting to trickle back to the deposit boxes of Dollars Corner.

The FBI set up a surveillance operation at the Value Motel, where the dye-spattered notes had originated. They immediately focused on two suspicious guests who had been renting a room by the month. Not only did the pair insist on paying cash, but they had explicitly told the manager that they didn't want maid service. The agents were puzzled by the two men. These suspected bank robbers dressed in flannel shirts and overalls and left the motel every morning with a boat trailer joined to their red pickup truck. When one of the suspects tossed something into the motel Dumpster, an FBI agent went over to retrieve the item: an empty salt box. The following day, the agents tailed the suspects to the local Federal Express office. After the men left, the agents inspected the airbills and found the packages were destined for Bergenfield, New Jersey. When the clerk at Federal Express mentioned that the two men were regulars and that they always stank of fish, the FBI agents realized that the suspects who they had been trailing for days were not bank robbers at all.

They were sturgeon poachers. Over a period of five years, the two men had caught hundreds of sturgeon illegally and made over three thousand pounds of white sturgeon caviar, which was then shipped through FedEx to Hansen-Sturm in New Jersey. The white sturgeon population had been decimated during the nineteenth-century caviar rush. Although fishing was banned in the beginning of the twentieth century, the species still hadn't rebounded. But there was enough white sturgeon around for the state to permit sport fishermen to cast for the big fish with a hook and line. Fishermen could do whatever they wanted with their catches, except sell them.

When Hansen-Sturm found out that most sport fishermen were throwing away the roe, he was as appalled as his ancestors were when they first arrived in New Jersey in 1873. Emulating his forebears, Hansen-Sturm found a couple of fishermen who were willing to sell him the roe and taught them how to prepare caviar. Pretty soon, they were shipping him large quantities of excellent white sturgeon caviar.

Hansen-Sturm knew he couldn't trade openly in white sturgeon roe, so he labeled it as osetra. Since it was good quality, it easily passed for one of the two most expensive caviars in the world. The deception enabled Hansen-Sturm to sell the fishermen's caviar for as much six hundred dollars a pound to exclusive clients such as the Rainbow Room and the Waldorf-Astoria Hotel in New York. At that price, Hansen-Sturm's three thousand pounds of illegal caviar must have netted him close to $2 million.

The FBI investigators turned the case over to the National Marine Fisheries Service, which had no trouble tracing the operation to Hansen Caviar. In the end, the poaching charge was the least of Hansen-Sturm's crimes. Once he got wind of the federal investigation, he began frantically pulling incriminating documents from his files. But the meticulous record keeper triumphed over the criminal. Instead of destroying the evidence, Hansen-Sturm decided to hide the account books in the trunk of an employee's car. Hansen-Sturm's deception was so transparent that a field agent for the marine fisheries service soon uncovered the records. Hansen-Sturm was charged with obstructing justice and lying to a grand jury, both serious felonies, as well as poaching.

When I asked Hansen-Sturm about the case, he claimed he was naive. "We thought we were doing everything according to the law, but we couldn't prove it at the trial," he insisted. He had used the same defense in court. But he had a hard time explaining to the jury why he paid the fishermen in cash and mailed the money to a post office box.

Hansen-Sturm was eventually sentenced to eighteen months in jail. His punishment might have been harsher, but the jury downgraded the poaching charge from a felony to a misdemeanor. This is typical. Most American juries don't consider crimes against wildlife serious enough to warrant a lengthy prison sentence. The only reason Hansen-Sturm went to jail at all was because of his bungled attempt to conceal his records and thwart the workings of justice. Hansen-Sturm and Hansen Caviar Company got off with less than $20,000 in fines, less than 1 percent of the value of the illicit caviar sales.

Even the damage to the Hansen family name, which Hansen-Sturm had fought so hard to preserve, was minimal. Almost as soon as he was released from prison in 1996, Hansen-Sturm returned to the fray, reopening the Hansen Caviar Company in the same Bergenfield warehouse where he had started it. With all the cheap Russian caviar pouring into America, Hansen-Sturm knew that there was still plenty of money to be made.

8

The Sturgeon's Fingerprint

We have the luxury of vodka. We have the luxury of caviar. But time, that luxury we do not have.
—BOB HOSKINS AS NIKITA KHRUSHCHEV,
IN ENEMY AT THE GATES

*T*he struggles of the old caviar houses were a symptom of a much greater problem. The flood of cheap caviar had ruined Dieckmann & Hansen and weakened Petrossian. But the deluge was also hastening the sturgeon's demise.

None of this was evident in 1991 when a Russian sturgeon expert named Vadim Birstein immigrated to New York. The slaughter in the Caspian and the Black Sea was just getting under way and Birstein's work on the sturgeon's genome was still on the fringes of scientific inquiry. But in the course of his research, Birstein began to comprehend what was happening to the sturgeon. He became determined to alert the world about the impending catastrophe and to galvanize environmentalists into action. Saving the sturgeon would become an all-consuming obsession for Birstein.

Birstein's original reasons for coming to America had nothing to do with sturgeon, however. In the Soviet Union, Birstein had been both a respected geneticist, as well as a prominent dissident. Because of those interests, he was invited to the United States to attend a scientific conference on ethics in genetics. He expected to spend just a few weeks in the United States, but ended up falling in love with an American woman.

Desperate to find a way to stay in America without resorting to driving a taxi, Birstein began calling every scientist he knew. In Russia, he had worked at one of Moscow's top research institutes. The closest equivalent in New York was the American Museum of Natural History. Since he was staying in New York, Birstein went to see a fellow geneticist named Rob DeSalle at the museum.

"Birstein just showed up on my doorstep," DeSalle recalled. For someone who needed help, Birstein was not the least bit deferential. DeSalle said that he didn't ask for a job, he demanded one. He handed DeSalle his CV as if it were a gift. In the Soviet Union, Birstein had navigated a successful career as a scientist despite repeated run-ins with the Communist authorities over his various dissident causes. He displayed an air of lordly entitlement that was common among Russian scientists who came up through the exacting meritocracy of the Soviet academies. As DeSalle scanned the pages of Birstein's résumé, he saw that his credentials matched his arrogance. Birstein had published dozens of papers and had made a significant discovery about the peculiar arrangement of chromosomes in the sturgeon.

At the time, DeSalle wasn't particularly interested in the ancient species. His specialty was fruit flies. Sturgeon hadn't yet become one of the hot species for geneticists to study, and the caviar rush that would decimate the Caspian Sea sturgeon was still a few months off. DeSalle, who was then thirty-five and given to wearing Converse high-tops to the lab, searched for a nice way to say no to this imposing Russian scientist. "I felt bad about not being able to give him a job," DeSalle said. "It was a typical Russian émigré story. He was immensely well educated, really smart, and a good scientist. If he had done all that work in the U.S., he would have been the chairman of a department." DeSalle tried to explain to Birstein that there was no opening at the museum worthy of his experience. But Birstein refused to be put off. His battles with the Soviet authorities had taught him persistence. After his first meeting with DeSalle, he returned every few days to see if anything had come up. By their third or fourth conversation, DeSalle could no longer resist. He offered Birstein a position as a visiting scientist in his lab.

The job was exactly what Birstein was looking for except for one thing: there was no salary. But the appointment would entitle Birstein to an office at the museum, access to DeSalle's laboratory, and the free labor of eager graduate students. Like many American researchers, Birstein would have to scrounge for grants to fund his work.

The two scientists took some time getting used to each other. Although DeSalle held a prestigious research position at the museum, he was still just starting out in his career. He had grown up in the Midwest and had never spent time with anyone like the Russian geneticist. Birstein was a graying veteran of searing academic and political wars in Russia. He was cultured, cosmopolitan, and equally at home in literary and scientific circles. "He was a god in Moscow and I was just this punk who had resources," DeSalle said. But both were dogged and scrupulous researchers. DeSalle tended to be more easygoing about

things and more open to different approaches, while Birstein believed
there was only one right way to do things. Whenever Birstein was
around, there tended to be a lot of yelling in the lab.

Birstein had only been at the museum a short time when he began
nagging DeSalle to let him conduct DNA studies on sturgeon. When he
came to America for the conference, he had brought his collection of
tissue samples, which he had gathered from all over Russia. "Sturgeon
aren't interesting because of caviar," he told DeSalle. "They're interesting biologically. They're a group of living fossils." DeSalle was still
more interested in fruit flies, but Birstein kept up the pressure. "It's a really neat system. Let's look at it," Birstein would say. Sturgeon were
also easier to study. While there are three thousand different kinds of
fruit flies, there are only twenty-seven species of sturgeon. It would
take several careers for DeSalle to examine the DNA of all those in-
sects, while the two could study all the sturgeon in a couple of years.
Birstein kept pestering. Sturgeon, he told DeSalle repeatedly, are an
especially intriguing species because they are the largest animal living
in fresh water, and because they arrived so early in the evolutionary
chain of vertebrates. Birstein wheedled and pleaded, until he succeeded
in wearing DeSalle down once again. Soon the two of them were mixing bits of Birstein's tissue samples with organic chemicals and separating out their DNA in DeSalle's lab in the musty sixth floor attic of
the Victorian museum, then running the sequences of chromosomes
through computers.

In Russia, Birstein had been a lot more than a scientist. He was an
active opponent of the Communist system, a true, KGB-hating dissident. He joined Amnesty International during the stifling years of
Brezhnev's rule, and supplied the group with the latest news about fellow dissidents who had been arrested, tried, or sent to psychiatric hos-
pitals. When I asked Birstein what prompted him to challenge the

all-powerful government, he smiled a little, and said, "Why was I a dissident? It was my personality. Just bad genes, I guess."

Birstein began his rebellion at an early age, while he was still a biology student at Moscow State University, the Harvard of Russia. He and some other students had come to believe that Soviet industry was devastating the environment. They knew there wasn't much they could do then to stop the government from draining the Aral Sea, or dumping nuclear wastes in populated areas. Instead, they focused on saving Russia's wildlife from human predators. On weekends they would travel to the Volga River to search for sturgeon poachers. When they found them, they took away their nets and called the fisheries police. In light of today's ferocious, high-tech poaching activity, such a gesture seems both prescient and quaintly naive.

After Mikhail Gorbachev came to power in the 1980s and began tantalizing Russians with the promise of democracy, Birstein was emboldened. He became interested in uncovering the dirty secrets of the Soviet past. In 1990, Birstein was named to a committee to investigate the disappearance of Raoul Wallenberg, a Swedish diplomat who had saved hundreds of Hungarian Jews during World War II, and had been given access to secret state files. Wallenberg had vanished mysteriously after the Soviet Army rolled into Hungary. Birstein was determined to prove what many suspected: that the KGB took Wallenberg back to Moscow and killed him.

Birstein continued to live a two-track life during these years. While he was spending several days a month in the Soviet archives, trying to piece together the final events of Wallenberg's life, he was also working in his lab, poring over sequences of sturgeon chromosomes, trying to piece together the fish's genetic code. Then, in one impetuous moment, he decided to abandon what had been his life's two great projects and start over again in America.

. . .

THE JOB at the Museum of Natural History enabled Birstein to return to one of these obsessions. By the middle of 1992, DeSalle and Birstein were immersed in the painstaking process of sequencing the portions of the DNA for all the known species of sturgeon. Each set of genes yielded vast amounts of information about the fish and its ancestry. The two scientists were trying to compile a library of every species' genetic history. By running the sequences of genes through a computer and comparing the differences, DeSalle and Birstein were creating a family tree that would show the order in which each species had evolved and its relationship to its various cousin sturgeons. In a very short time, they had accumulated a tremendous amount of information. Neither knew then where their research might lead. It was just fascinating to understand the connections among species. DeSalle was becoming as excited about sturgeon as Birstein.

One of the things they learned was that sturgeon are genetically unpredictable. To the human eye, one Russian sturgeon may look much like any another Russian sturgeon, but their collection of genes can be quite different. The two scientists spent a lot of time comparing these gene sets, trying to decide which genes were the key indicators of each species. Humans have a lot of genetic variety as well, but all belong to the same species of *Homo sapiens*. Sturgeon can look similar, yet belong to a different species.

One reason for the wide-ranging genetic variation in sturgeon is that local populations don't mix all that much. Sturgeon tend to stay loyal to a single river system. A Russian sturgeon native to the Volga River will rarely swim up the Ural River to spawn. Over time, the Russian sturgeon population in the Volga develops local characteristics that distinguish it from the Russian sturgeon population in the Ural

River. If enough time elapses and enough differences occur, those different characteristics might turn the two populations into different species. That was the way that all new species had diverged from their ancestors.

Because sturgeon were prone to variation, DeSalle and Birstein had to be careful to use large samples. Whenever they studied the genome of a particular species, they would sequence the DNA from dozens of different fish. They also made a point of examining samples from as many different river systems as possible. In this way, they hoped to come up with a reliable set of sequences for each species.

Much of this kind of genetic work is about making lists. Scientists make lists of DNA sequences, which they use to compile lists of different species. As a result of all their careful comparisons, DeSalle and Birstein came to believe that the standard taxonomic list classifying sturgeon was flawed. The original list had been assembled over several centuries by naturalists, starting with the great botanist Carolus Linnaeus, who was the first to categorize the world's diverse species. When those naturalists first began to classify the world's plants and animals, the only real tool they had for distinguishing among closely related species was their eyes. Now scientists had more advanced tools that allowed them to look inside a cell and examine its molecular composition. With these methods, and their new understanding of DNA, they could make much finer distinctions among species. Their discoveries inevitably required changes in the taxonomic lists.

Even before they started comparing DNA sequences, the scientists had suspected that some of the twenty-seven species of sturgeon would probably not stand up as full-fledged species. The prime suspect was the Persian sturgeon, or *Acipenser persicus*, which was found in the southern part of the Caspian along the Iranian coast. It looked almost exactly like the Russian sturgeon, or *Acipenser gueldenstaedtii*, which lived in the northern Caspian. The caviar from both fish was traditionally called osetra. After examining dozens of samples from each fish, DeSalle and Birstein concluded that they were indeed the same species. At the same time, they realized that there might be other distinct species that had never been identified and named, meaning there might be more than twenty-seven kinds of sturgeon. It was just a matter of time before they identified these previously unknown species.

But the Russian sturgeon continued to fascinate the two men. As they reviewed the DNA information they had extracted from Birstein's numerous samples, their results became stranger and more erratic. They kept producing oddball DNA combinations that didn't match either the Russian or its false cousin the Persian sturgeon. They tested osetra eggs from various areas of the Caspian, but a portion of the results always came out with a different sequence.

These oddball sequences, Birstein eventually became convinced, actually matched those of Siberian sturgeon—*Acipenser baerii*. How could that be? The Siberian sturgeon was a purely freshwater fish whose range was limited to Lake Baikal and Siberian rivers such as the Lena and the Ob, and Birstein's samples came from the salty waters of the Caspian. He had seen the fish and tasted its caviar. It looked just like the Russian sturgeon and the eggs tasted very much like osetra.

There were two plausible explanations, and both would have profound implications for both the caviar trade and the course of the scientists' careers. Approximately eight thousand to ten thousand years ago, at the end of the Ice Age, a vast freshwater lake had spanned the breadth of Siberia, connecting Lake Baikal and the Caspian, as well as the Black Sea and the Mediterranean. As the earth warmed, the waters receded and the basins were separated. What happened, Birstein believed, was that a population of Siberian sturgeon remained in the Caspian. As salt water invaded the Caspian, transforming it from a large freshwater lake to a small saline sea, the surviving populations of Siberian adapted to the new conditions, as did the Russian sturgeon.

DeSalle didn't really buy this explanation. He thought the reason was simpler. There were Siberian sturgeon in the Caspian because Russian scientists put them there. The hatcheries along the Volga had always been notoriously sloppy. They would collect buckets of sturgeon eggs, fertilize them, and dump the fingerlings back into the sea without keeping careful records about their origins. For instance, Russian scientists now admit that they bred almost all the beluga from four or five parents. That means that the descendants now swimming around the Caspian have dangerously little genetic variation. Given such a lax history, DeSalle was convinced that the hatcheries had released Siberian sturgeon into the Caspian just a few decades ago.

The issue wasn't really why there were Siberian sturgeon in the Caspian. It was their presence in the Caspian that mattered. Until DeSalle and Birstein began looking through the microscope at sturgeon chromosomes, no one had any idea that there were Siberian sturgeon living in the sea. Now they had evidence that this freshwater fish had adapted itself to the salty environment. But even after they presented their results in scientific circles, it would be a long time before anyone involved in regulating the caviar business believed them.

WHEN BIRSTEIN and DeSalle set out to study sturgeon, their work seemed to be the purest kind of science. It was research for its own sake. But as their results took them down unexpected paths, they began to wonder how they might put their DNA findings to use.

For fun, DeSalle suggested that they test caviar in New York shops to see whether the dealers were selling what they claimed. The two went around to the most famous caviar stores in New York and bought one of every kind of caviar. When they returned to the lab, they scooped out a few eggs from each tin, mixed them with their chemicals, and applied their test to see whether they were accurately labeled as beluga, sevruga, and osetra. Birstein especially enjoyed the exercise, sampling a little from each tin. DeSalle, ever his opposite, never learned to like caviar. But both were startled when almost a third of the tins came up wrong. Someone was pulling a fast one on the consumer, either the producers or the dealers. The scam was a natural for the papers. Their sensational findings won DeSalle and Birstein a few minutes of fame as newspapers investigated the "Fishy Business." When the headlines faded, they still weren't sure whether there was a use for their test outside of their genetics work, but they asked the museum to have their method patented anyway.

In the meantime, Birstein was already hearing stories of the decimation of sturgeon taking place in the Caspian; even before arriving in America, he had been aware of the fish's precarious existence. He knew better than most scientists how much their survival depended on the hatcheries and the Soviet Union's strict control of fishing. His father had been a zoologist and had worked extensively in the Volga delta during the 1930s. When Stalin first proposed to dam the river, his father and his colleagues lobbied hard to ensure there would be provisions made to protect the sturgeon. At the time, their main concern wasn't the loss of spawning grounds. They were more worried that the dams would alter the water levels in the Caspian, killing the crustaceans and worms that formed the main part of the sturgeon diet. As a boy, Birstein heard his father describe how the scientists imported a hardy worm from the Sea of Azov and placed it in the Caspian to ensure that the sturgeon would not go hungry after the dams were built. The worm, combined with the hatcheries and other protective measures, helped the sturgeon to survive. By the 1980s, catches were approaching their record levels from the turn of the century even though fewer and fewer fish were being born in the rivers.

Birstein arrived in America with his collection of tissue samples, only a few months after the rigid framework of state authority that had successfully protected the sturgeon for seventy years collapsed. By late 1992, he noticed that it was getting easier to buy caviar in New York for his DNA tests. It was cheaper, too. When he spoke with his colleagues in Astrakhan, they told him that every man in the delta had taken up sturgeon fishing. Birstein was thousands of miles away from the Caspian, but he understood the consequences of such unregulated fishing. The Atlantic sturgeon in the Delaware and the European sturgeon in the Elbe and the Rhône were already commercially extinct; the Caspian species would surely be the next to go. In 1993, he finally put these fears down on paper. With his colleagues, he published an article in an environmental journal called *Conservation Biology*. Unless the sturgeon was protected, he warned darkly, there would soon be none left.

Birstein's call to arms was written in the cautious language of scientists, but the message was clear enough to be heard by environmentalists and bureaucrats. As they began to focus on the fate of the sturgeon, Birstein became the spokesman for the endangered fish. Overnight, it seemed, he had become the most important sturgeon expert in the world. Officials at the World Conservation Union, an international environmental agency known by the letters IUCN, called Birstein and invited him to chair the Sturgeon Specialists Group, an international committee responsible for assessing the threat to the sturgeon.

Birstein was well placed to promote the plight of the sturgeon. He started publishing his own newsletter, *The Sturgeon Quarterly,* which included short scientific papers along with the latest news on the crisis in the Caspian. A year after the article in *Conservation Biology* appeared, he, DeSalle, and John Waldman organized a major conference on sturgeon at the American Museum of Natural History. The theme, "Biodiversity and Conservation," was aimed at saving the "living fossils" that were "now fast disappearing from our planet." The conference drew all the top sturgeon specialists in the world to New York, and won the museum a reputation as a center of sturgeon research.

After the meeting, Birstein began working on collecting population statistics, catch records, DNA samples, and other materials for the World Conservation Union. While he was assembling the scientific portion of the study, the Conservation Union decided to send researchers from one of its associates, TRAFFIC, to the Caspian to assess the poaching situation firsthand and to strengthen its case for putting the sturgeon on the list of endangered species. The researchers, Caroline Raymakers and Thomas De Meulenaer, spent several weeks traveling around the Volga River Delta, stopping at small towns and fishing tonyas. They could see that sturgeon fishing was among the only remaining economic activities in the desperate region. If the fish wasn't yet commercially extinct, it was on its way.

When TRAFFIC released its final report, the group wasn't sure what sort of response it would get. Environmentalists know too well that endangered species aren't all treated equally in the press. Cuddly and photogenic creatures such as dolphins and whales do much better than small and slimy ones like worms. Given the sturgeon's ungainly snout and armor-encrusted body, it wasn't an obvious candidate for prime-time coverage. But the threat to the caviar trade made the TRAFFIC report on sturgeon irresistible. Stories about the sturgeon's plight hit the news all over the world.

By then, there were plenty of scientists who agreed with Birstein that the sturgeon should be listed as an endangered species. The German environmental ministry took up the cause. They were especially concerned because so much of the illicit caviar coming overland from Russia was being sold in German shops. The Germans thought that the best way to stanch the flow was to impose international trade restrictions on caviar which would require the agreement of all the Caspian states. The only agency with enough clout to bring the former Soviet republics and Iran to the bargaining table was an international bureaucracy known as the Convention on International Trade in Endangered Species of Flora and Fauna, or CITES, the same people who had successfully outlawed the international trade in elephant ivory and restricted the sale of rare orchids from the tropical forests of Belize.

CITES is the closest thing to a worldwide environmental protection agency. More than one hundred nations are members. When a new country joins, it signs a treaty agreeing to follow CITES decisions and procedures on the export and import of its protected species. The logic behind CITES is simple. If poachers can't sell their products in lucrative foreign markets, then they lose their incentive to poach. But since CITES was formed in the 1970s, its record has been mixed. The most common criticism is that the agency focuses too much on controlling trade and not enough on the factors that threaten species in the first place, such as habitat loss, cultural traditions, and lack of other jobs for poachers. Despite being an agency dedicated to saving endangered species, CITES does nothing to stop slaughter or overuse. It merely makes it more difficult to transport products across international boundaries. In theory, if a country agrees to restrict the export of an endangered species, that means that it is also willing to crack down on its exploitation at home. But not all countries have the will or the means to follow through.

The Russians knew it would be difficult for them to stop the poaching. They had just lost a humiliating war in the Caucasus against the Chechen rebels, who controlled part of the illegal caviar trade. Just as

Russian negotiations with CITES were nearing a conclusion, a huge bomb destroyed an apartment building in neighboring Daghestan that was occupied by border guards who policed the caviar trade. The sixty-eight deaths were a chilling warning of the difficulties that lay ahead. There was a lot at stake for the local population if caviar was no longer traded freely. Thousands of families would be deprived of their only income, and Boris Yeltsin's shaky government feared social unrest.

In 1996, after intense pressure from CITES, Yeltsin and his cabinet reluctantly agreed to accept limits on its caviar exports. By then, the question was no longer whether to list the Caspian sturgeon as an endangered species; it was how to list it. CITES has three rankings that it assigns to some thirty thousand species. The least restrictive is Appendix III, which is given to species that are not in immediate danger of extinction. They can be freely traded. But if the population begins to crash, it is moved to Appendix II and put under international watch. Should the population decline continue, the species is put under the strictest regime, Appendix I. That designation means it is no longer commercially viable. All trade is banned.

All during the negotiations with Moscow, it had been assumed that the Caspian sturgeon would be listed under Appendix II and that caviar could continue to be exported. But not everyone saw things that way. Some sturgeon specialists believed the situation was so desperate that a complete ban on sales was necessary. They believed the sturgeon was heading for commercial extinction and wanted it listed in the strictest category, Appendix I.

The American representatives disagreed. They argued that unless the Russians and Kazakhs knew they could make money selling beluga caviar, they would have no incentive to invest in hatcheries that would restock the sea with hatchlings. The same logic followed for all the endangered Caspian species. "For CITES to work, people felt there had to be trade as an incentive to conservation," recalled Rosemarie Gnam, an official at the Fish & Wildlife Service who was then the U.S. liaison with CITES. Caroline Raymakers, whose report for TRAFFIC led to the trade controls, felt the same way. "We didn't want to drive the trade underground. We wanted to provide incentives for good management," she argued. The underlying assumption during the discussions was that Russia would eventually get its act together and rev up its hatcheries. Then everything would be all right again.

The Russians also fought to keep all three species listed on Appendix II. Even so, many officials remained skeptical about the whole idea. How was CITES going to distinguish between legal and illegal caviar? A total ban on caviar sales would have been relatively easy to enforce. It would mean that not a single tin of caviar could be taken out of Russia. The ban on elephant ivory had worked partly because it was a blanket ban. Of course, it was much easier to keep track of elephants, since their herds could easily be spotted from a satellite. But sturgeon populations were difficult to count. And the caviar trade was a much bigger business than the trade in elephant ivory. If some caviar was legal and some wasn't, the Russians wanted to know, how would CITES be able to tell the difference?

Birstein and DeSalle had the answer. In 1996, they had published their findings about the sturgeon's genetic makeup in the prestigious journal *Nature*. "Sturgeon are so similar looking that only with molecular information can you get a reliable idea of the species," Birstein said. "The Russians kept saying, we can't introduce restrictions because there is no method of discriminating between species. So Rob and I adapted our DNA test for the three main Caspian species." When Birstein met with CITES officials, he explained that the test could be used to fingerprint caviar. The same kind of genetic test was already being used in American courts to identify criminals. In those cases, evidence of a DNA match is considered irrefutable. Birstein suggested that a batch of caviar could be tested before it left Russia and given a set of identity papers similar to a passport. Just like a human traveler, the shipment would have to present a passport when it arrived at customs. It would then be tested again to see if the DNA matched. The system would enable all the Caspian states to keep track of their caviar exports.

Encouraged by the DNA work Birstein and DeSalle had done, the United States agreed to sponsor a resolution listing sturgeon as an endangered species. All three Russian varieties were ranked under Appendix II. When the resolution was put to a vote at the CITES general meeting held in Zimbabwe in June 1997, all 143 members unanimously agreed that the caviar trade should continue, but on a restricted basis. It seemed to Birstein that at last there was hope for the sturgeon.

IT IS HARD to date the end of Birstein's honeymoon with CITES bureaucrats, but their falling out probably began at the Zimbabwe meeting. All the representatives received a thick book with the scientific descriptions that Birstein had so laboriously compiled of every sturgeon, its habitat, and its environmental status. CITES would use this information as the foundation of its strategy for saving the sturgeon. But when Birstein inspected the book, he was insulted that no one from CITES had bothered to include his name on the document. He thought it was the least they could do, since they weren't paying him for the research, which had occupied months of his time. Scientists who did such work were usually supported by their universities or institutes and by grants. But Birstein was still only an unpaid visiting scientist at the natural history museum with little grant money to support his research.

The long debate over how to list the sturgeon had especially troubled Birstein. The people working for the sprawling international agency often reminded him of Soviet officials. He also worried that they didn't fully appreciate what was happening in the Caspian. "CITES is a giant bureaucracy," he reflected later. "They didn't want to confront the root of the problem. None of these international people wanted to hear the word 'Mafia'."

It wasn't long before Birstein started sparring with the U.S. Fish & Wildlife Service, which enforces the CITES regulations in America. Once the CITES controls went into effect, Fish & Wildlife would have to make sure, using Birstein's DNA test, that caviar poachers didn't try to slip their illegal haul through U.S. customs. If the caviar had been harvested legally, the DNA results would match the CITES passport. If the batch failed the DNA test, then it meant that the caviar was probably poached. It would be Fish & Wildlife's job to seize any shipment that failed the test.

What happened next is lost in the haze of recriminations. Fish & Wildlife says that it offered to buy the rights to Birstein's DNA test, but he imposed so many conditions that they gave up. "We had lots of discussions with Dr. Birstein. We were going to use Vadim's test. But there were too many complications with him, over where the test would be done and who would do it," said Rosemarie Gnam, who was running the CITES program. Whenever she talked about Birstein, it was always in a slow, modulated, precise way. The main problem, she said, was that "he wanted to control the test." Fed up with the Russian scientist, the service announced that it would develop its own DNA test instead.

But DeSalle and Birstein say that was not the way it happened at all. The Russian scientist merely wanted the government to pay him a fair price for his collection of sturgeon samples that formed the basis of the DNA test. "Vadim didn't want the royalties for himself," said DeSalle, who is listed as a co-inventor with Birstein on the patent. The money would have been paid to the museum in any case, because it owned the rights to the patent. "Vadim told me if we get royalties, then we can do more research."

But once Fish & Wildlife broke off negotiations with Birstein, it found itself in a jam. The CITES caviar inspections were due to start in April 1998. The service would have only a few months to compile the DNA sequences for all the sturgeon, while DeSalle and Birstein had taken years to do the same work. The deadline was only half the problem. Fish & Wildlife didn't even have the tissue samples for many of the species.

One way around this difficulty was to use the results that DeSalle and Birstein had published in journals. Those sequences were in the public domain. But many of their findings were still scrawled in their notebooks. Without the complete results, Fish & Wildlife wouldn't have enough time or tissue samples to create a valid test.

If Birstein wouldn't help, maybe DeSalle would. Fish & Wildlife asked DeSalle if they could use his notes, but he was reluctant to give them up. The service then approached his supervisors at the museum, which was now in a difficult position. It had gone to the trouble of hiring an attorney to patent the sturgeon DNA sequences, the first time in the museum's history that it had ever been awarded a patent. Should it now hand over those trademarked results for nothing? On the other hand, the federal government was a major source of scientific grants, and the museum could hardly afford to get itself on the bad side of the government agencies that provided significant amounts of funding. DeSalle said the museum told him to hand over his notes to the government. Caught between his loyalties to Birstein and to the museum, DeSalle decided in favor of the museum. He gave Fish & Wildlife everything they wanted.

Birstein was furious with the U.S. government. "It was just like the Soviet Union. DeSalle was put under tremendous pressure. He nearly lost his job," Birstein complained. Birstein himself was no longer welcome at the museum. In the course of his dispute with Fish & Wildlife, he had fallen out with nearly everyone connected to CITES.

Using DeSalle's notes, the data that appeared in scientific journals, and some of its own research, the government managed to fashion a DNA test. Birstein believed it had to be seriously flawed. Even with DeSalle's research notes, he claimed that they still didn't have enough tissue samples to make the test statistically reliable. What's more, the U.S. government has never accepted his discovery of Siberian sturgeon in the Caspian. Because government scientists had never published their findings in a peer-reviewed journal, Birstein believed the test had never been verified. He charged that Fish & Wildlife's test was unreliable, soon after making these claims, Birstein lost his position as head of CITES' Sturgeon Specialists Group.

While many of Birstein's colleagues thought he was on the mark about the government's test, they were still aghast at his behavior. Even as a newcomer to America, he should have known the rules of academia. He should have kept quiet and gone along with Fish & Wildlife. He would have at least been able to keep his position at the museum. But other scientists quietly admired him for sticking to his principles. "A lot of us tend to worry more about our careers," said Phaedra Doukakis, who did research for her doctorate at the museum. Birstein served as one of her thesis advisers. "If Vadim believes in something, if he believes he is right, he speaks up for that position no matter how much he might alienate someone," she said. DeSalle also continued to admire Birstein's commitment to principles. "He's fearless. I just wish he weren't so misunderstood," DeSalle said. At the time he told me this, DeSalle hadn't seen Birstein for nearly eighteen months, not since he was banished from the museum. With the luxury of time, it was easier to reflect on what had happened. "There is no doubt," DeSalle said, "that Birstein's dealings with the Russian authorities may have led him to be more unyielding with Fish & Wildlife than he should have been."

Birstein was certainly intractable. He was impolitic and a pain in the neck. But by all accounts, he was a good scientist. DeSalle said that Birstein is right about the flaws in Fish & Wildlife's test. Phaedra Doukakis is also convinced the test is inaccurate. Its main failing, they agreed, is that it does not take into account the presence of Siberian sturgeon in the Caspian. The sequences that the government culled from journals and DeSalle's notes weren't enough to create a good DNA test, DeSalle insisted. "Their database wasn't nearly as good as ours," he said. To create a reliable DNA test, "you need fifty samples of beluga, fifty of osetra, fifty of sevruga. You need samples from different rivers. They didn't have that." If the government's test was wrong, that meant they weren't going to be catching poachers. Instead, they were going to be punishing dealers who followed the rules.

The dispute over the DNA test had begun in the lab, but it would soon move from the abstract realm of scientific journals to the real world of the court system. As their disagreement with Fish & Wildlife grew more bitter, CITES' plan to save the sturgeon would be put to the test.

9

Caviar from
a Suitcase

*The bread can be white or brown, but the caviar must be
black.*

—CASPIAN FISHERMEN'S SAYING.

*W*hen a caviar smuggler arrives at Kennedy International Airport in
New York, one of the first things that he has to do is to find a luggage
trolley. Smugglers like to pack their caviar in the kind of large, un-
wieldy suitcases that travelers often choose for long vacations. One
large suitcase can hold sixty kilogram-sized tins of Russian caviar and
weigh 132 pounds, making it too heavy to carry or roll. There is another
reason to be careful with such a suitcase. Depending on the type of
eggs, dealers in New York will pay about $20,000 for the suitcase con-
tents. By the time the caviar is repacked into small jars and distributed
to gourmet shops, the roe will be worth over $100,000.

Caviar had long been an expensive luxury, but once CITES began to limit the supply in 1998 it also became a valuable item of contraband. Within a year after controls were introduced, the retail price for a pound of good beluga passed the thousand-dollar mark, making it the equivalent of several ounces of gold. Even the cheapest Russian sevruga cost over $300 at that time, more than a meal for two at many three-star restaurants. These prices caused some dealers to overlook the fact that it was now a felony to smuggle caviar into America.

The U.S. Fish & Wildlife Service wanted caviar dealers to understand that it was serious about enforcing the CITES regulations. Right before the new rules went into effect in April 1998, it invited all U.S. dealers to a meeting at St. John's University in Queens, New York. Fish & Wildlife officials made a point of asking all the dealers to sign in when they arrived, so that no one could later claim ignorance of a change in rules. Rosemarie Gnam, who had helped write the new CITES regulations, gave the main presentation, which was part seminar and part warning. From now on, she told the dealers, all caviar coming into the country needed a CITES certificate. Fish & Wildlife intended to do a DNA analysis of every shipment to confirm that the caviar inside the containers matched the information on the documents. Gnam said the government would give everyone a little time to get used to the new procedures. But after that, she said, gazing sternly around the room through half glasses, Fish & Wildlife would begin prosecuting anyone who tried to get around the CITES regulations.

A few months after Fish & Wildlife began policing the caviar business, I went to see Edward Grace, a special agent for the service who was assigned the sturgeon beat. He worked in a low, glassy office building on Long Island, close enough to Kennedy Airport that he could zip over any time customs agents found something fishy. Grace was eager to talk about his new specialty and invited me to see some recent hauls. We went into a storage room that was furnished with a variety of metal cabinets. Some were the kind of tall, narrow lockers found in high school gyms, but confiscated pelts from endangered animals such as zebras and leopards dangled from the hooks. Another evidence locker was heaped with dozens of alligator bags. Against one wall was a restaurant-style refrigerator. As Grace opened the stainless steel door, he was wreathed in plumes of frost. The refrigerator was stuffed with ice-crusted containers of caviar, the rewards of his latest seizures. Many of the tins and jars had amateurish labels with obvious misspellings and inaccuracies, and contained caviar made by poachers.

Most of the tins had been taken from tourists who had unknowingly brought home more than the allowable limit of 250 grams. But there were also regiments of neatly stacked cans that had been found concealed in smugglers' suitcases. Grace had recently busted a Georgian national named Albert Bazazashvili, who had arrived at Kennedy Airport with eleven large suitcases in tow. Given that he had carried all those suitcases from the Caucasus, the mountainous wedge of land between the Caspian and Black Seas, he might as well have been wearing a sign with the word *smuggler* written on it. On his customs declaration, Bazazashvili had checked "no" next to the question that asked whether he was carrying any "fruits, plants, meats, food, soil, birds, snails, other live animals, wildlife products [or] farm products." The customs officer processing Bazazashvilli's luggage must have rolled his eyes before he popped open the first suitcase. The suitcases were was indeed crammed with food—some sixty caviar tins. Bazazashvili, of course, had no CITES certificate. By the time the customs inspector had gotten to the eleventh suitcase, he had counted 659 pounds of caviar, worth about $500,000 retail. When Bazazashvili was asked what he was going to do with all that caviar, he explained that he had a dealer in Brooklyn waiting for it. Bazazashvili ended up pleading guilty to smuggling and spent ten months in jail.

For every smuggler as bumbling as Bazazashvili, Grace knew there were a dozen who were far more discreet and clever. Fish & Wildlife had just four agents assigned to Kennedy Airport, who were expected to be on the lookout not just for caviar, but for products made from all sorts of endangered species, such as soft woolen scarves woven with the hairs of the shatoosh, a Tibetan antelope, and jewelry boxes carved from the tusks of African elephants. Grace said the agents were lucky if they were able to check 20 percent of the passengers coming through the airport. Because caviar was a priority, the agents tended to concentrate their energy on flights from the former Soviet Union and Eastern Europe. "I could work an Aeroflot flight and make three or four seizures on each one," Grace told me.

It didn't take long for smugglers to realize this. They began taking indirect flights to the United States, especially those that originated in innocuous, land-locked countries such as Switzerland. They also chose to fly to secondary cities such as Miami or Baltimore. Some smugglers gave up the suitcase trade altogether. They found it easier to bribe foreign officials to provide them with the CITES documents they needed to export caviar legally. Tons of caviar were legally exported this way from countries such as Turkey, Poland, and the United Arab Emirates, even though none has a sturgeon fishing industry. This was another loophole in the CITES system. The environmental agency in any country could issue what were called re-export permits. Grace said that his job soon became "like looking for a needle in a haystack."

• • •

BRINGING CAVIAR in by the suitcase was a common practice during the early 1990s, before the CITES rules were adopted. As more and more people got into the caviar business, dealers proliferated and prices tumbled. The competition for supplies became cutthroat. A good many caviar dealers in the United States would buy their product from anyone who showed up at their door with a suitcase full of tins. Suitcase caviar was more or less legal, so long as it was declared at customs and accompanied by a health certificate—it just wasn't the best stuff.

Many dealers didn't care as long as the caviar was cheap, yet they boasted about the freshness and quality of their product. Customers were told that the caviar was hand picked on the shores of the Caspian, that it was lovingly protected from the moment it left the fish's belly, that the eggs had never been damaged by freezing. From the catalogue descriptions some dealers wrote for the products, you might imagine a strict foreman standing on the shore of the Volga, inspecting each fish as its belly was opened, and saying, "That one. Not that one." You might also get the impression that caviar was extremely difficult to come by in the 1990s. The Petrossian catalogue was typical in describing its "prized liaisons" in Russia that helped it to secure the best caviar.

But if fresh caviar was transported in a suitcase for a dozen hours, it couldn't possibly be good. Ideally, fresh caviar needs to be kept at twenty-six degrees Fahrenheit at all times. Because of the salt, the pershable roe will neither freeze nor spoil at that magic temperature. Should the thermometer drop just one degree, however, the caviar will begin to freeze. When it comes time to thaw the fragile eggs, their casings will crack, turning the product into mush. Even when fresh caviar is stored at precisely twenty-six degrees, it will remain at its peak for only six or eight months. Many dealers prefer to buy pasteurized eggs. When the roe is warmed slightly for about an hour and packed in vacuum-sealed jars, it can withstand the most grueling travel conditions. It could sit on a shelf unrefrigerated for two years or more and still be edible. But the taste of pasteurized caviar is as much like the real thing as powdered milk is like milk from a dairy.

Caviar smugglers faced the same transportation challenges as Ioannis Varvarkis did in the eighteenth century. They solved the problem by freezing their caviar rock hard so it could survive a ten-hour flight, stored in a suitcase in the underbelly of the plane, where the temperatures went from steppe-like heat to tundra-like cold. I asked Adam O'Hara, another agent for Fish & Wildlife, about the caviar shipments that he had inspected during those years, and he told me that a lot of the claims about freshness were hard to believe. "There's this romantic temperature. Caviar has to be kept at such and such temperature and consumed right away. But we're getting caviar that has been run around in the back of an Izuzu truck, without refrigeration for who knows how long," O'Hara said. "People tell you all about the texture and the taste. I see garbage coming into this country. It's repackaged under different names, and people are buying it like crazy."

AS SMUGGLERS' tactics became more sophisticated, Ed Grace began to worry that he would never be able to put a dent in the deluge of illegal caviar. But he underestimated the competitiveness among thieves.

In the fall of 1998, someone telephoned the U.S. Customs Service in Germany with a tip about a Polish smuggling operation. The customs official who took the information called the customs office at Kennedy Airport, and the airport officials called Ed Grace. The tipster had provided unusually precise details about the smuggling scheme. He advised customs officials to be on the lookout for seven Polish citizens traveling from Warsaw on Finnair Flight 003, and then listed each of their names. They would be carrying suitcases full of contraband eggs, the tipster said. Three were stewardesses for the Polish airline LOT. One was Warsaw's deputy police chief and another was a Warsaw police officer. The caller also promised that the ringleader would be there to meet them.

Grace and three other agents, including one who spoke Polish, waited for the group to come through customs. The tipster had been so accurate that it took only minutes to pick out the seven couriers and go through their luggage. Among their sixteen suitcases, they were carrying about a thousand pounds of caviar, worth around $800,000 in retail shops. The caviar appeared to have been frozen. But it had thawed during the trip, because a salty slime was leaking from the dented tins into the cardboard boxes, then into their suitcases. Grace assumed the seven were just mules who were paid to carry the suitcases to America. On the other side of the customs area he hoped to find the mastermind behind the operation.

Grace convinced three of the couriers to carry their suitcases out to the waiting area and to act as if nothing had happened. They were immediately greeted by two people, Wieslaw Rozbicki and Helena Koczuk. They bantered for a moment in Polish, then Rozbicki pulled several envelopes out of his jacket and handed them to the couriers in exchange for their suitcases. Each envelope contained five hundred dollars in cash. As soon as the deal was completed, Grace and the others swooped in, flashing badges.

Rozbicki immediately began to protest that he was just an employee who had been sent to pick up an authorized shipment. That didn't explain why he had paid the couriers in cash, but it did make Grace believe that others were involved in the scheme. Rozbicki said he worked for a caviar importer called Gino International, owned by another Polish immigrant, Eugeniusz Koczuk, who was Helena's husband. In the span of a few years in the 1990s, when unlimited amounts of caviar could be bought cheaply, Gino had become one of the largest importers in the United States. Koczuk's firm now supplied retailers such as Zabar's, Caviarteria, and Urbani Truffles, well-known New York names that distributed caviar around the country.

It wasn't until Grace was permitted to search Koczuk's modest ranch house in Stamford, Connecticut, a few days later that he appreciated the scale of Gino's operation. As he combed through the house and inspected Koczuk's well-kept blue Mercedes, he found logbooks detailing the company's purchases and sales. Inside the garage were several refrigerators. Cartons of empty tins and jars were piled on a table. Grace understood then that the case was a lot bigger than the one involving Bazazashvili, the amateurish suitcase smuggler. Grace suspected that the delivery he had witnessed at Kennedy Airport wasn't the first time that Koczuk and Rozbicki had tried to bring illegal caviar into the United States. But it would be a challenge to prove that they were running a major smuggling operation.

Koczuk and Rozbicki continued to insist that they ran a clean business and that the incident at the airport was simply the result of a paperwork mixup. As proof, they gave Grace several CITES certificates. They had attended the CITES seminar at St. John's, so they were aware that special documents were required to import caviar. Grace was surprised at first to see Gino's CITES permits. But when he studied them carefully, he saw that the dates didn't correspond to the shipment he had intercepted at Kennedy. As Grace put more details of the scheme together, he realized that those documents were an essential component. Gino International had obtained CITES permits, all right, but had never used them to import caviar. Rather, the permits were kept in reserve to use as a cover. If any of their suitcase imports were questioned, they would wave the permits. When cautious retailers would ask to see their CITES documents, Koczuk and Rozbicki would also fax them one of the unused certificates. Unless the buyer carefully examined the dates, he might not realize that the document was a fake.

Still, if Grace was going to prove a conspiracy, he would have to document a chain of events that started in Warsaw and ended in Stamford. The breakthrough for Grace came using the most mundane modern technology. Few people realize that every time they drive through a tollbooth using an E-ZPass or park in an automated airport garage, their license plate is photographed. To get from Stamford, Connecticut, to Kennedy Airport in Queens, Grace figured that the pair must have driven through the tollbooths at either the Tri-Boro or the Whitestone Bridge. Grace requested the computer records from the authorities that managed the bridges and airport parking lots and ran a search for Koczuk's license plate. Within minutes, the computer showed that the Poles had made the trip from home to the airport, and back home to Connecticut, thirty-six times between April and November 1998. Over the course of that same year, Grace found records showing that Gino International had sold 28,000 pounds of caviar with a retail value around $21 million. Almost none of the caviar had any documentation, Grace found. After that discovery, all his other cases looked small.

The case was also a window onto the interconnected world of caviar smuggling. Gino International was able to move huge amounts of illicit caviar and become the biggest U.S. importer because of its connections in Poland. The only reason that Koczuk wasn't at the airport during the bust, Grace learned, was that he was in Poland buying caviar and arranging for couriers to take it out of the country. One of the couriers who was arrested was Andrzej Lepkowski, the Warsaw deputy police chief. Because of his position, he could circumvent Polish customs. It also helped that Lepkowski's wife, Katarzyna, was a flight attendant for the Polish airline who recruited her colleagues to carry caviar-laden suitcases. Not only didn't they have to pay for their tickets but they were able to stroll past customs without submitting to the usual checks.

Grace believed that Lepkowski was more than just a courier. He was the only one in the group who wasn't handed an envelope full of cash that day at the airport. Grace was also convinced that Koczuk and the deputy police chief worked in tandem: Koczuk acquired the caviar and Lepkowski used his police connections with the customs service to help get it out of Poland. Lepkowski, who testified against Koczuk and Rozbicki in exchange for a reduced sentence, also admitted that he supervised the mules during their smuggling trips. Grace succeeded in having Koczuk sentenced to twenty months in prison, an unusually long sentence for a wildlife crime.

How the caviar was brought to Poland in the first place was another matter. It had probably traveled along a smuggling route that went from the Caspian to Belarus and Poland. But Grace knew that he would never be able to pursue the case much beyond that. Polish police didn't bother pursuing the scandal, which involved their own members. The names of those who produced the tons of illegal caviar and transported it to Poland would remain a secret buried in the depths of Russia.

THE GINO International case was a big coup for Fish & Wildlife, for CITES, and for Grace, yet the success of the investigation did not leave him feeling confident about stopping the flow of illegal caviar. As smugglers go, Koczuk and Rozbicki were relative amateurs, relying on luck to get their suitcase caviar past customs. Even so, they were only caught because someone was angry enough at them to tip off the authorities. Grace wondered what kinds of methods more sophisticated smugglers might employ. It wouldn't be long before his colleagues in Baltimore discovered an even darker side of the caviar business.

By late 1998, the industry was in such turmoil that even respectable dealers would occasionally play loose with the CITES rules and buy caviar that they knew was illegal. They did it because they were short on supplies, or because they were tempted by a bargain price. Experienced dealers still tried to stay clear of suitcase caviar; the risks were too great, both for them and for the future of the caviar business. But there were others who were determined to buy the cheapest caviar they could find and would resort to any means to secure it. U.S. Caviar & Caviar was that kind of company.

Caviar & Caviar came into existence in 1995, at the height of the caviar rush. It was founded by two Iranian-Americans, Hossein Lolavar and his brother-in-law Ken Noroozi, who opened an office in Rockville, Maryland. Both were veteran dealers, but they had never seen a time when there was so much caviar on the market. The glut had changed the pace and style of doing business. They now had to compete with dozens of other importers who were all selling the identical product. Some dealers, such as Petrossian, could trade on their reputation for impeccable quality. U.S. Caviar & Caviar chose instead to emphasize its low prices, which meant buying caviar from poachers.

Even before CITES began regulating the caviar trade, U.S. dealers were required to buy caviar approved by local health officials in the Caspian. But poachers obviously couldn't submit poachers' caviar to the government health inspector. U.S. Caviar & Caviar got around this problem by using forged labels printed with the required health stamp, in Russia's Cyrillic script. The fake labels were made in the United States and sent by Federal Express to poachers in the Caspian. The round sticker was designed to fit perfectly into a depression on the lid of the caviar tin. When the shipments arrived in the United States, harried customs officials would usually just glance at the labels to see if they matched up with the pictures of legal brands supplied by the Russian government. If the labels were the same, the official would usually approve the shipment. The fake label scheme enabled Caviar & Caviar to offer caviar at prices 20 to 30 percent below those of its competitors. In just a short time, the new company became one of the largest U.S. importers, with an impressive list of clients that included American Airlines and Fresh Fields supermarkets. Little did these customers know that much of the caviar had been made in the poacher's kitchen using untreated water from the polluted Volga.

The introduction of tougher CITES trade restrictions threatened to end Caviar & Caviar's successful run. Lolavar and Noroozi knew that their only advantage over other dealers was price. If they had to buy caviar from approved producers they would lose their competitive edge. But if they tried to use couriers to carry in illegal caviar, the chances of being caught like Gino International were high. So they decided to modify the scheme that was already working. They developed a plan that would enable them to import illegal caviar as easily as if it were approved by CITES.

CITES may not be the most efficient way of protecting endangered plants and animals, but the agency's controls nevertheless had an immediate effect on the illegal caviar trade. The Caspian poachers had to work much harder to move their product to the lucrative markets of America, Western Europe, and Japan. Bribes, given to poorly paid Russian border guards helped clear the way. But once poachers succeeded in getting their caviar out of the Caspian region, they still needed something better than suitcase couriers to get it into the United States. The answer came from corrupt environmental officials in Turkey, Poland, and the United Arab Emirates.

Noroozi decided to open an office in the Emirates in 1995, which he incorporated as Kenfood Trading. The Emirates were well known as a clearing house for all kinds of smuggling. Because of the huge array of cheap goods offered for sale there, they had also become a regular stop in the 1990s for Russians making what was known then as "shopping tours." Since Russia still lacked a distribution system to deliver goods to stores around the country, individual couriers did this work. They would fly to wholesale markets in the Emirates or Turkey, load up on consumer goods such as curtain rods or T-shirts, then fly back home to deliver them. Very often, the shopping tourists would make a little extra money by bringing a few pounds of caviar with them. After the CITES rules were established in 1998, local merchants had to use their connections in the environmental ministry to obtain CITES export permits for this caviar. Typically, merchants obtained the permits by supplying Emirates officials with prostitutes. In a pinch, cash would do.

Still, a CITES export permit was only the beginning. Caviar & Caviar needed either a Russian, Kazakh, or Azeri health certificate to bring the caviar into the United States. Noroozi was still pasting fake labels on the tins, but these were no longer enough by 1998. As part of the effort to protect the sturgeon, U.S. Customs started asking to see actual health certificates. Lolavar solved this new problem by having a rubber stamp made that was identical to the one used by Russian health officials. With the stamp, he could turn out as many forged health documents as he needed.

Lolavar seemed to have thought of every angle. But the more illegal caviar Lolavar smuggled in to the United States, the more corners he looked to cut. Rather than declare the full value of his caviar shipments, he started cheating U.S. Customs. Lolavar used fake shipping manifests that misrepresented the kind of caviar in the shipment. A ton of beluga became a ton of less valuable sevruga. The deception worked so well that Lolavar figured he could do the same with his American customers. When he ran short of Caspian caviar, he would often pass off low-priced American paddlefish caviar as sevruga. Occasionally he would try to be honest with his customers about the origin of his caviar. He once asked American Airlines if they would prefer the cheaper paddlefish roe to sevruga. But when the airline insisted on having the real thing, Lolavar simply sent them paddlefish caviar anyway. Neither the airline nor its customers ever recognized the difference.

But Fish & Wildlife was beginning to notice. In December 1998, an inspector in Baltimore asked to look at four of Caviar & Caviar's shipments. When he picked up one of the tins, he noticed that its label was curling up at the edge. Using his fingernail, he peeled the label back, revealing another label imprinted on the metal. The original imprint lacked the required government markings. To confirm his suspicions, the inspector sent samples from the four shipments to a Fish & Wildlife lab in Oregon. Using a version of the DNA analysis that Vadim Birstein had first developed, the government concluded that the caviar in the tins didn't match the description on the CITES permits issued by the United Arab Emirates. Fish & Wildlife seized the four shipments and launched an investigation.

Lolavar and Noroozi knew they were under suspicion for smuggling, yet they kept looking for ways to get illegal caviar into the country. Hoping to avoid more scrutiny, they directed their next shipment to Miami and listed a different company as the importer. They were so bold that they instructed their Miami shipping broker to hide the Baltimore fax number that appeared at the top of some of their permits. "Here are the shipping docs," they instructed in a separate fax. "*Do not forget* to white out the ID on the top of the pages."

But now the tower of deceptions had begun to topple. By the time the Miami shipment arrived in Maryland in March 1999, it was too late.

Investigators had obtained warrants to search their Rockville offices. They found the Miami shipment in Caviar & Caviar's refrigerators. The DNA analysis again showed that the contents didn't match the documents. It took months for investigators to dissect the company's intricate ruses, but when they did they calculated that Lolavar and Noroozi had smuggled in 32,200 pounds of sturgeon roe from the Caspian in 1998 alone, worth around $24 million.

The two smugglers Gino International and Caviar & Caviar between them had brought in roughly ten tons of caviar during the first year of the CITES controls. That was more than Russia's entire legal quota.

CAVIAR & CAVIAR'S scheme was uncovered by an attentive investigator, but it was science that proved the case. As caviar smugglers became more skilled at crossing borders, the government's DNA analysis became a crucial weapon in the fight to save the sturgeon. Flush with success, the government put aside the questions that Vadim Birstein had raised about its methods. Then something happened that would elevate the controversy from merely an obscure academic disagreement.

In the summer of 1998, Evgeny Aptekar's fishing company Karon shipped close to a ton of osetra from its Astrakhan packing plant to Caviarteria in New York. The caviar arrived at Kennedy Airport and quickly passed through the border formalities, just as Caviarteria's products had done hundreds of times before. Caviarteria was a seasoned New York importer, a company that had supplied caviar to several generations of New Yorkers. The firm had ordered its latest batch of caviar from one of the most scrupulous licensed producers in Astrakhan, Karon, which had won its right to fish for sturgeon in the Volga at a public auction and was certified by CITES as a legal producer. After the shipment checked out at customs, Fish & Wildlife told Caviarteria's owners, Eric and Bruce Sobel, that they could take the osetra to their Queens warehouse, while a sample went through the formalities of being tested at the service's forensic lab in Oregon.

This time, the samples didn't match their CITES documents. The Oregon lab found trace amounts of Siberian sturgeon in the osetra. On November 12, Fish & Wildlife agents arrived at Caviarteria's warehouse and announced they were seizing that shipment, as well as a second shipment that also failed the DNA test. Eric Sobel, who was the more high-strung of the two brothers, exploded. He began screaming at the agents. As the confrontation escalated, agents saw Sobel reaching for a gun. The situation seemed to be turning into more than a routine customs seizure. The agents tried to calm him down. They asked Sobel to keep his hands planted firmly on his desk. After a few moments, he settled down enough to call his lawyer and the agents decided not to press gun charges.

Fish & Wildlife couldn't actually seize the suspect caviar anyway—the service didn't have a refrigerator big enough to store it all. Everyone agreed that it would remain at Caviarteria under lock and key until the matter was sorted out. When Evgeny Aptekar heard what had happened, he offered to take the caviar back and refund Caviarteria's money. Aptekar told me later that he was baffled and embarrassed by the DNA analysis. His fishermen worked only in the Volga, he protested. "I couldn't catch a Siberian sturgeon there if I tried," he added. "Why would I try to do something illegal? I'm interested in providing a good product and developing a good reputation. I won't ship anything that isn't approved by CITES." At the time, neither Aptekar nor Sobel knew that Vadim Birstein had discovered a population of Siberian sturgeon in the Caspian.

Fish & Wildlife refused to let Aptekar take the shipment back. If the caviar was from poachers, they reasoned, why should he be allowed to resell it? Instead, the government began forfeiture proceedings. Sobel, who was still furious at the government, counterattacked. His lawyer had heard about Birstein's DNA work and filed a lawsuit claiming the government's test was inaccurate and illegal. Birstein, who had crusaded to save the sturgeon from overfishing, agreed to take the side of the caviar dealers, the people who drove the trade. He became Caviarteria's expert witness.

With Caviarteria, the Fish & Wildlife Service was no longer dealing with a thuggish, fly-by-night organization. The Sobels were second-generation dealers. Caviarteria had been started by their father, Louis, in 1950. Having grown bored working in a Madison Avenue advertising agency, Louis Sobel decided to put his skills of persuasion to use by selling fish eggs. The name of his first shop, Caviar on Third, did not reflect any particular skill at salesmanship. But Louis would eventually prove that he could give his product its own particular aura. His ambition was to demystify caviar, to present it as a product that any middle-class person could afford. Unlike those in other stores selling caviar, his tins were not hidden away but stacked openly on shelves where customers could pick them up and feel their weight. Louis eventually hit on the perfect concept for his democratizing project. His shop would be as accessible as a cafeteria. He finally came up with the right name, too: Caviarteria.

This approach worked fine until Petrossian arrived in New York. Instead of promoting middle-class accessibility, Petrossian was intentionally swank. Its shop and restaurant just off Central Park were decorated with sensuous Erte etchings and deep black marble paneling. Tuxedoed waiters stood on alert at the diners' elbows, ready to whisk away cool toast and replace it with a fresh batch. Caviarteria responded by opening its own marble-paneled restaurant on 59th Street, near

Madison Avenue, but theirs was bright and unpretentious. You could sit at the bar and sip a flute of champagne as you watched people stroll pass the uncurtained shop window. More Caviarteria bars followed in Las Vegas and Miami, and each one strove to marry a streamlined glamour with maximum accessibility. Caviarteria still saw itself as un-Petrossian.

The 59th Street restaurant still felt like a cross between a deli and a small bistro when I arrived to talk to Bruce Sobel. Although it was midafternoon, he seemed sleepy and unfocused. Every time I would explain that I was interested in Caviarteria's efforts to discredit the government's DNA test, he would jump up from the table to call his wife or his mother. Once he left me alone while he went to have some photographs developed. I sat there following the progress of a large fly as it guided itself along the mirror above the banquette. A young couple came in and ordered a large portion of caviar, which arrived nestled in ice on a silver cake tier. When Bruce returned, he brought over a 100-gram jar of beluga for us to share. Bruce handed me a plastic spoon, which dealers use to avoid oxidizing the eggs. Then he unscrewed the lid and dug in, as if it were a pint of ice cream. He stopped for a moment with his spoon in midair, admiring the taste of his product. Then he passed the jar to me across the black marble table.

Bruce began to boast about Caviarteria's high sanitary standards. I passed the beluga jar back to him, swatting a fly away. Bruce told me he had made all his employees attend a course on "bacteria-ology." He warmed to the theme, describing Caviarteria's state-of-the-art refrigerators, which were wired with alarms designed to ring if the temperature rose above twenty-six degrees. The fly dived toward Bruce's spoon. I swatted again. "New York health inspectors are awed by our cleanliness," he said, and licked the last of the beluga off his spoon, oblivious to the fly that seemed at odds with his claims of purity.

Whenever I brought up any questions about business issues, Bruce would tell me to ask Eric. I decided to do that. Eric worked out of Caviarteria's warehouse just across the East River, in the shadow of the 59th Street bridge. He was thinner than Bruce and more deeply tanned. Like Bruce, he had deep blue eyes that seemed a little too big for their sockets. The warehouse was even less glamorous than the restaurant. The offices felt like temporary quarters, even though Caviarteria had been there for years. Boxes for the printers and computers were piled around as if the equipment might have to be packed up and moved at any minute. Eric's desk was covered with stacks of paper, empty caviar jars, an assortment of electronics. Where Bruce had been casually vague, Eric was determined to answer every question with written proof. If he couldn't quote a number from memory, he would shuffle his papers until he came to one that illustrated his point. Eric wasn't keen to talk about the lawsuit, though. When I raised the subject, he handed me a sheaf of faxes from various producers offering to sell him caviar, as evidence of how difficult it was to choose an honest broker. It was becoming harder to find good-quality legal caviar, he complained.

As he said this, he began to chortle and clap his hands. "If there is a shortage, that's better for me . . . I've just bought the entire catch of Black Sea beluga, seven hundred kilos," he announced. "I'm going to sell it for twenty dollars less an ounce, too. All our competitors have been buying Black Sea beluga for years and calling it Caspian. I'm the only stupid one who's honest . . . ha! This year I took every egg of Black Sea they could produce. This is going to be a bad year for beluga. The price can only climb . . . everyone in the industry is a liar except for me. There are only a couple of major players left . . . in Astrakhan no one knows who Petrossian is . . . but they all know what I'm looking for."

After a few moments like this, he ran out of words. He slumped back into his chair, brooding. In the months since Fish & Wildlife had impounded his shipment, the ton of caviar from Karon had spoiled.

Proving the government wrong had now become more important than the costly loss. "I had to go into the market and pay top dollar for replacement caviar," Sobel said. "Thank God I have the guts and the resources to teach the government a lesson."

Sobel slumped again into his chair. I decided not to press again on the lawsuit. I figured I could always ask his lawyer, Walter Drobenko. Over the next few months, I spoke to Drobenko on several occasions. Each time I called, he would tell me that the Caviarteria case was almost ready to go to trial. He felt confident that Birstein's testimony would highlight the flaws in the government's test. Several other dealers had also raised questions about the validity of the test. A respected forensic expert was also prepared to testify about problems with the government's method. I was curious to know how a jury would deal with the scientific complexities of the case.

It was late in the spring of 2001 that I called Walter again to check on the date of the trial. The court hearing, which promised to settle the dispute over the government's DNA test, had been postponed, perhaps indefinitely.

Eric Sobel had committed suicide.

THE CAVIAR business had changed enormously by then. Between 1999 and 2001, the number of U.S. dealers had been cut in half. Gino's owners were in prison. So were the principals of U.S. Caviar & Caviar, who were also ordered to pay a $10.4 million fine—an immense figure for a wildlife crime. The owner of Caviar Russe, a tony New York caviar bar, had pled guilty to having an unregistered gun when Fish & Wildlife agents showed up at his warehouse to inspect a suspect shipment. Bruce Sobel was struggling to keep Caviarteria going. Dieckmann & Hansen, the oldest caviar house in the world, had closed its operation. Petrossian was one of the few big importers to survive with an unblemished record. Fish & Wildlife officials pointed to the firm as an example of a company that had scrupulously complied with CITES and still flourished. But for smaller dealers, surviving in the caviar business remained a daily struggle.

Joel Assouline was among the few smaller dealers who had made it into the new millennium. His company, Caviar Assouline, had been selling caviar for more than a decade when the rush of the 1990s began, and his experience helped him ride out those tumultuous years. By the time the CITES rules were adopted, he had successfully transformed his company from a small restaurant supplier into a mid-sized retail chain. He bought an old factory building in Philadelphia's trendy gallery district, located his packing plant on one of the upper floors, put offices in the middle, and opened a large, sunny shop on the ground floor. He kept shops in the downtown office district and at the airport. He also did a substantial catalogue business.

I met him in his new shop in the gallery district, which he had stocked with a large assortment of gourmet foods that had nothing to do with caviar. Because of the turmoil in the caviar business, he had begun to diversify his business. Now customers could buy a jar of duck confit or some French sea salt along with a jar of caviar. Or they could sit at one of the café tables, sipping coffee and enjoying the sunshine.

Assouline explained that what helped him endure the difficult years was both a knowledge of food and a knowledge of business. Born in Morocco, into a French-Jewish family, he had come to Philadelphia to study at the prestigious Wharton business school. Food always came first for Assouline. He worked his way through school by waiting tables at Le Bec-Fin, Philadelphia's Michelin-starred restaurant, then went off to start his own French restaurant. In the early 1980s, he closed his restaurant and began selling caviar. He rode out the worst of the

Iranian embargo, when supplies of caviar dried up, and the Soviet collapse, when the country was flooded with cheap caviar.

But the trade restrictions imposed by CITES were by far the most trying. Although his company had grown substantially during the 1990s caviar rush, Caviar Assouline was still a mom-and-pop-sized operation. Assouline didn't have the staff to investigate the background of every broker who offered him a shipment of caviar. "The rules have completely changed," he explained. "We used to make the rules. We used to say this is how much caviar we want and we'll pay you later. Now the suppliers say, this is how much we'll give you and you have to pay upfront. When the Soviet Union was around, everyone was on an equal footing."

Like many dealers, Assouline welcomed CITES. He knew the sturgeon were in trouble, and he was convinced that the trade restrictions were the only way to save the caviar business, even if it meant more headaches for him. But the headaches now often kept him up at night. Every time a supplier faxed him an offer, he would wonder: "Is it legal? Will I go to jail if I buy this?" The first thing he always told the salesman was, "Send me your CITES permit." Once a pair of Turks arrived at his packing plant carrying four hundred tins of caviar. They had a CITES permit, but the caviar was in bad shape, as if it had been left unrefrigerated for a few hours. He tasted a few eggs from each tin before agreeing to buy sixty tins. Yet even with their CITES permit in his files, he still worried that he could be held liable if Fish & Wildlife later discovered the caviar was not really legal. As much as he believed in the CITES mission, he thought that too much responsibility was being placed on the dealers. How were the dealers supposed to identify illegal caviar when the smugglers were so good at forging their CITES permits? "You have Fish & Wildlife, who are on a mission. They feel if they catch a few people they have done their job."

Almost on cue, a government official walked into his shop. He wasn't from Fish & Wildlife, but from the FDA. He wanted to inspect Assouline's packing operation. Go ahead, he told him with a wave. He led the inspector up to the packing floor and then returned to continue our conversation. Assouline said he was confident that he would get a clean bill of health.

What worried him more, he confided, was a recent attempt to import Russian caviar. He had received a call from a friend at another caviar company, asking if he wanted to split 1,100 pounds of osetra that was going through Holland. It was August and Assouline was having trouble finding enough caviar for the Christmas season. He told his friend, Alfred Yazbak of Connoisseur Caviar, that he would gladly split the shipment. The Dutch company faxed Assouline its CITES permit, and Assouline in turn faxed it to Fish & Wildlife to get a second opinion. As far as he could tell, it seemed legitimate.

Since Yazbak was traveling to Europe, he told Assouline that he would stop in Holland to inspect the caviar. A few days later, Yazbak called Assouline to tell him that the caviar was not worth buying. Assouline was disappointed, but he trusted Yazbak's taste buds. In fact, the caviar was very good, so good that Yazbak had lied to Assouline and bought the entire shipment for himself. This was Yazbak's bad luck. When the caviar arrived at Kennedy, a DNA analysis found traces of kaluga from the Amur River mixed in with the osetra. The entire shipment was seized. Yazbak was sentenced to two years in jail and fined $185,000. "Alfred's greediness was my saving grace," said Assouline, but he saw no poetic justice in the outcome. The same thing could just as easily happen to him. A few days later, an unfamiliar supplier sent him an express-mail package containing a 125-gram sample of caviar. Assouline refused to sign for it and sent it back unopened. It was just too risky.

Rather than continue to take chances, Assouline decided to transform his company once again. He had always been interested in regional American cooking. Why not sell American caviar? True, the quality was not as good as Caspian caviar, but perhaps he could help fishermen raise their standards. Assouline made a trip to the Mississippi, where fishermen were legally catching paddlefish. He brought them good French salt, taught them the best techniques for processing the roe, and arranged to buy their production. Rather than downplaying the origin of the caviar, Joel decided to make it an attraction. It would be the specialty that distinguished him from other dealers. The chalkboards in his shops boast seven regional American caviars, from what he calls Tennessee black paddlefish to Montana Yellow River paddlefish. Assouline supplemented his supplies with caviar from farm-raised paddlefish and sturgeon. He has also been buying the entire production of the Caviar d'Aquitaine farm in Bordeaux, which raises Siberian sturgeon.

Between American caviar and farm-raised caviar, Assouline felt that he was almost safe. But after what happened to Yazbak, he decided to stop importing Caspian caviar on his own and buy from bigger companies that could afford to take the risk. His profit would be lower, but his business would be safer.

Assouline still had plenty of cause to worry. The price of paddlefish roe had risen dramatically in a few years, as Caspian stocks declined. Environmentalists were warning him that the paddlefish could be endangered. Even as biologists spoke of trade restrictions, Assouline remained optimistic about the caviar business. "I have to," he said with a wry smile. "I wouldn't know how to do anything else."

But he was preparing himself for a day when the only caviar he sold came not from a river but a farm.

10

Saving
the Sturgeon

Caviar comes from the virgin sturgeon,
Virgin sturgeon is one fine dish.
Virgin sturgeon needs no urgin'.
That's why caviar is my dish.

—SONG BY DWIGHT FISKE

*C*huck Edwards led me into the dark warehouse and I followed, trying not to touch anything damp or slimy. As my eyes adjusted to the
moist gloom, I saw what could be a swimming pool showroom after
closing. Rows of vinyl pools stretched all the way to the back of the
building. There was the same steady gurgling of filters sucking the
dirty water out and pumping the oxygen in. Every once in a while, I
heard a rustling that reminded me of dry dog food escaping its bag. I
made out the shadowy forms of fish inside one of the pools. They were

endlessly crisscrossing its circumference. When I leaned over for a better look, a fish poked its snout out of the water and gazed at me like a puppy wanting to be petted. "Go ahead. You can touch her," Edwards said. The sturgeon's sandpaper hide grated lightly on my hand as I slid it along the fish's armored body.

As a zoology student, Edwards dreamed of being the next Jacques Cousteau. But instead of ranging across the seas on voyages of discovery, he now covers a smaller realm, stepping from tank to tank to check on the 100,000 or so white sturgeon that inhabit the Stolt Sea Farm in northern California. The sturgeon are grouped in pools by age and size, starting with nearly transparent hatchings that are still living off their egg sacks, and moving in stages up to the eighty-pound, eight-year-old females, in whose distended bellies resides a vault of ripening eggs. Edwards estimated there are more white sturgeon in Stolt's tanks today than there are next door in the Sacramento River, once home to behemoths weighing half a ton.

While the farm may lack the diversity and mystery of the oceans, Edwards and his staff consider themselves fortunate to be presiding over this hermetic sturgeon world, tucked among the flooded rice paddies of the San Joaquin valley. In its own way, raising sturgeon on farms is as much uncharted territory as the ocean depths. Sturgeon farming still hasn't proven itself a profitable business, despite more than a decade of trial and error, and millions of dollars in investment. Whether the farm succeeds has less to do with the fish biologists who work there, or the deep pockets of its owner, and everything to do with what happens to the sturgeon in the Caspian. Stolt is betting that the future of caviar lies on the farm, although he knows that the farm's success will be secured only when it is no longer worth catching sturgeon in the wild.

When I met him, Edwards was in his early forties, with a lanky build and the pensive calm of a fly-fisherman. He told me that he had moved around the aquaculture business a bit before settling down with sturgeon on the Stolt farm in Elverta, ten miles north of Sacramento. The Norwegian-owned company is one of the largest fish-farming companies in the world. A significant portion of the non-wild Atlantic salmon sold in the world's supermarkets is grown on Stolt farms. The company has diversified into other species such as salmon trout, Atlantic halibut, turbot, and sea bream. These are often sold in portion-sized pieces under the brand name Sterling. Raising those fish in captivity has become routine. But when Stolt first became involved with sturgeon in 1987, Edwards said, no one was really sure that caviar could be successfully produced on a farm.

To show me some of the problems the company faced, Edwards took me into another dark warehouse building that was known around the farm as the "500" building, because it can hold 500,000 pounds of fish. The sturgeon here were bigger than in the first building, about three feet in length, and they swam around large in-ground tanks. We could see thousands of sturgeon darting in all directions in the black water. Despite their size, they were only three years old—mere grade-schoolers in sturgeon years. Edwards told me that it takes eight to ten years in captivity before the eggs of a female white sturgeon are mature enough for caviar. This means that Stolt must feed and care for those 500,000 pounds of sturgeon, and all the rest of its fish on its farm, for almost a decade before it can realize any profit from them. (In contrast, farm-raised tilapia go to market in six months, salmon in about three years.) There is hardly a business in the world in which an investor will wait for ten years before he realizes any revenue, never mind a profit. When I visited the sturgeon farm, it had been in existence in various forms for eighteen years, and it was only just anticipating its first year in the black.

Sturgeon farming has turned out to be trickier than Stolt expected. Although the process of fertilizing sturgeon eggs was first developed in Russia in the 1860s, there were always too many fish in the sea to bother with farms. The hatcheries that were built in Russia and Iran after World War II were intended for restocking the sea, not for raising sturgeon babies to maturity. When Stolt's farm was started, no one was sure what to feed the sturgeon, or how many could live comfortably in a tank. They didn't know precisely how to distinguish the worthless males from the valuable females, or when the females would be ready to give up their roe. In the wild, female white sturgeon don't spawn for the first time until they are in their late teens. Stolt has reduced the age of maturity by almost half through selective breeding and a better diet, but ten years is still a long time to wait for caviar.

As Edwards and I stood in the darkness of the 500 building, we could see the complex system that Stolt had introduced to keep the sturgeon happy and healthy. Because the fish live in close quarters, the water is constantly filtered to remove fish feces, uneaten food, and other waste. Computer sensors track the water temperature and oxygen content. If either level should vary too much from the prescribed range, the computers sound an alarm. Computers had also mechanized the feeding of the sturgeon. A basket containing pellet feed rumbled along an overhead metal track, dropping measured portions into the tanks at timed intervals. The fish would lunge toward the surface, as if they, too, were computer controlled. But after a few minutes of frenzied consumption, they would lose interest and drift to the bottom along with the pellets.

All the sturgeon on Stolt's farm are descended from the same twenty wild white sturgeon that were taken from California's northern rivers in 1982, and the company tries to follow the natural rhythms of the wild sturgeon on the farm. Around the same time of year that their wild cousins would be swimming upriver to spawn, a small group of

Stolt's farmed sturgeon are selected as brood stock. The females are stripped of their eggs, the males of their milt, the ichthyological term for fish sperm. Then these two ingredients are combined with water in something that looks like a blender, shaken for a couple of minutes, and poured into trays. The fertilized eggs are continually washed by water to imitate the natural current that brings oxygen to the developing hatchlings. After only a couple of days, the babies will be about a quarter inch in size, big enough that you can make out the form of an adult sturgeon, with its pronounced snout and sharklike tail. The young sturgeon have a frisky cuteness that seems completely out of character with the adult sturgeon's sluggishness. Before a sturgeon's face becomes jowly and its hide thickens, it resembles an otter, especially as it splashes playfully around the tank. The sturgeon's front fins are parallel with their bodies, like airplane wings, enabling the fish to speed through the water like a torpedo.

From the time the babies are hatched, a good part of work on a sturgeon farm involves the sorting of fish. The sturgeon are measured and grouped into tanks according to size. When the fish are three years old, Edwards and his staff are finally able to determine the sex of the fish using a blood test. This is the end for the males. They will be culled for meat in order to reduce the number of unnecessary mouths that must be fed. Some females will also be slaughtered. "We keep only the best-looking ones," Edwards said, winking at the joke. He was actually serious. Fish biologists believe that beautiful sturgeon produce beautiful eggs that can be made into beautiful caviar.

THE DAY after we toured the farm, I found Edwards peering into a large vinyl pool that had been set up outdoors next to the 500 building. He appeared outwardly placid, but he was smoking, a sign of controlled nervousness. His staff would be taking roe from two hundred adult sturgeon, and Edwards was anxious for a good harvest. If the farm could produce four tons of caviar over the next few days, it would turn its first profit ever. Since early morning workers had been transferring mature eight-years-olds from Stolt's ponds to the outdoor holding pool. The water temperature had been reduced to near freezing. The cold would make the normally docile sturgeon even more submissive. The fish had also been given a hormone injection to cause their eggs to ripen, a shot similar to the kind women are given to induce labor. Inside the 500 building, a crew in white lab coats had assembled in the processing room, their knives sharpened and ready to go.

The end came swiftly and efficiently—a mallet to the head, a swipe of antiseptic across the stomach. Then a worker raised his knife and made a clean lengthwise slit across the china white belly. As the skin was pulled back, another worker snipped out the two ovaries. The grayish sacks, which were about the size and color of old canvas sneakers, were placed in a bowl and rushed next door to the kitchen to be turned into caviar.

Edwards followed the bowl into the kitchen. Three men hovered over the tiny eggs, picking out bits of tissue and dabs of blood. They rinsed the eggs in cold water and gently massaged the mass over a sieve to separate the beads. The eggs were still grayish, but with the addition of salt they seemed to ink up right before our eyes. When the salt content was judged to be about 4 percent, the American ikryanchiks spread the fresh black caviar over a plastic sheet for Edwards to inspect.

Taking a small plastic spoon, Edwards transported a cluster of eggs to his mouth and rolled them over his tongue. His lips barely moved. He stayed silent, deep in thought, while the ikryanchiks stood by waiting for the verdict. Edwards handed me a spoon and I imitated him, scooping up a few eggs and letting them settle in my mouth. Most dealers say that caviar needs to sit a few weeks to be at its best. As the eggs absorb the salt, the individual globules plump up, and the taste becomes stronger and more complex, like wine aging in oak. But at that moment, as waves of just-salted eggs pounded my tongue, I believed that the substance in my mouth was the most perfect caviar I had ever eaten. Edwards, less effusively, pronounced it merely good.

THE HISTORY of the caviar farm had been so troubled that Stolt had never bothered to give its product a brand name. But in late 1999, the company realized that the farm had crossed the line from an experimental operation to a commercial producer. Edwards was predicting the farm would turn its first profit in the spring. Everyone agreed that having a widely recognized name would help Stolt command a higher price for its caviar, just as the Petrossian name did for its brand of caviar. Stolt thought about using Romanov, the surname of the former Russian royal family, but it was too close to the famous Romanoff label. It considered the ridiculous Stoltinski, the Norwegian-sounding Nelson's, and the over-caffeinated Jacob's Choice. Edwards listened quietly while company officials bandied around those vaguely foreign-sounding names, then he launched his own argument: American caviar should have an American-sounding name.

Rather than obscure the origins of Stolt caviar, he thought that the company should trumpet them. "I wanted to sell not only the best caviar, but the best American caviar," he recalled. It was also crucial that people know the caviar came from real sturgeon, and not from its cousin, the paddlefish, which produced less succulent eggs. Since Stolt's other fish products were sold under the trade name Sterling, Edwards suggested selling the white sturgeon caviar under the same brand. Much to Edwards's surprise, he carried the debate. Along with the Sterling name, the words "White Sturgeon Caviar" were printed on the lids and tins.

The notion of a fine American caviar appealed to many food purveyors, particularly in California, where fresh ingredients and fine cooking had been forged into a distinct cuisine. And yet, liking the idea of American caviar and actually buying it turned out to be two different things. The farm had the misfortune to harvest its first caviar in the middle of the 1990s, when the United States was glutted with cheap Caspian caviar. It was hard enough for farmed caviar to beat the price of the bootlegged import, but it was impossible to beat the reputation of the wild Russian eggs, even when they had been frozen and carried to market in a suitcase. The problem, Edwards complained, is that "people think the best caviar is Russian caviar."

While Sterling's caviar drew high praise from food writers, who marveled at how much the white sturgeon eggs tasted like osetra, many caviar dealers remained skeptical. "Farmed caviar grows too fast. It has a sweetwater taste. Like any farmed fish, everything tastes the same," Susanne Schwerdtfeger, the former head of Dieckmann & Hansen, told me. While wild sturgeon enjoy a diet that varies constantly, farmed sturgeon eat the same processed pellets every day. Farmed sturgeon live in fresh water, not the salty brine of the sea. When I asked Armen Petrossian whether he would ever sell Sterling, he said it was unlikely. Why not? "The taste," he sputtered through a grimace. I frequently heard that farmed caviar was too bland, but it was always difficult to tell whether the complaint was objective, or part of the same caprice that had elevated caviar beyond mere fish eggs in the first place. One day in the fall of 2001, Edwards telephoned me to say that Sterling had come out the favorite in a blind tasting by the *Wall Street Journal,* beating all the Caspian varieties. He sounded overjoyed—and a little doubtful.

Despite resistance from the old-school dealers, Sterling was starting to make inroads among American purveyors by the late 1990s. Edwards started getting orders from chefs who had once refused to take his phone calls. But despite Sterling's growing popularity, the farmed caviar still wasn't able to command the same price as the Caspian roe. Chefs and dealers bought Sterling because it was cheap; the fact that it was also good was secondary. Even when Russian osetra hit forty and fifty dollars an ounce, Sterling was obliged to keep its retail price fixed around thirty dollars.

Until Sterling could compete equally with Caspian caviar, volume would help the bottom line. Edwards was hoping to harvest four tons of caviar in 2000, but the farm's sturgeon population was growing so fast that he projected a day when Sterling caviar might produce ten or even fifteen tons of caviar. In every Caspian country but Iran, CITES harvest quotas were being reduced. If Russia's quota kept falling, Edwards saw a chance for Sterling's farm-raised caviar to become a sizable part of the market at a comparable price. His challenge now was to make sure people believed that the quality of farmed caviar would always be as good as the wild kind.

While I was hanging around Edwards's office, Rod Mitchell, a major East Coast fish supplier, called in an order for his Browne Trading Company. Mitchell was a good customer and Edwards wanted to inspect the caviar himself before it was sent out. Grabbing a fistful of plastic spoons, he called over a couple of his men and asked them if they would mind eating some caviar.

As we walked from the office to the 500 building, Edwards explained the farm was having a big problem with spoilage. Most producers can keep their caviar under refrigeration for a year or more, but Stolt's eggs barely lasted a couple of months in its refrigerators. He wondered whether this meant that farmed caviar had a shorter shelf life than the wild kind. Or was it the water? One year, he had made the mistake of using pond water in the tanks instead of well water, and the eggs smelled of mud.

In a wine chateau, this kind of tasting would be organized in a cool underground cellar. At Stolt, it was done in the supply room next to the refrigerators, amid the shelves of empty jars, sterile gloves, and plastic spoons. Edwards took several 1,800-gram tins out of the fridge, most of it harvested about six months earlier, and passed around the spoons. The men all scooped out a few eggs and swirled them around on their tongues. Edwards was the first to speak:

"I'd like to flush this down the toilet."

What they were looking for, Edwards explained, was the slightest evidence of imperfection, a hint of fermentation or a bitter aftertaste. Fermentation signals that the caviar is growing mold. Caspian caviar may take a beating on its way over here, but its reputation was already solid. Sterling's quality, Edwards was convinced, needed to be superior if the company hoped to knock down the resistance to farmed eggs. People who eat caviar just once a year are unlikely to notice a bit of fizz or muddy aftertaste, but the experts surely would. Sterling caviar couldn't afford one bad review.

Edwards opened another tin and bent over to smell the plateau of eggs. "I smell sour," he announced.

Joe Melendez, who was known to have the best taste buds on the farm, wasn't happy either. "It tastes like fresh mortar," he proclaimed after taking a sample from another tin. Melendez, a big, jovial man who worked as a processor on the farm, usually had the most colorful descriptions for bad caviar: "Sour apples." "Dirty." "Cidery." "Roquefort." "Tastes like beer."

But after a couple of bad tins, the kidding around stopped. Edwards grimaced a lot and flicked his used spoons in the trash. Out of the sixteen tins the group had sampled, twelve were deemed unsaleable.

"Throw it out," Edwards ordered after the last one, then abandoned the room while the others cleaned up.

It was after five P.M. and most of the office staff had gone home. Edwards had been at the farm since six-thirty in the morning, but he went to his desk to go over some papers. While he was trying to decide whether to stay or go home, his manager, Peter Struffenegger, came rushing in, holding a caviar tin in his outstretched palm. Smoke was seeping from the bottom of the tin. Edwards started laughing. "Are you suggesting we should burn the place down?" he asked darkly.

But Peter wasn't concocting a practical joke. "Look at this," he said, pointing to the tin. There was a cigarette burning inside. "It would make a good ashtray," Edwards said.

"Don't you see? Peter said, smiling. The smoke is leaking. This is why the caviar is going bad. It's the tins!"

Although the tins were the industry standard, the batch that Stolt bought was poorly made. Where the sides should have been sealed airtight to the sides of the cans, there were small openings around the base. In an effort to follow the traditions of the caviar industry, Stolt packed its wholesale caviar in the same kind of cans that had been used for the last century, ever since replacement of the lime wood barrel. Tins were one of the caviar business's inviolable traditions, but Edwards saw that the tradition was failing Stolt. The company was losing caviar because of the faulty tins. Stolt was going to have to abandon some of caviar's traditions.

Edwards had been looking at some new packing equipment. At a trade show, he had seen a machine that could pack fresh caviar in jars with a vacuum seal. Now that Stolt had proved that farmed caviar could be a good business, Edwards decided it was time to make the investment.

· · ·

WHEN STOLT bought the sturgeon farm in Elverta, the company knew a lot about aquaculture but not much about making caviar. The people who taught Stolt how to make caviar were Mats and Dafne Engstrom.

The Engstroms live in San Francisco, in a neighborhood of elegant pastel Victorians overlooking a wide expanse of blue bay. Caviar paid for the view.

Both Mats and Dafne were impossibly tall, impossibly handsome Swedes who had fled their homeland in the 1960s because they were bored. Mats originally came to America to study business at Harvard, although it was really California that beckoned them. Mats eventually took a job as an investment banker in San Francisco, but both his personality and the times were unsuited to such buttoned-down work. The Engstroms saw their friends getting involved in alternative careers, such as health food stores and solar energy, and both Mats and Dafne loved good food as much as the good life, so when Mats gave up banking, they started a gourmet foods business. Dafne, who taken time off to raise the kids, was eager for a new challenge. It was only a matter of time until Mats and Dafne realized there was a market in America for caviar.

In the 1970s, caviar was not an easy sell, not even in California. "We arrived in the U.S. in the time of porterhouse steaks," Mats deadpanned with a wry, lopsided smile. When people did think of caviar, it was always the Petrossian brand. Petrossian wanted people to think they had a monopoly on caviar." Since it was difficult for a newcomer to get a contract with the Russians for black caviar, the Engstroms started packing lumpfish roe under the label Tsar Nicoulai. By the beginning of the 1980s, the Soviets had loosened up. The Engstroms established themselves as a major West Coast supplier of Caspian caviar.

Caviar became a staple of their business, which they named California Sunshine, in honor of their adopted home.

The Engstroms loved all kinds of outdoor activities, from skiing to boating. One afternoon when they had come back from an excursion on the water, Mats got to talking with a sport fisherman on the dock. The fisherman told him he had caught a female white sturgeon and was taking the roe home to his cat. Engstrom found the image of a cat lapping up the precious eggs immensely funny. Here he was begging the Russians for black caviar while this American fisherman was throwing it away. For weeks afterward, he couldn't get the story out of his mind. Commercial sturgeon fishing had been banned in California since 1917, but he wondered whether there might be some way around this restriction—like fish farming. Mats and Dafne decided to drive up to Davis, about an hour north of San Francisco. The University of California had an agricultural college there that had helped transform the fertile Napa Valley into one of the world's most important wine growing regions. Mats thought they might also be interested in cultivating fish.

As it happened, Davis was very interested in fish. The college had just started an aquaculture department with the intention of encouraging fish farming in California. One of the first professors hired was Serge Doroshov, a Russian who had just defected from the Soviet Union. Figuring that a Russian ichthyologist must know something about caviar, the college sent the Engstroms to see Doroshov. He had worked in the prestigious Russian Federal Research Institute of Fisheries and Oceanography, where Igor Burtsev had learned to milk caviar from live bester sturgeon. But, Doroshov knew nothing about sturgeon. His specialty was striped bass and other marine fish. He had eaten caviar perhaps three times in his life.

The Engstroms weren't the only ones who had asked Doroshov

about raising sturgeon. Several California fish farms were also looking into the business. When the university started its aquaculture program, it figured it might investigate oysters or catfish. But the university prided itself on working with native California species, and sturgeon certainly qualified. Doroshov promised the Engstroms that he would find out what he could about farming sturgeon.

Doroshov began reading everything he could about sturgeon aquaculture. Nearly all the work had been done by Russians. But he also learned a few things from the work of Maurice Fontaine, one of France's best-known fish experts. Fontaine was famous among ichthyologists for convincing the Soviet government in the late 1970s, to give France an aquaculture starter kit of live sturgeon. The French had dreamed of reviving the caviar industry in the Gironde region, which had once turned out tons of the delicacy from its native sturgeon, the *Acipenser sturio*, or common European sturgeon. Since European sturgeon was no longer commercially viable, the French wanted to raise Siberian sturgeon on their farms instead. The Soviets were naturally reluctant to share their trade secrets. Caviar was one of the few Soviet products that the world coveted, and the delicacy was a source of national pride. But Fontaine persisted. He offered to trade France's expertise with trout for sturgeon. Eventually, Fontaine's charm won the Soviets over. The offspring of that diplomacy is the Caviar d'Aquitaine farm in Bordeaux, one of the most successful sturgeon farms in the world.

Just because Caviar d'Aquitaine had succeeded with Siberian sturgeon in France didn't guarantee that white sturgeon could be raised in captivity in California. Siberian sturgeon spend most of their lives in fresh water, while the white sturgeon of California only enter the fresh water of the rivers to spawn. And Siberian sturgeon mature much earlier than white sturgeon. Doroshov wasn't sure whether the California fish could survive in the artificial environment of a farm. Doroshov's other problem was collecting eggs and milt to spawn the trial generation.

In 1982, California's Department of Fish and Game agreed to let the Engstroms take twenty fish from the Columbia and Sacramento Rivers, but only on the condition that the specimens be returned to the river once their eggs and milt had been removed. Mats went around to the local bars trying to find fishermen who would bring back live sturgeon for the experiment. The fishermen couldn't understand why he was so particular about having live sturgeon, but they complied. They found it even stranger when the Engstroms came back with the same sturgeon and let it go.

Mats once observed that raising sturgeon on a farm to produce caviar was the equivalent of planting a forest to start a paper mill. Getting the sturgeon farm established took far longer than the Engstroms had first expected. Initially, they set up their tanks in an old warehouse in Sacramento. But just as the fish were gaining size, the warehouse caught fire and all the sturgeon died. After that experience, they moved the operation out among the rice farms of Elverta. The fire had made them excessively cautious, and they installed the latest monitoring equipment to prevent another accident from devastating the farm. They also bought an expensive treatment system to filter the water. The system was designed to remove the fish waste and recycle the water in an environmentally responsible way, but it cost a fortune. They weren't producing a lot of caviar, but with Russian caviar so cheap in the mid-1990s, it didn't matter. No one was interested in their fish eggs. The Engstroms were forced to bring in new investors to help keep the farm going. Eventually, they were forced to sell out their share. Stolt, which had already experimented with sturgeon on another farm near Sacramento, bought the Elverta operation in 1995. The Engstroms stayed on just long enough to teach the staff how to process the roe into caviar.

It was a bitter experience for the pair. But the Engstroms couldn't get caviar out of their minds. When the sturgeon population in the Caspian began to crash, they put together all the money they could raise and in 2000 started another sturgeon farm to compete with Stolt.

THE SPRING catches in the Caspian were dismal in 2000, far worse than anyone ever expected. The Volga fishermen had pulled in only 40 percent of the sturgeon they had caught just a year earlier. Evgeny Aptekar had been right to worry about his fishing company being able to fill its quota.

The scientists and conservationists who had placed so much store in the power of export controls a few years earlier were deeply disappointed in CITES. The agency had imposed all kinds of quotas and rules, but the bootleggers were still able to slip their caviar out of the Caspian. The Russian government also seemed to lack the will to save the sturgeon. While I was in Astrakhan, the minister of the interior swept into town to announce a new crackdown on poaching. Local television coverage over the next few days showed the police seizing illegal nets and snast lines, arresting poachers, and leading the pitiful, sunburned creatures away in handcuffs. But when I strolled over to the neighborhood grocery store down the street from my friend Mira's apartment, caviar was freely available and selling at prices cheaper than in the mid-1990s.

While the crisis was growing in Russia, the alarms were going off in the United States. America's appetite for caviar had only grown since CITES had introduced trade restrictions, and it was now the biggest caviar-eating country in the world. One result of caviar's popularity was a rising demand for the eggs of previously despised species such as the American paddlefish, and the species was already beginning to show the strain. The environmental catastrophe in the Caspian was no longer just a regional event. The shock waves were felt wherever sturgeon struggled to swim upriver to spawn, from the Amur River along the Chinese-Russian border, to the Danube in Romania, to the Mississippi in America.

As the gloomy harvest reports filtered in from the Caspian, several American conservation groups began to voice concern over CITES' inability to stop the poaching. In the fall of 2000, three groups decided to join forces—the Natural Resources Defense Council, the Bronx Zoo's Wildlife Conservation Society, and SeaWeb—to pressure CITES into taking stronger measures to save the sturgeon.

The problem was goading the sluggish CITES bureaucracy into action. The trio of environmental organizations decided to issue a report to the media detailing the sturgeon slaughter in the Caspian, just as TRAFFIC had done in 1996. The new report, titled "Roe to Ruin," covered much of the same ground, but came to more radical conclusions. Arguing that the existing trade controls had failed to stop the slaughter, they demanded an immediate ban on beluga caviar. The beluga is the biggest, best known, and most ancient of the sturgeon. By the report's estimate there were less than 1,800 mature fish left in the Volga River.

For maximum impact, the coalition arranged to release its report during a major CITES meeting. The event was being held, conveniently enough, in the United States—at the Fish & Wildlife's training center in the rolling hills of Shepherdstown, West Virginia, an hour's drive from Washington. At the coalition's urging, CITES agreed to consider the beluga ban during the meeting.

As the delegates assembled in the lobby of the faux-rustic lodge, the words "ban" and "beluga" seemed to ripple across the room. CITES meetings are usually taken up with mind-numbing recitations of rules, regulations, and statistics. But this time the visitors' gallery was packed and everyone seemed to have multilingual headsets affixed to their ears. The meeting also had the air of a reunion. Caroline Raymakers, who wrote the TRAFFIC report, and Rosemarie Gnam, who had left her job at Fish & Wildlife to take a position at the American Museum of Natural History, were both sitting with the delegates. In the gallery, Mats Engstrom and Armen Petrossian huddled with sturgeon scientists such as David Secor, from the Chesapeake Biological Laboratory, and Ellen Pikitch from the Wildlife Conservation Society. Noticeably missing was Vadim Birstein, who was no longer on speaking terms with anyone at CITES. What was more surprising—and worrisome—was that Kazakhstan had failed to send a representative to discuss the proposed ban, despite having the largest population of beluga in the world.

The stars of the meeting were the two Iranian delegates, Mohammad Pourkazemi, the head of the state caviar company, Shilat Trading, and its managing director, Mohammad Hosseini. They were greeted like returning heroes. Only a few months earlier, the United States had lifted a thirteen-year-long embargo of Iranian caviar. Not only did their presence at the CITES meeting signal a warming of relations with the United States, it gave CITES a chance to boast about its one success story. Iran was seen as the only Caspian state that wasn't driving its local sturgeon population to extinction. It had organized its fishery to ensure that there would always be sturgeon to replace those caught in the fishermen's nets. By stocking the sea with millions of baby sturgeon and keeping careful catch records, Iran had managed to stabilize the sturgeon population in its waters. U.S. and European officials hovered around the two Iranians as they described their hatcheries and fish-tagging program, occasionally proffering a respectful question. Once condemned as an international pariah, Iran was hailed at the CITES meeting as a model citizen.

Although much had changed in the three years since sturgeon were listed as an endangered species, the arguments over banning beluga continued to circle around the same territory. The passionate conservationists complained that it was immoral to sell the delicacy when there were so few sturgeon left. The more pragmatic types countered that the lucrative caviar trade was necessary to give the Caspian states a financial incentive to save the sturgeon. "We don't want to drive the trade underground," Marinus Hoogmoed, the gruff Dutchman who was chairing the discussion, reminded the delegates. "We want to provide incentives for good management."

But Liz Lauck, from the Wildlife Conservation Society, told me later she thought that it was too late to cajole the Caspian countries into being responsible. "The idea of using trade as incentive for conservation is a powerful argument. But with species so endangered as the beluga, you can't afford to take one more fish," she argued. The ungainly beluga had already disappeared from the Adriatic, the Sea of Azov, the Po River in Italy, the Morava River in the Czech Republic, and the Danube in Hungary. Its existence in the Volga was almost entirely dependent on hatcheries, and Iran and Kazakstan were the last places left where the beluga continued to spawn naturally. I asked Sue Lieberman, who represented Fish & Wildlife at the CITES meeting, what the United States would do if it was home to a fish in the same condition as the beluga. It would ban fishing, of course, she answered quickly. "Certainly, if we had the same situation with the beluga as they have in the Caspian, we'd close the fishery. We've already done that with other species that are in much less dire straits than the beluga."

After listening to the various points of view, the delegates appeared more confused than divided and Hoogmoed seemed to be growing impatient. He complained that the sturgeon problem was too complex for such a big group of delegates and suggested a small working group be formed to hash out a compromise. The working group would be open to anyone with a stake in the caviar trade, from producers to scientists. It was already midafternoon and people were getting tired. As the delegates stood up from their seats for a brief recess, Hoogmoed reminded everyone that participants in the working group needed to register with him.

I strolled out to the lobby for coffee, and I noticed two men standing off by themselves, who were speaking Russian. No one was lining up to talk to them, so I introduced myself. The shorter man, who wore a dapper tweed jacket, was Vladimir Shevlyakov, the fisheries attaché at the Russian Embassy in Washington. Next to him towered a member of the Russian Fisheries Commission, a giant in an ill-fitting blue suit named Sergei Nikonorov. Neither had said anything in the meeting, so I was eager to hear their take on the sturgeon crisis. I told them I thought it would be sad to see Russia lose something so important to its culture as caviar.

"Caviar isn't important to Russian culture," Shevlyakov shot back. "Oil is important to Russians."

I was taken aback by his bluntness, and I suppose Nikonorov was, too. Later, when we were talking alone, Nikonorov told me he had been born in Astrakhan. His father had been a fish biologist and he had followed him into the profession. It was very painful now for him to watch oil take precedence over sturgeon. He said a big Russian oil company had already sunk a well in the shallow northern Caspian, an area that served as a nursery for young sturgeon. "I'm sure it will have a very negative effect on the sturgeon," he sighed heavily. "Now it's a choice between oil or biological resources." There was no question of which he thought would win. The best thing Russia could do now, he suggested, was to assemble a collection of sturgeon embryos and put them in a deep freeze. "After a hundred years, when the oil in the Caspian is exhausted, we can use them to restart the biological resources."

Shevlyakov returned a few minutes later and I asked him what he was going to propose to the working group. He said he hadn't heard anything about a working group. That struck me as odd, since Hoogmoed had gone on at length about forming one, and Shevlyakov's English was perfect. I told Shevlyakov and Nikonorov that they needed to register if they wanted to take part in the discussion on the beluga ban. "Oh, yes, I must do that," Shevlyakov said, nodding vigorously.

After the meeting had resumed and the delegates started filtering back, I glanced out the lobby window and saw the two Russians crossing the parking lot. They got in their car and drove away. Of the three nations where the beluga still existed, only one, Iran, cared enough to participate in the effort to save the ancient fish.

As it turned out, the working group didn't accomplish much. The group met, talked, argued, and broke up, without adopting a ban on beluga caviar. Few of the delegates had the stomach for a complete ban. Many believed that it would be unfair to Iran, which seemed to be working hard to protect its sturgeon. So instead of imposing a ban, CITES once again asked the Caspian states to reduce the size of their catch quotas. It was less threatening than banning beluga completely.

But four of the five Caspian states refused. The four former Soviet states insisted that the existing quotas were perfectly reasonable. CITES officials were baffled by the resistance. The four were concerned that the quotas had simply been pulled out of the hat, without any scientific evaluation of the fish populations in the Caspian. CITES asked the four states to conduct a sturgeon census. Once the Caspian states knew how many fish were really left in the sea, CITES explained, *then* they could make an informed decision about how many should be caught each year. The argument went back and forth for months, until CITES began to take on an exasperated tone. "I've never had this level of miscommunications or misunderstandings," a frustrated CITES official complained to a *Wall Street Journal* reporter in the spring of 2001.

When the 2001 fishing season started, the quotas were still the same. The fishermen returned to their tonyas on the Volga and Ural Rivers and dropped their nets once again. The poachers resumed their midnight efforts. The catches would continue to fall, just as they had the year before. Only the caviar farms of California and France offered any hope for the future of the sturgeon.

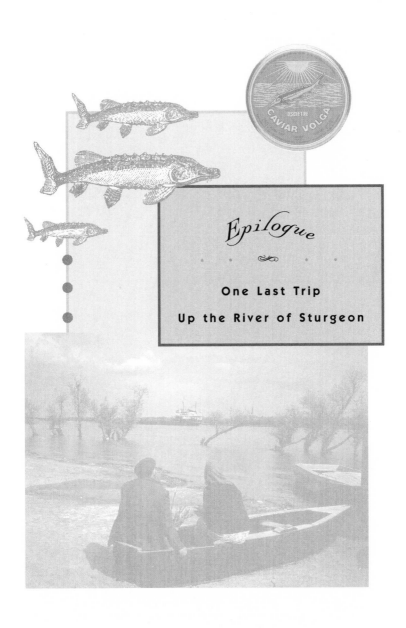

Epilogue

One Last Trip

Up the River of Sturgeon

Caviar for peasants is a joke,
It's too good for the average man.

—SONG BY RICHARD RODGERS AND LORENZ HART

Behind the tower the sea began, the utterly faceless,
leaden, unfathomable Caspian Sea, and beyond, the
desert—jagged rocks and scrub: still, mute,
unconquerable, the most beautiful landscape in the
world.

—KURBAN SAID, ALI AND NINO, 1937

*T*he spring fishing season in the Volga was nearly over. The winds that rattled the steppe in the spring had been replaced by the torpid air of summer. It was rare now to see a sturgeon doing backflips in the net that the fishermen heaved out of the water. All the fish from the spring run had either been caught, or had somehow eluded the gauntlet and continued upriver to their spawning grounds. At the tonyas, fishermen started drifting back to their villages to work in their gardens and rice fields. I returned to Astrakhan to look for a taxi driver who would take me north to Volgograd, where I had arranged to spend a couple of days at the local sturgeon hatchery.

The road from Astrakhan to Volgograd runs parallel to the straight, placid Volga River during much of the three-hundred-mile trip, and as we headed north I realized that we were pacing the few sturgeon that had escaped the fishermen. Two centuries ago, when sturgeon would swim all the way to Kostroma, in Russia's medieval heartland, this part of the Volga would have been crowded with migrating sturgeon. At Volgograd, the sturgeon would have completed a mere third of their river journey.

We could smell Volgograd before we could see it. The city exuded a vague alkaline scent. After Stalin blocked the river with his immense hydroelectric dam, the old tsarist outpost became the industrial powerhouse of the steppe. As we drove, chemical plants and factories reared up before us like ancient turreted fortresses. The factories crowded near the river and deposited much of their waste into it. There were still clusters of brightly painted wooden houses along the road, too, as if they hadn't realized how the neighborhood had changed. The country houses soon gave way to the first of the Soviet apartment blocks. Volgograd is a long strip of a city that hugs the west bank of the river, and the apartment towers seem like links in an extended chain. We eventually turned inland to the center of the city, an empty square flanked by various official buildings, and parked in front of the Intourist Hotel, which was done in Stalin's preferred Gothic wedding cake style, a squat version of the skyscraper towers in Moscow.

Sergei Maltsev arrived at the hotel in his green Niva jeep. When I had telephoned to request a tour of the hatchery, he told me I would need several days in Volgograd to see the operation and generously offered to be my host. Maltsev had thick tinted glasses that sometimes made it difficult at first to get a fix on his expression, but he was unfailingly gracious. He virtually hugged me when I introduced myself. He was so gentlemanly and courteous, I was afraid he might bow as he opened the door to let me into the Niva.

Maltsev was the deputy chief of the Volgograd hatchery, which was located on an island in the Volga just below the dam. The hatchery was organized much like the Stolt sturgeon farm, except the fish were sent sluicing into the river when they were only a few inches long. At that size, they were too big to be eaten by the voracious sterlet, a river sturgeon, and could fend for themselves. The Volgograd hatchery was producing millions of fingerlings a year, although not as many as before the Soviet collapse. After its government funding was cut in the early 1990s, the hatchery tried to raise money by selling fertilized sturgeon eggs to fish farms in Uruguay, Sri Lanka, Hawaii, and Australia, an option that was once banned in order to preserve the Soviets' deeply guarded secret of sturgeon cultivation. But the hatchery now could not care less about foreign competition, gladly selling fertilized eggs to anyone who will pay five thousand dollars a kilogram—about ten times the wholesale price for virgin eggs. "Anyone can start a sturgeon farm now," Maltsev said, sounding amused. All the places he mentioned were in the Southern Hemisphere, where there had never been any native sturgeon. Farms had their place, Maltsev said, but "the much bigger problem will be to preserve the sturgeon's natural spawning grounds. We must prevent the species from reaching some critical minimum, otherwise it will never be able to recover. We have almost passed the point of no return already."

We were driving north again along the river, toward the massive Volgograd dam. Maltsev wanted to show me the hatchery's latest project. Along the way, he pointed out some of the factories that lined the river. The pollution levels had fallen because so many companies had gone bankrupt after 1991. Now some were starting to revive their operations. This was good for the people of Volgograd, but not so good for the fish, which retain PCBs and heavy metals in their fatty tissue. Maltsev tended to dismiss the role of pollution in the sturgeon's current troubles, just as he tended to discount the effects from the dam and the poachers. "Something mysterious is going on. Fifteen years ago we had dams, we had pollution, we had poachers, but we still caught 25,000 tons of sturgeon." Several years ago, his hatchery had dumped rocks around a small island at the base of the dam to create an artificial spawning ground for the sturgeon. In the spring, divers would swim through clouds of hatchlings. This year, however, divers found the water clear of wriggling sturgeon babies.

Maltsev left out one of the main reasons behind the sturgeon's demise: caviar had gone mainstream. Originally a food for peasants, the sturgeon's eggs were later appropriated as a delicacy by wealthy connoisseurs. But in the last century, as the pleasures and conveniences of the wealthy became available to more people, so did caviar. With the collapse of Communism's controlling cartel, it was caviar's turn to be democratized and transformed into a mass-marketed delicacy for the middle class, sold to commuters rushing through train stations and airports. Now, both unemployed peasants working hook lines in the night, and middle-class office workers dining in candlelit restaurants, chase their dreams of wealth in the eggs of the sturgeon.

The problem, is that there aren't enough sturgeon in this one region to support the appetite of the whole world. Nature intended local sturgeon populations to feed local people. It is the same story with many plants and animals. Most can't survive as mass market commodities unless they are rigorously domesticated and farmed.

The Niva climbed a winding road until we reached the base of the dam. Although it was only three miles to the other shore, it was impossible to see the other end of the structure. Maltsev parked the car in

front of a mural of workers striding into a beautiful future, and motioned me to follow him into a door behind their legs. We entered a
stairwell and began descending several long flights of steps. I could
hear a rumbling noise as we climbed down, something like the roar of
the ocean when you hold a shell to your ear. The rumbling grew louder
with each flight. The light inside the dam was murky and damp, just as
it was in the warehouses at Stolt. When we reached the bottom, we saw
a row of glossy red machines perched on spidery legs: the turbines in
the belly of the dam. The dull roar was the sound of the river itself,
pressing uselessly against the 54 million tons of concrete.

We passed into a large room, empty except for several large tanks.
Maltsev gestured proudly. Those were for baby sturgeon. His hatchery
was planning to start a caviar farm inside the dam. The moist heat was
perfect for raising fish, Maltsev explained, and the hydroelectric company didn't need the space anymore. Since economic collapse had swept
the former Soviet Union, this section of turbines had been shut down.
Inside the beast that had devoured so many sturgeon, Maltsev envisioned a day when new ones would be born. The dam would save the
sturgeon.

It had all been worked out. The Russian government had even
agreed to contribute some money to the project, and so had the hydroelectric company that runs the dam. Maltsev was hoping foreign investors would join them. One level below the sturgeon tanks, Maltsev
had set up an entirely different farm for growing worms. He planned to
feed his sturgeon the same diet they enjoyed in nature, so that their eggs
would taste of the sea. No ground fish meal compressed into pellets for
them. When the sturgeon became too big for the tanks, they would be
moved outside to floating pens in the river until they reached maturity.

The biggest problem facing the new farm, Maltsev told me, is the
lack of wild fish for brood stock. By his calculations, the farm needed

eggs from at least five hundred wild female sturgeon to get started. In the past, the Soviets made do with five or ten. Stolt had used twenty fish to start its farm. But Maltsev was convinced that a wider genetic pool was necessary to breed healthy fish. He had no idea how he was going get the five hundred female fish. Fishermen weren't about to give him their egg-laden fish and buying the cows was beyond the hatchery's budget.

The lack of money and resources didn't seem to stop Maltsev from making grand plans for the sturgeon farm. Given its location on the Volga, the mother of sturgeon rivers, he felt an obligation to create a farm that would mimic nature as much as possible. In some ways, though, such environmental rescue operations are almost as damaging to nature as the poachers they seek to circumvent. As the farm grows and Maltsev adds more sturgeon to the floating pens, the feces and un-eaten food will form a sizable garbage heap at the bottom of the river. The waves will carry the refuse out to sea, further polluting the sturgeon's natural habitat. Some farm-bred sturgeon will very likely escape from the pens and breed with the wild fish, creating genetic extremes and spreading disease. In humanity's feeble attempts to protect and pre-serve the plodding sturgeon, we are reminded that we can't help alter-ing the natural world even when we try our best to rescue it.

Maltsev views these dangers as a small price to pay for saving this piece of the world's aquatic patrimony. The sturgeon will no longer be the "pilgrim of the most illustrious waves" that Ovid saw frolicking off the Black Sea shore, but a captive animal, dependent on human care and intervention for its survival. Our hunger for the sturgeon's luscious eggs may turn out to be our burden.

Caviar may be nothing more than raw fish eggs, yet there is some-thing about this delicacy that still inspires people to inchoate dreams of other worlds and other identities. No one is ambivalent about caviar.

Those who loathe it, loathe it viscerally. Those who crave it will go to extreme lengths for the sensation of eggs bursting like fireworks in the mouth. If we lose this experience, and the fish that is responsible for it, we are destined to lose a part of ourselves. The sturgeon is our connection to a time when the world was new. All we need is one taste of caviar and we are suffused with the whisper of an ocean breeze that recalls that primal moment when we, like the prehistoric sturgeon, were enveloped in the womb of the sea.

Acknowledgments

*

$\mathcal{T}$his book could not have been written without the indulgence, enthusiasm, and good will of many people.

I was lucky to have many multilingual friends who helped enrich
this book by tracking down foreign books, translating official documents, and guiding me through Russia's labyrinthine bureaucracy. Mira
Bergelson and Volodya Sverdlov jumped at the chance to wander
around the Volga River Delta in search of sturgeon poachers and trans-
lated their words effortlessly. Valentina Markova made phone calls,
arranged interviews, and pulled all the right strings for me. My Russian
friends took me into their homes, fed me, and made me feel welcome
during my stay in Moscow.

In Philadelphia, my friend Mika Tsekouris became so excited by a
Greek sea captain's role in the development of the caviar trade that she
researched the details of his life story. Beate Hemmann patiently read
German history aloud to me.

I am grateful for the hospitality of several people I met during the
course of my research. Susanne Taylor, *née* Schwerdtfeger, graciously
welcomed me in Hamburg, as did Armen Petrossian in Paris. David
Secor at the Chesapeake Biological Labs set me straight on many scien-

tific points. Ellen Pikitch graciously agreed to review this manuscript and guided me on several scientific issues. Mats and Dafne Engstrom shared memories of their caviar days. Chuck Edwards allowed me access to a working caviar farm. Sergei Maltsev, besides being a generous host and dedicated scientist, provided me with invaluable archival material. I am also indebted to the Calvert Marine Museum for sharing letters and photographs from their archive. The New Jersey Coastal Heritage Trail provided me with much useful information. The Salem County Historical Society and the Greenwich Township Historical Society were invaluable resources.

Thanks also go to my agents, Neal Bascomb and Christy Fletcher, for finding a home for this book, and to my editor, Charles Conrad, for shepherding it through to completion.

I would never have finished this book if my editors at the *Philadelphia Inquirer* had not tolerated my frequent absences with grace. Robert Rosenthal, Anne Gordon, and Jeff Weinstein gave me the time I needed to complete this project. I also want to thank all my observant friends and colleagues who pointed out every mention of caviar in print and on screen during my writing of this book.

Most of all, I am grateful to my husband, Ken, a lifelong fish hater who made sure I had the time to write, endured my sturgeon-centered worldview, and baby-sat our balky printer; and to my daughter, Sky, who drew pictures of sturgeon, accompanied me on sturgeon-hunting expeditions, and joined me in dreaming of caviar.

Bibliography

Aczel, Amir D. *The Riddle of the Compass: The Invention That Changed the World.* New York: Harcourt, 2001.

Allen Brigid, ed. *Food: An Oxford Anthology.* New York: Oxford University Press, 1994.

Asimomytis, Vassilis. *Ioannis Varvakis.* Athens: Kaktos, 2001.

Astrakhan, Time and the City. Astrakhan: Nova, 1998.

Barrett, Thomas M. *At the Edge of the Empire: The Terek Cossacks and the North Caucasus Frontier, 1700–1860.* Boulder: Westview Press, 1999.

Beebe, Lucius. "The Costliest Food." *Holiday* (September 1955).

Bemelmans, Ludwig. *La Bonne Table.* Boston: David R. Godine, 1989.

Birstein, Vadim J., John R. Waldman, and William E. Bemis, eds. *Sturgeon Biodiversity and Conservation*, Dordecht/Boston/London: Kluwer Academic Publishers, 1997.

Birstein, Vadim J., ed. *The Sturgeon Quarterly* 5, nos. 1–2 (June 1997).

Birstein, V., P. Doukakis, and R. DeSalle. "Polyphyly of mtDNA lineages in Russian sturgeon, *Acipenser gueldenstaedtii*: forensic and evolutionary implications." *Conservation Genetics*, 1: 81–88, 2000.

Borodine, N. "The Ural Cossacks and their Fisheries." *The Popular Science Monthly*, no. 6 (October 1893): 767.

Boss, Kit. "The Great Northwest Caviar Caper." *Pacific* (March 13, 1994). (magazine of the *Seattle Times*) p.12.

Burk, John. *The History of Virginia, from Its First Settlement to the Present Day*. Petersburg, Va.: Dickson and Pescud, 1805.

Chamberlain, Lesley. *Volga, Volga: A Journey Down Russia's Great River*. London: Picador, 1995.

Chang, K. C., ed. *Food in Chinese Culture*. New Haven: Yale University Press, 1977.

Clarke, Edward Daniel. *Travels in Various Countries of Europe, Asia, and Africa. Part the First. Russia, Tartary, and Turkey*. 1811. Reprint, New York: Arno Press, 1970.

Cobb, John N. *The Sturgeon Fishery of Delaware River and Bay. Report of the Commissioner*. Washington: U.S. Commission of Fish and Fisheries, June 1899. Part XXV, Government Printing Office.

Coleman, Charles Washington. "Sturgeon Fishing in the James." *Cosmopolitan* (1892).

Connor, Bud. *Great White Sturgeon Angling*. Frank Amato. Portland, Oregon, 1996.

Cresson, W. P. *The Cossacks: Their History and Their Country*. New York: Brentano's, 1919.

De Custine, Marquis Astolphe. *Empire of the Czar: A Journey through Eternal Russia*. Reprint, New York: Doubleday, 1989. Original date 1839.

De Hell, Xavier Hommaire. *Travels in the Steppes of the Caspian Sea*. London: Chapman and Hall, 1847.

De Meulenaer, T., and C. Raymakers. *Sturgeons of the Caspian Sea and the International Trade in Caviar*. Cambridge, U.K.: TRAFFIC International, 1996.

De Rohan-Csermak, Geza. *Sturgeon Hooks of Eurasia*. Chicago: Aldine, 1963.

Dieckmann & Hansen. *125 Years, 1869–1994*. Hamburg: Dieckmann & Hansen, 1994.

Dodds, Richard J. S. *Solomons Island and Vicinity: An Illustrated History and Walking Tour*. Solomons Island, Md.: Calvert Marine Museum, 1995.

Dorsey, Hebe. *The Age of Opulence*. London: Thames and Hudson, 1986.

Dumas, Alexandre. *Adventures in Czarist Russia.* Trans. and ed. A. E. Murch. London: Owen, 1960.

———. *Le Grand Dictionnaire de Cuisine.* Vol. 3, *Poissons.* 1873. Reprint, Payré, France: Edit-France, 1995.

Feodoroff, Nicholas V. *History of the Cossacks.* Commack, N.Y.: Nova Science, 1999.

Forster, George. *A Journey from Bengal to England through the Northern Part of India, Kashmire, Afghanistan, and Persia, and into Russia by the Caspian-Sea.* Vol. 2. London, 1798. Reprint, Languages Department Punjab, 1970.

Friedland, Susan R. *Caviar: A Cookbook with 100 Recipes, A Guide to All Varieties.* New York: Charles Scribner's Sons, 1986.

Gemelin, Samuel. *Travels in Russia in Three Domains, Cherkass to Astrakhan, 1769 to 1770.* St. Petersburg, Russia: St. Petersburg Academy of Sciences, 1773.

Georgacas, Demetrius J. *Ichthyological Terms for the Sturgeon and Etymology of the International Terms for Botargo, Caviar and Congeners: A Linguistic, Philological, and Historical Study.* University of North Dakota Press, 1978.

Georgi, Johann Gottlieb. *Russia: Or a Compleat Historical Account of all Nations which Compose the Empire.* Trans. William Tooke the Elder. Vol. 4. London, 1783.

Glants, Musya, and Joyce Toomre, eds. *Food in Russian History and Culture.* Bloomington: Indiana University Press, 1997.

Glavin, Terry. *A Ghost in the Water.* Vancouver: New Star Books, 1994.

Godecken, Horst. *Der konigliche Kaviar.* Hamburg: Heinrich Siepmann Verlag, 1969.

Goode, George Brown. *The Fisheries and Fishing Industry of the United States.* Washington: Government Printing Office, 1884.

Grigson, I. *Fish Cookery.* London: Penguin Books, 1973.

Hanway, Jonas. *An Historical Account of British Trade over the Caspian Sea, with the Author's Journals of His Travels from London through Russia into Persia and Back Again through Russia, Germany and Holland.* London, 1754.

Herodotus. *The Histories.* Trans. Aubrey de Sé Incourt. Baltimore: Penguin Books, 1954.

Hildebrand, Samuel F., and William C. Schroeder. *Fishes of the Chesapeake Bay*. Bulletin 53. U.S. Bureau of Fisheries, 1972 Reprint by Smithsonian.

Holmes, William Richard. *Sketches on the Shores of the Caspian, Descriptive and Pictorial*. London: R. Bentley, 1845.

Hosmer, Dorothy. "Caviar Fishermen of Romania." *National Geographic* (March 1940).

Ian, Vasilii *Batu-Khan; A Tale of the 13th Century*. Trans. Lionel Erskine Britton. London: Hutchinson International Authors, 1945.

Ivanov, V. P. *Biological Resources of the Caspian Sea*. Astrakhan: KaspNIRKH, 2000.

Khlebnikov, Velimir. *Collected Works of Velimir Khlebnikov: Letters and Theoretical Writings*. Trans. Paul Schmidt. Ed. Charlotte Douglas. Cambridge; Mass.: Harvard University Press, 1987.

Khodarkovsky, Michael. *Where Two worlds Met: The Russian State and the Kalmyk Nomads, 1600–1771*. Ithaca: Cornell University Press, 1992.

Kraft, Herbert C. *Lenni Lenape: Archaeology, History, and Ethnography*. Newark: New Jersey Historical Society, 1986.

Krasinski, Count Henry. *Cossacks of the Ukraine*. London: Partridge and Oakley, 1848.

Kurlansky, Mark. *Salt: A World History*. New York: Walker, 2002.

———. *Cod: A Biography of the Fish That Changed the World*. New York: Walker, 1997.

Lazlo, Pierre. *Salt, Grain of Life*. Trans. Mary Beth Mader. New York: Columbia University Press, 2001.

LeBrun, M. *The Present State of Russia. Vol. 2, part 6. Observations on his Journey through Russia and Persia*. Reprint, New York: Da Capo Press, 1968.

Lord Kinross. *The Ottoman Centuries: The Rise and Fall of the Turkish Empire*. New York: Morrow, 1977.

Mathisen, Ole A., and Donald E. Bevan. *Some International Aspects of Soviet Fisheries*. Columbus: Ohio State University Press, 1968.

May, Col. John. *Journals, relative to a journey to the Ohio Country*. 1789, Archives of the Pennsylvania Historical Society.

Molokhovets, Elena. *A Gift to Young Housewives.* Trans. Joyce Toomre. 1897. Reprint, Bloomington: Indiana University Press, 1998.

Norman, Barbara Makanowitzky. *Tales of the Table: A History of Western Cuisine.* Englewood Cliffs, N.J.: Prentice Hall, 1972.

Olearius, Adam. *The Travels of Olearius in Seventeenth-Century Russia.* Trans. and ed. Samuel H. Baron. Stanford: Stanford University Press, 1967.

Oliphant, Lawrence. *The Russian Shores of the Black Sea.* 1853. Reprint, Cologne: Könemann, 1999.

Parkinson, John. *Tour of Russia, Siberia and the Crimea, 1792–1794.* Ed. William Collier. Reprint, London: Frank Cass, 1971.

Perry, Captain John. *The State of Russia Under the Present Czar.* 1716. Reprint, London: Da Capa Press, 1967.

Popkin, Susan A., and Roger B. Allen. *Gone Fishing: A History of Fishing in River, Bay and Sea.* Catalogue of Exhibition, Philadelphia Maritime Museum, 1987.

Putnam, Peter. *Seven Britons in Imperial Russia, 1698–1812.* Princeton: Princeton University Press, 1952.

Radcliffe, William. *Fishing from the Earliest Times.* Chicago, ARES, 1921.

Raleigh, Donald J. ed., and A. A. Iskenderov, comp. *The Emperors and Empresses of Russia: Rediscovering the Romanovs.* Armonk, N.Y.: M. E. Sharpe, 1996.

Ramade, Frédéric. *L'Univers du Caviar.* Paris: Editions Solar, 1999.

Riasanovsky, Nicholas V. *A History of Russia.* New York: Oxford University Press, 1963. First published 1963, my edition 1984.

Riddervold, Astri, and Andreas Ropeid, eds. *Food Conservation: Ethnological Studies.* London: Prospect Books, 1988.

Rieber, Alfred. *Merchants and Entrepreneurs in Imperial Russia.* Chapel Hill: University of North Carolina Press, 1982.

Rostovtzeff, M. *Iranians and Greeks in South Russia.* Oxford: Clarendon Press, 1922.

Royle, J. F. *On the Production of Isinglass along the Coast of India.* London: Wm. H. Allen, 1842.

Ryder, John A. *The sturgeons and sturgeon industries of the eastern coast of the United States, with an Account of Experiments bearing upon Sturgeon Culture, pages 231–328.* Bulletin of the U.S. Fish Commission, 1888. Washington Vol. VIII

Rundquist, Jane. "Fishing and Utilization of Sturgeon by Aboriginal Peoples of the Pacific Northwest." Private paper written for Sierra Aquafarms, Inc., 1994. San Francisco.

Shulz, A. Ya. *Researches into Fishery Conditions in Russia.* Report to the State Properties Ministry, St. Petersburg. Vol. 4. 1861.

Sebold, Kimberly R., and Sara Amy Leach. *Historic Themes and Resources Within the New Jersey Coastal Heritage Trail.* Washington: U.S. Department of Interior, 1995.

Secor, D. H., and R. Waldman. *Historical Abundance of Delaware Atlantic Sturgeon.* Transactions of the American Fisheries Society. 1999.

Shephard, Sue. *Pickled, Potted and Canned: How the Art and Science of Food Preserving Changed the World.* New York: Simon & Schuster, 2001.

Sim, Mary B. *Commercial Canning in New Jersey: History and Early Development.* Trenton: New Jersey Agricultural Society, 1951.

Skinner, John E. *A Historical Review of the Fish and Wildlife Resources of the San Francisco Bay Area.* California Department of Fish and Game, June 1962.

Smith, R.E.F., and David Christian. *Bread and Salt: A Social and Economic History of Food and Drink in Russia.* Cambridge: Cambridge University Press, 1984.

Sobel, Dava, trans. *Letters to Father: Suor Maria Celeste to Galileo, 1623–1633.* New York: Walker, 2001.

Somerville-Large, Pater. *Caviar Coast.* London: Hale, 1968.

Speer, Lisa, et al. *Roe to Ruin: The Decline of Sturgeon in the Caspian Sea and the Road to Recovery.* National Resources Defense Council, Wildlife Conservation Society, and Sea Web, December 2000.

Sternin, Vulf, and Ian Dore. *Caviar: The Resource Book.* Moscow: Cultura, 1993.

Stockard, Charles R. "Our New Caviar Fisheries." *Century Magazine,* July 1908.

Stoddard, Charles Augustus. *Across Russia: From the Baltic to the Danube*. New York: Charles Scribner's Sons, 1891.

Stutz, Bruce. *Natural Lives, Modern Times: People and Places of the Delaware River*. New York: Crown, 1992.

Tannahill, Reay. *Food in History*. New York: Stein and Day, 1973.

Taylor, William W., and C. Paola Ferreri, eds. *Great Lakes Fisheries Policy and Management: A Binational Perspective*. East Lansing: Michigan State University Press, 1999.

Thomazi, Auguste. *Histoire de la Pêche, des âges de la pierre a nos jours*. Paris: Payot, 1947.

Tompkins, Calvin. *Living Well Is the Best Revenge*. New York: Viking Press, 1971.

Toussaint-Samat, Maguelonne. *A History of Food*. Trans. Anthea Bell. Cambridge, Mass.: Blackwell, 1994. My edition, 1992—See U of Penn catalogue.

Tower, Walter Sheldon. "Passing of the Sturgeon." *Popular Science Monthly*, October 1908.

Ure, John. *The Cossacks*. London: Constable, 1999.

Vaisman, A., and V. Gorbatovsky, eds. *Wild Animals and Plants in Commerce in Russia and CIS Countries*. Moscow: TRAFFIC Europe, 1999.

Volokh, Anne, with Mavis Manus. *The Art of Russian Cuisine*. New York: Macmillan, 1983.

Waldman, John R., and David H. Secor. "Caviar Trade in North America: An Historical Perspective." *Proceedings of the Symposium on the Harvest, Trade and Conservation of North American Paddlefish and Sturgeon*. Washington: TRAFFIC North America and World Wildlife Fund, 1999.

Weigley, Russell F., ed. *Philadelphia: A 300-Year History*. New York: W. W. Norton, 1982.

White, William C. "Fishy Breezes from Soviet Astrakhan." *Asia*, October 1931.

Wildes, Henry Emerson. *The Delaware*. New York: Farrar & Rinehard, 1940.

Williamson, Douglas F., George W. Benz, and Craig M. Hoover, eds. *Proceedings on the Harvest, Trade and Conservation of North American Paddlefish and Sturgeon*. Washington: TRAFFIC North America and World Wildlife Fund, 1999.

Index

●

About the Author

A reporter for the *Philadelphia Inquirer* for the past fifteen years, Inga Saffron has split her journalistic career between foreign affairs and domestic culture. She spent four years as the *Inquirer*'s correspondent in Moscow during the chaotic, post-Soviet period of the mid-1990s. The job enabled her to travel extensively around the former Soviet Union, and she was a frequent visitor to the Caucasus region and Central Asia.

Before, after, and between stints abroad, she was a member of the *Inquirer*'s features staff, specializing in design and culture. After returning from Moscow in August 1998, she was named the *Inquirer*'s architecture critic.

Before joining the *Inquirer*, she spent several years as a student and freelance journalist in Dublin and Paris. She lives in Philadelphia with her husband, novelist Ken Kalfus.